Optimising Distressed Loan Books

Optimising Distressed Loan Books

Practical solutions for dealing with non-performing loans

By John Michael Sheehan

Hh

HARRIMAN HOUSE LTD

3A Penns Road
Petersfield
Hampshire
GU32 2EW
GREAT BRITAIN

Tel: +44 (0)1730 233870
Fax: +44 (0)1730 233880
Email: enquiries@harriman-house.com
Website: www.harriman-house.com

First published in Great Britain in 2011

ISBN: 978-0-85719-129-8

British Library Cataloguing in Publication Data
A CIP catalogue record for this book can be obtained from the British Library.

Set in Minion and Gotham Narrow

Printed and bound in the UK by CPI Antony Rowe.

Hh Harriman House

Contents

About the Author

John Sheehan's introduction to this subject was undertaking real estate advisory and collateral valuation of non-performing loan portfolios. From here he moved into loan pricing, portfolio negotiation and acquisition from financial institutions and governments. Ultimately, he progressed into loan servicing, establishing and managing large work-out platforms, specialising in new jurisdictions.

His early career was spent in the UK and western Europe. He worked in Asia Pacific after the 1997 crisis until 2005, before moving to Europe, and then moving to Latin America, gaining global experience through loan transactions in Hong Kong, Singapore, Malaysia, Indonesia, Thailand, the Philippines, Taiwan, Korea, India, Australia, Brazil, Columbia, Portugal, Spain, Germany, Poland, the Czech Republic, Greece, Turkey and Israel.

Increasingly concerned with the perilous state of the banking sector in 2008, John left Lehman Bros. 21 days before they went bankrupt. He embarked upon a new career, by lecturing and presenting on the global financial crisis in order to provide businesses with a more informed view of what was occurring in the world and how this would impact their commercial future. He is a popular speaker in Europe and Asia.

John now advises financial institutions, administrators and investors on the subject of distressed debt and organises specialised training courses for loan work-out units and distressed debt asset managers. He can be contacted at **www.distresseddebtservicing.com**.

Acknowledgements

A number of people have provided me with the opportunity for writing this book, and have therefore contributed to the ideas and concepts within.

In particular, I would like to thank Alex Kirk, Guy Moar, Tarun Jotwani, Carl Everett, Brian Prince, and above all John Paterson.

Preface

This book seeks to condense two decades of international distressed debt work-out history into a brief, easily understood, concise format. The specific subject is non-performing bank loan books and portfolios, collateralised by real estate. The primary focus is on larger loans and tougher borrowers, as these represent the greatest resolution challenge.

It is written predominantly for financial institutions in a way that should appeal to everyone from executive to officer level. Within banks, it should have resonance with credit, debt work-out, auditing, product control and risk management functions. It should also be of interest to banks' third-party advisors, particularly in law, real estate, and loan servicing, and with government sponsored entities tasked with cleaning up distressed loans and the banking system. Investors, accountants, administrators and rating agencies should find this book to be a useful source of reference, whilst regulators, academics and students may also find it will better their understanding of the distressed debt problem and therefore the financial system.

The book identifies and analyses practical solutions for dealing with distressed debt, both from the loan and the property collateral level, based upon past experiences. It is not designed to be read once; it is planned as a practical, reference, working and training manual that can be referred to when needed or appropriate. It is divided into three main parts:

Part I, the first two chapters, examines the reasons why many banks fail to maximise distressed debt recoveries.

Part II, the bulk of the book, identifies detailed, workable solutions for maximising collection or mitigating loss from collateralised non-performing loans (NPLs).

Part III includes lessons from previous crises and considers methods for improving all-round distressed debt performance in the future.

Throughout the book you will spot a series of note boxes. These provide examples of real situations I have been involved in, where I think lessons can be drawn (grey boxes), and emphasise key points (black boxes).

Due to the cyclical nature of distressed debt there are not many, if any, books on this subject. This is therefore a pioneering effort and it is sincerely hoped that it will benefit everyone involved at the professional end of debt recovery, deleveraging and loan monetisation.

Introduction

Since the late 1980s, speculative investors all over the world have raised billions of dollars to purchase distressed debt from banks and enormous profits have been made from these investments. The investors include investment banks, hedge funds, sovereign wealth funds, pension funds and even commercial banks themselves. Many of the principals running these organisations have made colossal personal fortunes that have been used to buy indulgences like racehorses, luxury yachts, private jets, castles or even tropical islands.

For every winner though, there is a loser. Distressed debt is not a win-win situation; it is a zero-sum game. Simply put: I win, you lose. The gain of the investor is the loss of the bank. There may be other losers too. In more severe instances it can also be the loss of central bank deposit insurance funds, or the government treasury itself, and ultimately the taxpayer. The expression: "You make your profits when you buy, not when you sell," has rarely been more appropriate.

Distressed debt portfolio transactions are normally conducted privately, with press restricted to positive spin around bank balance sheet clean-up and NPL ratios. Transaction details are normally limited or withheld. For banks to broadcast particulars of debt haircuts they may have given to borrowers, or the fact that they may have left hundreds of millions of dollars of potential upside on the table for loan book purchasers, would be extremely damaging. Similarly, it is not good for future potential business for buyers to publicise or brag about internal rates of return in excess of 40% that they may have made on their investments. As a result, hard facts and transactional information are hard to come by and the industry generally is shrouded in secrecy.

Some of the central questions posed by this book are how and why financial institutions fail where the distressed investor succeeds. How do investors turn the dredge of bank defaults into a treasure trove of gold? Why can't banks maximise proceeds the way an investor can for those same loans? How do sophisticated investors find value in bank loan portfolios that the banks themselves miss or cannot realise? How can such a fundamental bank arbitrage phenomenon be allowed to occur?

Whilst following financial crises around the world, I have met with presidents, politicians, central bank governors, regulators and bank owners. They all have one thing in common; they have absolutely no idea of what distressed debt is really about. To them, bad loans are an unfortunate number on bank balance sheets that leads to awkward questions around competence and poor performance.

Their lack of real understanding is not surprising though. The distressed debt industry is very small, private and usually only comes around to individual jurisdictions once every 10 to 15 years or so. Sharing what I have learned about this arcane subject is the purpose of this book, and the result is a manual of mechanics, techniques and processes used by the wily, deft, international vulture investor.

My work in the distressed debt industry

I started undertaking distressed debt advisory work in the 1980s. My first client was a London bank, who asked me to give them strategic advice regarding a development site they had repossessed. They mentioned that they always used a well-known appraisal firm in the City for valuation services. This surprised me as I knew that the firm in question had very limited experience in this sector. The reason they were employed was the need to sue for damages in the event of a negligent valuation. Ability or knowledge was secondary to the size, reputation and indemnity capacity of the appraisal entity.

This mind-set typifies how banks sometimes fail to gather accurate data and information that relates to the real-world dynamics of collateral, which ultimately seriously compromises their ability to properly assess resolution strategies. In other words, in the example cited, covering themselves took precedence over understanding, relevance and competence. The first lesson about distressed debt I learned was that the credit appraisal system did not provide the bank with sufficient information to make accurate property-related calls, but they didn't worry too much as long as they had someone else they could blame.

Asian experience

In 1993 I moved to Asia, working with an international real estate consultancy that was transferring Western technology to Asian development companies. At this time, the easy property pickings of the 1980s were drying up, the markets were much more challenging and development companies did not know how to compete. Asia's dynamics were the same then as now; enormous appetite for change, held back by fear of ceding control to outsiders. By 1996, it was plainly obvious that the Asian real estate and capital markets were overheating and in trouble, with very similar conditions to the forces that are building up in 2011.

In the wake of the 1997 Asian crisis, I joined a US investment bank as part of their distressed real estate underwriting and servicing team. They possessed top-flight expertise in distressed debt, but didn't have any local knowledge. I was hired to fill in the gaps that they couldn't find solutions for from within the local real estate industry. They recognised that buying NPLs and profitably monetising them demands three things: in-depth experience, proven capability and specific local market knowledge, and anything less than three out of three didn't work.

Over the next few years, I worked in various Asian jurisdictions where we bought a number of NPL portfolios. Bank management changes or consolidation often occur after credit markets fail, which opens the door for new management or regulators to sell off loans, take the losses and move on with new business.

Bank capital structures and the regulatory environment were pretty much the same everywhere. NPLs devour precious bank capital, whilst regulators, rating agencies and shareholders detest them. If NPL ratios rise above their peer group, banks are viewed as sub-standard. If NPLs for the banking sector rise too high, investors get nervous about the economy as a whole. A general lack of confidence in dealing with NPLs and a prevailing attitude of treating them like toxic waste are at the heart of the bank arbitrage phenomenon. In my experience, banks tend to offload NPLs for the wrong reasons, which is when they give away the greatest value.

As Asia rebounded after the millennium, I transferred to the credit side, originating new loans collateralised by real estate. Very soon, it became clear that as long as my underwriting proposals were well presented, ticked all the boxes and had all the required support information, then the loan was approved. The box that was missing was 'is the real estate actually any good?'

It may have passed valuation requirements, but what were the prospects for getting all the money back in the event of default or market collapse?

Appraisal is undertaken at a given point in time, sometimes in different, historic market conditions, and is crystallised as a single number, which is insufficient for complete credit evaluation. There was no real system for understanding whether a piece of collateral would lose money, recover at par, or even make money for the bank in the event of downturn, default and liquidation. The credit world does not expect mass defaults to occur, and therefore does not have a reliable system for determining what the real collectability prospects are in distressed real-estate markets. This inadequacy shows up in the event of a major crash when a high volume of distressed collateral needs to be sold.

The inadequacy of banks when dealing with distressed loans

At this time I also got involved in loan servicing and work-out. I was shocked by the high returns we were able to make on distressed loans. I could not understand why the banks who sold them were not prepared to commit additional capital and resources to earn the same profits. The problem for the banks is a system that structurally disadvantages them from earning back on what they have previously loaned upon. They tend to lose confidence after a market crash, which prevents them from taking further risks with distressed assets. Taking real estate onto bank balance sheets is discouraged by regulators, is frowned upon by rating agencies and investors, and receives very poor capital treatment. Lending more money against defaulted assets is considered bad business.

An investor, on the other hand, is not a market crash victim, and is not suffering the shock of loss. After buying an asset at a discount, they are comfortable investing more risk capital in order to increase profits. Using a poker analogy, banks cannot double down. They are structurally and regulatory set up to fold too early and leave the game, on almost every hand. Investors, on the other side of the table, are happy to twist, draw or increase the stakes for as long as they can hold their nerve.

By now, I was fully versed in the immense profit potential available from distressed-debt investment and decided to completely focus on this business. The bank transferred me back to Europe and I took charge of my first loan work-out platform in a new jurisdiction. I was already aware of the deficiencies around liquidating real-estate collateral but what surprised me was how little we knew about the borrowers beyond the superficial information in loan files. By the time you got around to addressing this, the borrower has already had a head start in hiding assets and camouflaging their real situation. Credit officers are generally ineffectual when it comes to leaving information on file that will help work-out teams afterwards. The credit origination system devised by banks, whether it is collateral or borrower information, is just not geared up for the challenge of market correction.

Like most people, I originally never knew much about the distressed debt industry; I certainly never planned to enter it, and arrived there as a result of circumstance. My background is real estate; I was a chartered surveyor who became a banker. My talent was precision with property; where others hoped and guessed, to me it was always crystal clear. When I moved over to banking, this enabled me to price risk extremely accurately. My success with NPLs was built upon an immediate grasp and detailed understanding of distressed collateral markets anywhere in the world, and an instinctive ability to successfully and easily manage the toughest, trickiest and testing borrowers. The rules for NPLs are the same, whether it is in Asia, Europe or the Americas. Repeated challenge, practice and experience directly impact personal performance. The problem is that distressed debt is a cyclical business, so there are very few people with top-flight proficiency available when most needed.

Converting bank default waste into gold

In the following chapters, I will develop the theme of how investors convert bank default waste into gold. At times, it may look as if I am being highly critical of banks. If this appears to be the case to the reader, that is not my intention and no criticism is intended. The problem is a system that struggles with complete change in the tools, information, approach and strategy that are needed when the market cycle suddenly and abruptly turns the wrong way. The reality is that bank processes, decision-making structures, and indeed management and investment philosophies, are designed for making money in buoyant markets. Unfortunately, in downturn, the same characteristics together conspire to destroy value in distressed assets, as opposed to optimising it.

Distressed debt is different to banking and there is no reason why banks should be particularly good at something foreign to their normal operations. Prudent budget control and competitive pressure do not allow institutions to waste excessive resources on something that only comes around occasionally. Banks are in the credit business, not the debt collection business, and we should always remember that when we judge them.

John Michael Sheehan
September 2011

PART I

THE DISTRESSED DEBT PROBLEM

1. HOW DISTRESSED DEBT ESCALATES OUT OF CONTROL

The 2008 Western financial crisis exposed fundamental structural problems with the prevalent banking model, particularly in relation to the increase in the concentration of risk to real estate. Technology and innovation had run ahead of the underlying risk fundamentals that drove the core business. Mathematical models and statistics prevailed over experience and common sense. The combination of a cyclical real estate crash, loss of confidence and an economic downturn was too much for the financial system to handle.

Widespread devastation of Western bank balance sheets made the task of maximising non-performing loan recoveries harder than anything that the current generation of banks had ever had to deal with before. It occurred after a decade of new technology had rasied the power of information to hitherto unseen, almost mystical levels. The crisis unmasked the danger of relying solely on past trends and exposed the need for institutions to change focus from the *power of information* to the *power of interpretation* and thereby respond better to different conditions and unexpected events. Making sense of this fundamental shift is exactly the circumstances for which this book is written.

How banks traditionally handle bad loans

Under normal market conditions, banks expect 2% to 3% of their property loan book to become delinquent with a 75% to 95% recovery rate on their principal. This is readily absorbed through their normal earnings cycle without too much difficulty. Real estate collateral is normally fairly straightforward to liquidate and in a rising market it is possible for banks to make a full recovery. Bank business models are built on this expectation, with an assumption of low single digit GDP increases and moderate rates of real estate market growth. Ratings for banks and mortgage-backed securities use similarly conservative macro-projections, incorporating techniques like standard deviation and probability theory, which do not contemplate extreme market changes.

When a cycle turns and markets fail, outlier results can occur. Dependant upon the severity of the crash, as much as 10% to 50% of a bank loan book can be negatively impacted. In the more severe recessions, real estate may drop by 50% and GDP may contract by 5%. Consequently, income, debt service and collateral value crumble across the entire loan book. In the case of 2008, extremely high leverage, carried unknowingly through questionable structured finance products, unexpectedly pushed the extent of loan impairment levels to hitherto unimaginable levels.

Changes to bank loan books since 1980

Banks were originally perceived as originators of relatively safe loan assets, earning revenues on the spread between their short-term funding rates and their lending rates. In more recent years, this has changed, whereby banks originated and held riskier assets, in order to distribute them through securitised bonds to third parties and earn fees. Historically, real estate loans constituted a much smaller part of bank balance sheets. Since the 1980s this has been fundamentally shifting.

The bank business model, borrowing short and lending long, is not as efficient as the securities market in financing the lowest risk, blue chip public companies, and consequently bank's corporate loans business has been gradually eroded. In its place, many bank loan books and structured portfolios were taken over, and dominated by real estate loans that are highly cyclical in nature. In the US, for example, Federal Reserve data for 1980 shows real estate exposure as being 20% of bank assets. By 1990 this had increased to 30% and by the time the cycle peaked in 2008 mortgage-backed securities and real estate loans together surpassed 60% of bank assets.

The root of the problem is therefore less in the operational system but more in banks' increasingly high-risk concentration in real estate. Capital markets voraciously demand bank growth and, for some, the only way they could do this was by bringing more real estate onto their balance sheets. Regulatory changes in the 1990s allowed banks to grow their loan book with minimal additional capital and carry real estate in structured securities that camouflaged the full extent of their exposure to the sector. Additional negative downdraft in 2008, as a result of valuable collateralised securities being marked to market at zero under the prevailing accounting rules, was for some institutions the final straw that broke the camel's back. The banking industry has been established on long-held loan-and-hold-to-maturity principles and mark-to-market really has no place on their balance sheets.

Real estate cycles

In the past, the principal of making high loan-to-value long-term loans generally worked well because real estate always went up and never fell in value. This has now been exposed as a myth by repeated property crashes. Some institutions blame the market, but it is the banks that knowingly drive and inflate the market through the provision of liquidity. When they pump up the market they improve the debt coverage on existing underwritten loans, but they are unable to recognise the stage at which their actions become self-defeating. The more they lend, the more they increase the amplitude of boom and burst cycles. At a certain point, adding further market liquidity stokes price inflation that exponentially increases downside risk for their loan book.

Real estate risk is lowest at the beginning of a property cycle and highest at the top, which usually coincides with the time when everyone has greatest market confidence. Banks follow the crowd, approaching risk the wrong way, and as long as government and regulators choose to ignore asset prices there is no reason why this approach should be frowned upon.

As a result, banks end up charging most when risk is lowest and least when risk is highest. When the competition for growth gets tougher, they increasingly take bigger risks at a lower margin. Benchmarks like the ratio of wage rises to property prices are overlooked, so banks end up lending more to people when they can least afford it. Loan-to-value percentages should in theory be gradually lowered as property prices rise, but in reality the opposite happens, thereby reducing the credit quality of loans. Confidence eventually outweighs caution.

For some financial institutions, extreme capital markets performance pressure effectively forced them to trust that the property market would keep rising indefinitely. They reassured themselves that when correction came it would develop slowly and manifest itself clearly in advance, waving a big red warning flag. Every crash in the past 30 years has been characterised by those with most to lose loudly proclaiming that there will be a *soft landing*, but there never is. They are wrong every time. If market growth in the decade prior to 2008 was spectacular, the inevitable correction was equally brutal.

Globalisation, rather than diversifying risk, unwittingly increased risk exposure further, where banks from one jurisdiction were exposed to the negative real-estate cycles of another; for instance European banks and the US sub-prime market. The cumulative effect of all these factors was an unprecedented Western debt overhang that will take many years to resolve, with emerging markets bracing themselves for their turn in an endless, contagious, global merry-go-round.

Problematic high volumes of distressed debt

Banks are the financial lifeblood of economies – over the course of modern history they have come to be regarded as a pillar of the financial system and *guardians of risk*. Whilst loan impairment is an inherent risk in a credit-originating environment, the concepts of credit mispricing, underwriting errors or bad judgement do not fit in with the prudent, carefully risk-managed image that institutions choose to cultivate. Distressed debt is their *dirty laundry*. NPLs are understandably resolved quietly and privately, with public disclosure limited to the small print in annual reports. Given NPL resolution is normally a tiny part of a bank's earnings activity, budgeted resources for work-out are minimal and work-out is usually carried out at a relatively junior level.

Individual bank NPL ratios are carefully studied by investors and analysts in order to compare the institution against its peer group. A high NPL ratio would suggest less credit competence by comparison with a competitor with a lower ratio. Central banks also quote sectoral NPL ratios, as a means of demonstrating the soundness of their financial system and, by association, the economy as a whole.

So, given that resolving NPLs is a normal activity in banks, why are high volumes of distressed debt such a problem for the banking industry? Let's use an analogy of a car manufacturer's mass production plant.

A manufacturing analogy

Under normal circumstances, our car manufacturer's plant functions efficiently and profitably, utilising a state of the art production line, high quality control, and an expert sales and dealership distribution network. A few cars are defective every month, in which case a special task force sells them off, without warranty, at a local auction. By and large, this deficiency system works well and in most cases the manufacturer can recover his material costs on defective vehicles, even though he doesn't make a profit.

Suddenly, the manufacturer is confronted with a massive defects problem affecting most of his inventory. This coincides with a market downturn, whereby his sales pipeline completely evaporates. The recovery task force is overwhelmed, to the extent that they have no idea where to start, or what to prioritise. Auctioning or selling off such a high volume of inventory in one go will result in the realisation of scrap or salvage value for the defective vehicles, and given that everyone else is in trouble at the same time, the manufacturer will end up receiving next to nothing.

Meanwhile, his production line has ground to a halt, the market for new cars has collapsed and his distribution network is redundant. All he can do is store the flawed vehicles on an adjacent vacant land plot in order to keep them out of the way, knowing that every day they sit there they are deteriorating, becoming more obsolete and their value is falling.

The manufacture appreciates that until he shifts his defective inventory, he cannot get back to focusing all his resources on the business of profit-generating mass car production again. The easiest way of maximising recovery and avoiding a huge fire-sale loss is to sell or auction off cars individually over an extended period of time. This is slow and cumbersome, but makes financial sense. It can be embarked upon instantly and is relatively easy to manage and monitor on the adjacent, vacant plot.

The manufacturer also realises that there are other options besides auction that are capable of producing higher recoveries. Some cars can be repaired or remodelled with a small amount of modification. Some are capable of being sold to competitors, if adjustments are made and labelling is changed. Others can be exported and sold in new, previously untried markets. For some models, the best price will be achieved by dismantling the vehicles and selling the spare parts whilst, for a few, the only realistic option is scrap or salvage.

The problem facing the manufacturer is that his workforce has only a limited idea and no experience of how to execute these alternative strategies. They are trained in working as teams to put cars together on a mass production line, following strict processes and procedures, but have never been taught how to remodel, repair or dismantle cars. Even if they tried, would they risk damaging parts by dismantling vehicles in the wrong order? Would they be sure of choosing the right strategy to resolve a particular model? Even if they get this right, the current distribution and sales support network is neither capable, nor properly resourced, to effectively support these new activities.

What is more, in order to undertake this exercise properly, he would need to make adjustments to his current manufacturing line that will require additional capital expenditure. Does he really want to do that and, if he does, will that handicap him in the event the market rebounds and he finds that part of his production line is tied up and prevented from responding fully to reawakened demand for his core products?

The crux of the bank problem

The problems facing banks in a bear market are similar to those outlined above for our car manufacturer. Distressed debt *contagion* usually follows a similar pattern. After a market crash, demand for new loans declines sharply. In its place is an urgent need for specialist debt collection execution, in response to a growing need to resolve high quantities of NPLs. At a later stage, when deleveraging peaks, and credit markets rebound and return to growth, the need for specialist operations gradually weakens and debt collection is ultimately absorbed back into mainstream credit operations.

As the need for wide-scale debt collection fades, so most NPL professionals or special servicers either retire, or find something else to do. By the time the cycle has revolved and a new crash occurs, there is hardly anyone left in the local credit markets with any experience of downturn that understands the business of resolving overwhelming volumes of delinquent loans. On top of this, the distressed debt industry constantly changes in response to advances made possible by computer technology and more complex debt securities.

Once recession takes hold, banks discover that the collection business is complicated, time-consuming and completely different to the prevailing bank marketing and distribution model. Banks are not geared up to be debt collectors and there are very few people around who really know what to do. Not only is there a huge shortfall in distressed debt proficiency within institutions, but also in all the associated and support competencies necessary to maximise monetisation of bad debts.

The idea that a bank can suddenly and dramatically switch its resources from *good bank* activities and become a successful *bad bank* is simplistic and naive. Top-flight distressed debt resolution is highly entrepreneurial but banks are not. Most in-house work-out divisions adopt a safe and systematic style, with a moderate collection performance, a bit like the car manufacturer analogy, slowly and steadily selling off inventory, one by one, from a vacant plot.

The difference between normal market conditions and conditions after a crash

In normal market conditions performing loans follow similar trends, usually based on the principle that the underlying collateral will be worth the same or more tomorrow. As a result, borrowers are highly predictable and, under these circumstances, banks' pooling of loans and taking a broad, generalised view of loan books makes sense. Distressed loans are the opposite, which is a constantly recurring theme in this book.

A quotation from the Russian writer, Leo Tolstoy, is particularly pertinent to this situation: "all happy families resemble one another, every unhappy family is unhappy in its own way." The message that we can take from this is that banks should not treat performing borrowers in the same way as delinquent borrowers. Each one is unique and should be managed according to their individual debt circumstances and their particular motivation in order to optimise recovery from their case.

The history of financial crises shows that the response by financial institutions, and particularly government, most influences the speed and strength of market upturn. Assets need to either be recycled or sold in order to lay the ground for market recovery. If this happens though, balance sheets will deteriorate further at a time when banks can least afford it. Not only will auctioned assets exacerbate bank losses, as a result of a collapsed market, but the more distressed assets that are sold, the more real estate values will continue to slide downwards. On top of this, most banks have neither sufficient resources nor experience to optimise recovery in terms of maximising prices, exploiting opportunity and retaining future upside.

The end result for the bank is a vicious, downward cycle of continuing capital destruction, with vast sums of money wasted through lack of experience, misunderstanding and indecision.

2. WHY BANKS FAIL TO MAXIMISE DISTRESSED COLLECTIONS

After a market crash, a high percentage of a bank's loan book may be impaired. In many jurisdictions, the provision of these loan books is unregulated. Rules and regulations vary in different countries, and even the term *non-performing loan* has different meanings around the world. Standardised classifications are applied to delinquent loans, but generally it is up to the individual institution to judge and calculate its exact provisioning needs.

The bank's main priority is then preserving capital and avoiding hits to its profit and loss account. Faced with sudden losses, negative headlines and a battle for survival, it is understandable that banks adopt a safe, low-risk, defensive posture. Confronted with the choice of either selling off the loan book at a deep wholesale discount or holding it and working through loans on an individual basis, most banks will favour the latter. The work-out exercise will then also be driven by saving cost, accountability and choosing the least expensive resolution strategy. As a result, the primary objective for most banks in loan work-out is to pursue low-risk strategies that minimise and delay loss recognition.

Generally, performance levels vary substantially amongst different work-out and debt monetisation entities. Some collection units seem to be able to consistently outperform their peers. It is not uncommon, for example, to find a situation where a bank's internal work-out department struggles to achieve, say, 70 cents on the dollar resolving a particular loan. Later, when the same loan is sold to a third-party investor, they eventually manage to resolve the loan at par, or even above.

Reasons why distressed debt resolution performance is variable

There are a number of possible causes, or combinations of reasons, why distressed debt resolution performance is so variable. These include:

1. Mispricing habits
2. Distressed debt fatigue
3. Communication breakdown
4. Strategic approach and rationale for servicing
5. Technical and organisational competence
6. Institutional philosophy
7. Alignment, motivation and remuneration

1. Mispricing habits

In the first instance, banks get into trouble through the mispricing of loans. They do this by providing too high advance rates, demanding too little debt service, offering too long a term, and accepting poor covenants and poor security. This occurs because of competitive peer pressure. If banks do not respond to aggressive, new initiatives by their opponents, they are left behind and criticised. If they compete on ever more risky enterprises ultimately a correction and collapse will occur, for which once again they are criticised. They are in a no-win situation, an issue that threatens to be repeated in every new cycle, unless the system or regulations are fundamentally altered.

However, mispricing can become a habit and once a loan goes bad banks tend to misprice collections too. After a market crash, banks particularly seem to struggle to come to terms with new pricing levels. Maybe it is a case of institutional resistance to change, or just unwillingness to accept new paradigms that erode capital. For whatever reason, delays in recognising new market realities cost time, neglect opportunity and therefore lose money.

Flawed and outdated valuation estimates

Bank collateral valuation estimates are frequently wrong and tend to be driven by past outdated appraisals. This can be particularly inaccurate in a sliding market, like the one shown in Figure 2.1.

Figure 2.1 – the effect of real estate valuation timing on loan pricing in a falling market

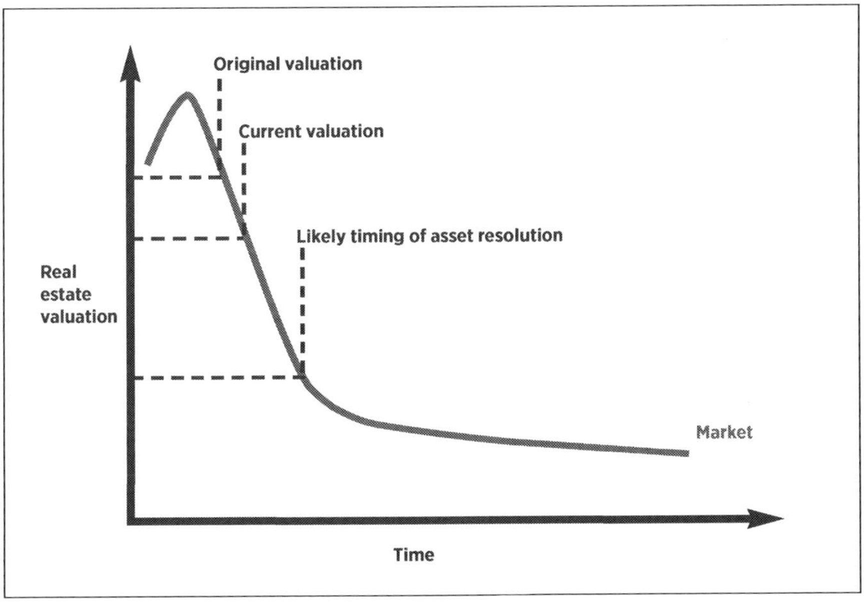

Since property appraisal is historic, in a sliding market, rather than adjust values downwards, most banks continue to adopt their last appraisal result. This can create a double problem where property is marked at an unrealistically high historic price with likely resolution timing occurring somewhere in the future, by which time prices will have fallen considerably further. Investors, or the market at large, will, on the other hand, likely mark the property to where the correct level should be. On top of this, when it comes to negotiating with potential buyers, not only do banks use the wrong collateral price but they tend not to apply the correct market discount rates either.

Concentration risk

Real estate concentration risk is a serious issue that credit professionals are understandably concerned about. Whether banks approach real estate concentration correctly when they are determining credit risk is another matter and not the subject of this book. As far as NPLs are concerned, concentration risk is a huge problem, which drives down collateral prices exponentially. Problems resulting from over-concentration are multiplied many fold when loan books turn delinquent. Liquidating a difficult property in a bad market is particularly challenging. Liquidating many of them can be extremely demoralising. When resolving distressed portfolios, this issue needs to be factored into resolution strategy plans and clearly reflected in pricing adjustments, but it rarely is.

Concentrating delinquent loan recovery through early enforcement and asset sale is a favoured approach by many bank work-out teams. They may not spend enough time on alternative strategies, or giving the borrower either the time or the opportunity to offer other solutions. The shift from relationship balance sheet lending to pooled structured lending has driven professionals and borrowers further apart, thereby limiting communication and potentially further handicapping resolution options. Works-out units are generally just too closely orientated towards legal resolutions.

Execution is a safe option that is easily tracked and monitored within a pipeline process. It can neither be legally challenged nor criticised, either at the officer or institutional level. It also avoids the need to pursue more risky strategies or increase operational costs that may produce higher recoveries. Creativity, new ventures and entrepreneurial approaches are taboo. As a result, banks run the risk of resolving their better collateralised NPLs too early at cheaper prices. They also do not spend enough time exploring or researching the tougher loan cases, which reduces their choices and limits collections.

Negotiated resolutions reduce collection leakage

In order to minimise collection leakage, banks need to put more emphasis on negotiated resolutions. For loans that can be revived or assets with upside, they need to consider finding new private equity partners who can put in further cash. Instead of shunning risk, banks should use what they have learned from the crash to accurately price new equity risk. For liquidation properties, in volatile or sliding markets, they should consider cryonic-type solutions, where real estate can be held in trust with levered real estate companies, which can be monetised later when markets rebound.

2. Distressed debt fatigue

In a boom market, banks are full of confidence, feted by investors and looked up to with respect. Graduates from the best schools queue to join them. When a major crash occurs, they can suddenly and dramatically go from being the darlings of the markets to the fall guys; from winners to losers. Politicians and the media have publicly and loudly blamed them for the 2008 crisis. Whether this is deserved or not is another debate, but the banks have subsequently been portrayed as financial pariahs.

Bank reactions to adverse public opinion

When public opinion is adverse, usually the best thing to do is to keep a low profile. After the shock of crash, fear of additional public criticism will likely drive banks to adopt a chastened, rational approach which of course includes debt work-out. However, it is the triumph of irrationality over rationality that normally causes market crashes and gets banks into trouble. Rather than harness similar alternative approaches and forces to boost recoveries, they tend to become introverted, go completely the other way, and overlook anything that might attract attention. The exuberant irrationality that caused the problem in the first instance is completely avoided and a conservative, safety-first culture takes over.

From this point forwards, typical human behaviour patterns as identified by behavioural science kick in. The banks' first response is fear: fear of making further embarrassing mistakes and fear of exacerbating existing deficits. Loss aversion is a widely debated field of behavioural economics. How appropriate it is to apply this to banks is conjecture, but is very clear from history that the first reaction to crisis for many institutions is to avoid selling assets at a discount so that they do not have to recognise an early loss on their balance sheets. Banks may also try to avoid restructuring loans and converting debt to equity, as this would both crystallise a loss and result in a higher capital charge against the new equity stake. This would adversely pressure their capital ratios at a time of weakness and capital famine.

When loans are performing, banks only need to hold a small amount of capital in reserve against loan losses expected during the normal course of business. This leaves the vast remainder of their capital free for additional loan-based revenue. At the other extreme, defaulted loan provisioning is a double whammy for banks. The significant amount of increased capital that is provisioned against a recognised loan deficit is not only tied up covering the shortfall, but they can no longer earn lending revenue from that same amount of cash.

The ambiguous loophole for the bank is that they are generally allowed to exercise their own judgement in determining how much capital is required to provision against a given loan. How they calculate this also varies in different jurisdictions. Collateral, for example, can be used to offset losses in some jurisdictions, in which case the lender can benefit substantially from overstated, unrealistic collateral valuations and mispricing.

Holding out until the point of capitulation is reached

Due to the rules for risk weighting and treatment for holding assets, institutions are structurally incentivised to hold out as long as they can before they recognise default. They are much better off keeping loans *alive* and holding the assets in the short-term in the hope of an early rebound, which hopefully will prevent pointless balance sheet damage. Under these circumstances, selling early to an investor or actioning enforcement proceedings would be disruptive. Whilst this is all playing out, the bank will be uncertain about which direction to move in and is therefore not motivated to do very much in terms of enhancing asset value or investing to improve future monetisation prospects for legacy loans.

Eventually though, in many cases, the bank's attitude changes. This could be due to any number of events or situations including, for example:

- Realisation that recession will drag on for longer than expected and the chances of an early rebound are evaporating.
- A brief upturn appears that gives optimism for selling distressed assets at a slightly higher price.
- A change occurs in top management, who want to sell off bad assets and move on.
- Further collapses in market prices cause the institution to sell bad assets in order to reassure investors, the markets or rating agencies.

For whatever reason, a point of capitulation arises that overcomes the fear of loss and distressed debt fatigue sets in. Losing money on the sale of assets somehow becomes more palatable after a respectable period of time has passed and people's memories fade. Once this occurs, banks seem to turn completely against the same assets that they were so keen to hold immediately after crisis. Asset management then recedes further into the background, defaulted borrowers are given less attention and collection discipline slackens. Asset sheltering turns to asset resentment and the overriding tendency is to want to get rid of bad loans as quickly as possible, like *hot potatoes*.

The worst thing that can then occur is lemming behaviour whereby a number of competing institutions capitulate on holding assets and follow one another to sell their loan books in a short period of time. The resultant sudden increased supply has the effect of driving down market prices further and merely serves to boost buyers' upside.

This is the instant that the patient, wily, distressed investor is waiting for; the moment when the selling bank is prepared to forgo financial benefit, discount out and hand over the upside. The new owner will then of course enhance the value with creativity, additional investment and more rigorous enforcement, and they will pocket the benefit.

3. Communication breakdown

Institutions have been criticised in recent years for depersonalising the credit process, whereby credit decisions are made according to scoring matrices, removed from personal judgement, involving minimal communication with the borrower. In the past decade there has been a growing shift away from judgement-based credit calls to data-based decision making. Some commentators consider this to be a major contributor to the scale of the 2008 crisis and clamour for a return to a more traditional approach to credit risk-taking, based on closer communication with borrowers and greater professional judgement from credit officers.

A parallel theme in this book is the necessity to communicate closely with debtors as individuals and to exercise personal judgement when making debt strategy decisions in order to maximise collections. Institutions that have previously contributed to their own demise by depersonalising the credit process can now also debilitate their own recovery by following a similar impersonal, bureaucratic approach to the distressed debt collections process.

4. Strategic approach and rationale for servicing

If a bank work-out division perceives its function as a processing unit cleaning up a mess, it will likely take a one-dimensional view of the collection, based on the history of the loan. As a result of the shackles of past experience, they are unlikely to detach themselves from the original lending decision and consider new directions and fresh solutions. Units directed by a good bank parent to adopt a particular stance with a debtor, in order to retain a positive customer relationship, are particularly handicapped in their ability to maximise collections.

NPL activities are given little attention and little budget

Many banks understandably tend to view their NPL work-out departments as a fringe area of the main business. This is then reflected in limitations in top management attention and low budget allocation. Given the choice between increasing budgets to expand or improve mainstream operations against increasing expenditure for more effective or creative NPL work-out, core profit-generating activities will prevail. Investing additional speculative cash into distressed assets in order to maximise returns is a difficult decision to approve and is generally viewed as placing good money after bad, even if it may have commercial merit. Bank NPL work-out departments are expected to operate on a minimalist budget and gradually reduce their costs as more loans are resolved.

This limited approach to work-out is sometimes highlighted when banks consider outsourcing collections to loan servicers. Generally, third-party servicers cost more than internal work-out divisions. Independent servicers will usually recruit suitably qualified specialists, effective in maximising performance within every skill-set division of the work-out process. This means that they are more likely to fully resource the different expertise required for optimising collections. If a bank work-out department is significantly cheaper, it usually means it is under-resourced. This is a case of paying for what you get and lower budgets are reflected in a corresponding reduction in collection performance.

Government involvement in NPLs

Government-sponsored asset management entities usually get involved in NPLs in order to restore order to a particularly chaotic situation, or in response to the need to demonstrate public accountability as a result of taxpayer bail-outs. They are usually newly set up, with no previous experience of servicing, and they report to civil servants. Officers with previous NPL experience may be recruited, but generally the bulk of their hiring is sourced from local credit markets where few people, if any, have any experience of dealing with distressed debt.

Historically, the principle of nationalising commercial problems or enterprises under the control of the civil service is not a good formula for achieving maximum efficiency or return on investment. Public entities are driven by accountability and are not geared up for creative profit generation. The commercial issue to be considered is that if banks cannot maximise recovery, what can government agencies do any better, given they are also one step further removed from the loan and the borrower? Past experience would suggest that government sponsored entities perform best either as regulators or overseers of bank work-out divisions, with commercial involvement limited to facilitating outright sale of NPL portfolios at the wholesale level to third-party investors.

NPL investors – speculating to increase returns

NPL investors, at the other extreme, exist to make as much money as possible from an investment and mispriced risk is their mantra. The structural and regulatory environment within which banks operate controls their ability to move away from narrow pricing guidelines. Investors are the opposite; for them, the fundamental notion of a loan is that it may be re-priced. There is no greater concept in the world of distressed finance than the ability to re-price a fixed-income debt instrument into an ownership instrument, thereby removing the cap on returns and allowing unlimited upside.

Buying portfolios of assets demands excellent administrative skills and the discipline to follow solid processes and procedures. Otherwise, successful distressed debt investment is a mixture of common sense, a strong risk appetite and an eye for opportunity. Repositioning and refinancing assets is central to the opportunistic investor's philosophy, and pocketing all the upside is their reward. Purchasing assets at a discount sometimes provides the opportunity to fully finance out their position. Taking out their investment basis enables them to convert all the upside into pure equity and effectively creates an infinite return on their investment.

Whereas the primary objective for most banks in loan work-out is to pursue low-risk strategies that minimise loss, NPL investors are prepared to invest and speculate as much as they think they need in order to increase returns. The words of John D. Rockefeller are particularly appropriate: "I always try to turn disaster into opportunity," he said. By nature investors are creative, aggressive and entrepreneurial. They view everything as a money-making opportunity which is generally reflected in higher collection results.

5. Technical and organisational competence

The credit process

The normal credit process typically follows an integrated cohesive process, held together and centred on a loan agreement, with a security charge over the collateral, as illustrated in Figure 2.2.

Figure 2.2 – the normal credit process

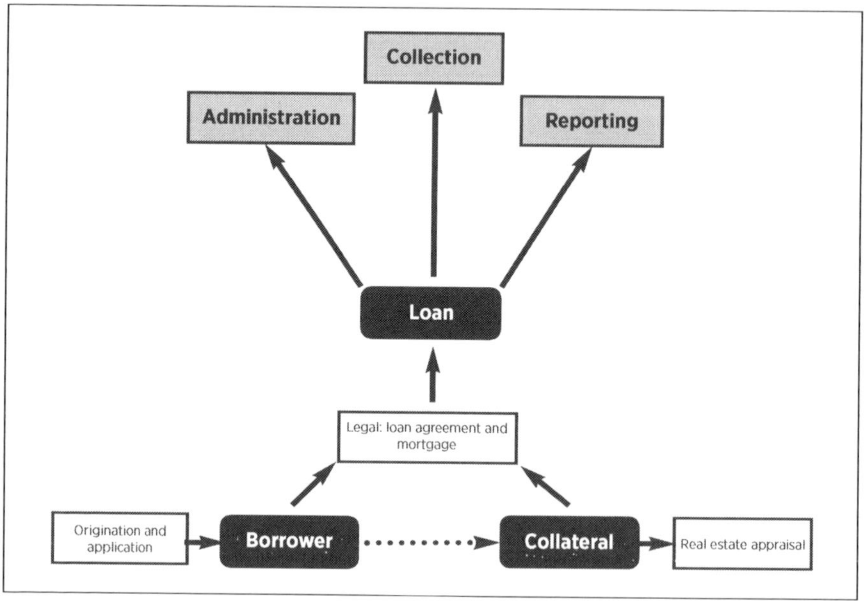

Simplicity, *cookie-cutter* repeats, predictability and low volatility make the perfect environment for the performing loan model to flourish in. The more that the principle of *one size fits all* can be followed, the greater efficiency will be and the higher the margin for the lender.

The NPL work-out process

NPL work-out, on the other hand, is a tough, unpredictable and a much more complicated business. Maximising recovery demands a simultaneous high standard of application across a far wider range of technical skills. Achieving this consistently in all skill sets at the same time is challenging. Metrics are difficult and oversight is an issue. It is not easy to find managing executives with a sufficiently broad range of diverse skill sets to cover all areas of operations and support functions that can drive performance throughout the organisation at an optimum level.

A further operational complication is that the requisite core skill sets for work-out are unrelated to one another. Taking the finance, legal and real estate fields as an example, they do not provide each other with mutual support and can only be linked in a linear rather than a modular fashion within an organisation.

When disparate skills compete with one another within a business unit the risk of inefficiency and miscommunication are high. A work-out unit can even make what appears to be a solid level of collection with deficiency or even absence of some functions. For example, servicing can appear to be operating perfectly well without, say, intelligence-gathering resources or with sub-standard property management resources, without anyone realising that the shortcomings are causing them to miss out on additional collections.

Compare the flowchart in Figure 2.3, illustrating the complications involved in the work-out process for a defaulted loan, with the flowchart in Figure 2.2, showing the typical performing loan process.

Figure 2.3 – the complications in the work-out process for NPLs

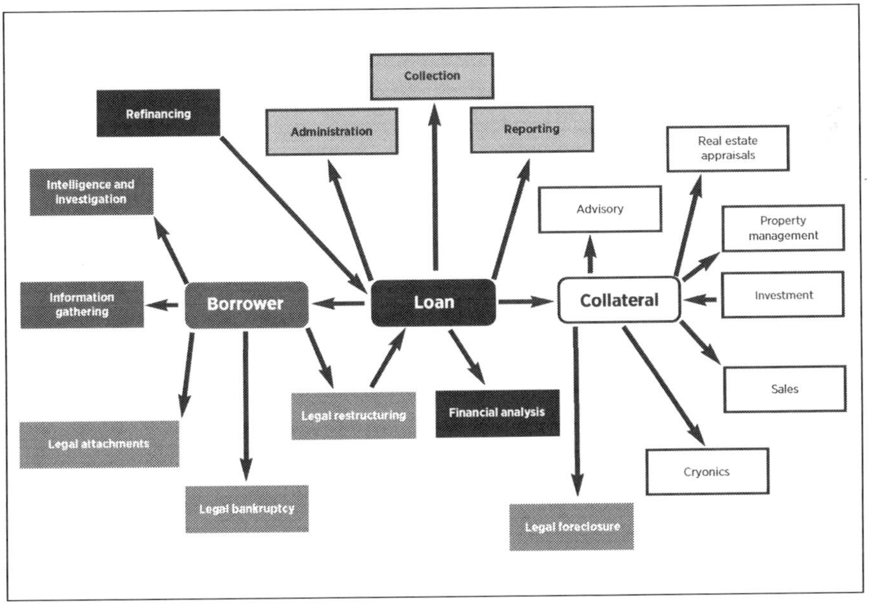

Figure 2.3 has many more disparate strands and tentacles by comparison with the performing loan model. The only common part is the need to administrate, collect and report on the loan. Implementing such a complex process flow like this, linked in such a brittle linear structure, at short notice, is extraordinarily challenging.

Collection performance is also driven by the accomplishments of third-party outsourced resources, whose execution standards can be extremely variable. As in any field of human endeavour, left unattended, people tend to cut corners and take the easiest and softest option. Monitoring and motivating third parties is therefore critically important, albeit extremely time consuming.

In order to be sure of optimising performance, at times servicers may need to set up in-house divisions in order to supplement or replace outsourced functions that fall short of their needs, either on a short or long-term basis. For example, in-house marketing or real estate brokerage functions. If servicers cannot set up their own property marketing division, or are precluded through budget constraints, as may occur within some work-out units, this can also limit collections.

So far, we have only illustrated procedures and functions. Outlining a process is one thing; applying it successfully is another.

6. Institutional philosophy

Institutional philosophy is governed by the following attributes:

1. **Culture**: Whether the recovery unit and asset managers within it are encouraged and motivated to view recoveries as a bureaucratic or administrative process, or an entrepreneurial opportunity.
2. **Approach**: Whether profit and collecting every last penny is the main objective or whether cleaning up a balance sheet by removing non-performing loans in an efficient and timely manner takes priority.
3. **Systems**: Whether systems are primarily focused on records, accountability and reporting only, or have the capacity to ensure that asset managers have tried every possible alternative to exploit collection opportunity options.
4. **Controls**: Whether the decision-making system allows or promotes initiative and creativity, or stifles it.

If a good bank fails to adapt all of these attributes sufficiently within its loan distribution structure it will almost certainly result in lower NPL collections.

Managing change is a fundamental challenge, not just in terms of institutional philosophy, but also due to a constantly fluid operating environment. Adjustments are required in economic, commercial and market conditions, allied to the need to transform strategies and core working practice. One of the biggest difficulties for banks planning to set up bad banks is one of culture and approach that is not geared up for unstable, volatile and hostile market conditions.

Human factors in performing loans

Figure 2.4 shows how the involvement of human factors varies throughout the life of a performing loan. Different roles and functions within a credit institution demand differing levels of innovation and creativity at one extreme, whilst other functions are totally process driven with no initiative. The left-hand line shows the varying influence of human factors. The line at the bottom traces a loan through marketing, origination into processing, and ultimately maturity.

Figure 2.4 – human factors in the life cycle of a performing loan

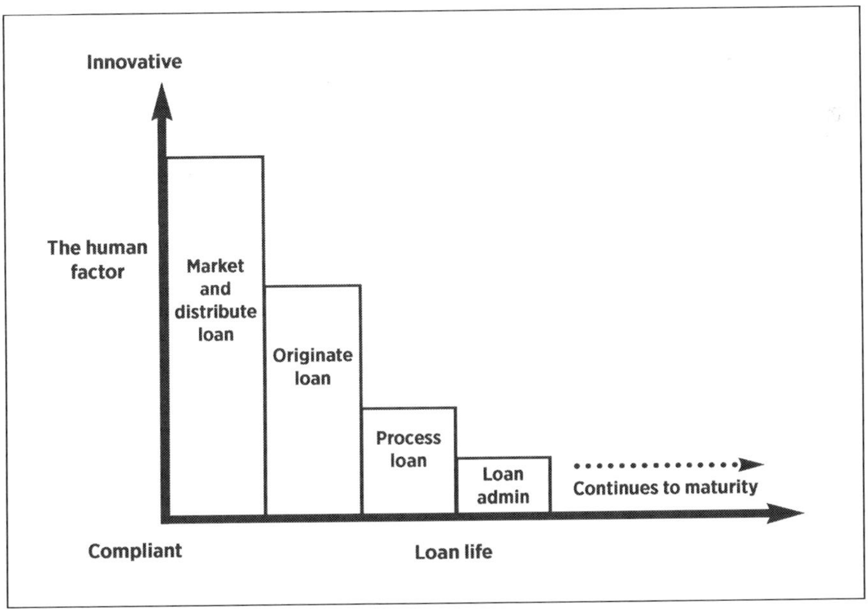

The traditional good bank distribution model benefits from a certain amount of initiative, particularly at the marketing and origination stages of a loan. Thereafter, the system is geared towards strict procedures and systems. Initiative, if any, is restricted to technical issues only. This attitude prevails through to maturity of a performing loan.

Human factors in a NPL

Once a loan defaults, the lender's situation fundamentally changes, even though the system is still locked into a normal passive compliant position. Staff within a financial institution are trained and accustomed to operating within this environment. However, if the passive compliant stance is continued going forwards, the chance of maximising debt collection is minimal at best. What is more, the passive work-out unit may have no idea on how much opportunity it may be missing out on. Figure 2.5 shows how the involvement of human factors varies throughout the life of a NPL.

Figure 2.5 – human factors in the life cycle of a non-performing loan

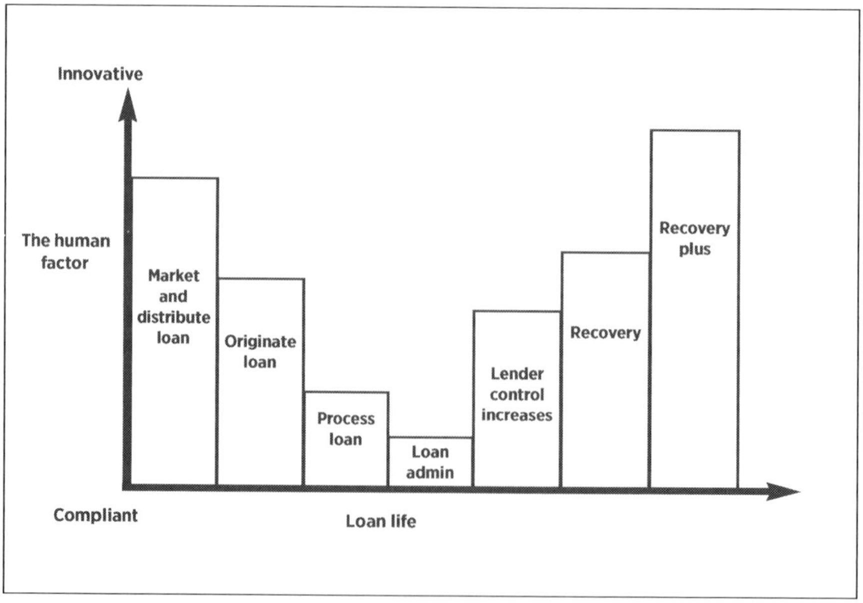

Immediately upon default, the lender needs to take control of the situation. Thereafter, the level of cash recovery will generally be dictated by the levels of initiative shown by asset managers. The greater the initiative, the higher the potential collection will be. *Recovery plus* demands top-flight asset management skills, communication and entrepreneurship.

A change in culture and approach is required

Maximising recovery therefore requires a radical change in culture and approach, and institutions trapped in the passive compliant groove will have difficulty transitioning successfully. It may be that the servicing entity is deeply rooted in a performing credit approach and may be unable to change. Some organisations may not see the need to change from an institutionalised approach. Government-sponsored or owned asset management entities, with an overriding need for transparency and public accountability, staffed by civil servants, may not want nor wish to change at all. Unless servicing entities can break the commercial side of their operations free from an institutional good bank culture they will generally struggle to maximise recoveries.

Computer technology has tended to foster an even more procedurally driven approach to the credit process. The introduction of structured lending, in place of traditional relationship lending, has further prioritised the requirement for rigid, impersonal, systemic compliance over individual innovation in loan origination.

An institutionalised approach to collections tends to be endorsed by rating agencies. Asset manager rating score cards are based on categories such as:

- Shareholding structure
- Experience
- Asset structure
- Corporate governance
- Risk management and controls
- Compliance
- Decision making process
- Investment administration
- Technology and data management

Resolution success is not part of the rating process. Subjects such as competitive commercial skills, incentivisation, collection innovation and adaptability, performance training, debt collection efficiency and, most importantly, cents on the dollar collection performance are generally omitted from their analysis.

Third-party servicers also tend to advertise an institutionalised approach to collections. Asset management and administrative systems are likely to be given promotional prominence over bottom line debt collection performance numbers. The primary focus tends to be on issues such as loan surveillance, stability, controls, procedures and disaster recovery.

Performance is correlated to experience. Training tends to comprise methodologies, procedures, compliance, market trends and property management. Individual collection performance skills generally do not get mentioned. This traditional approach to NPL servicing is likely to be insufficient in the future, and there is likely to be much more emphasis, both for organisations and individuals, on the need to excel at bottom line cents on the dollar collection performance. The challenge for servicers is to demonstrate a robust, institutional image to potential banking clients, whilst proactively pursuing innovative and alternative collection strategies that creatively improve collection results.

7. Alignment, motivation and remuneration

Aligned economics and incentives are critical to maximising debt recoveries. Servicers and asset managers, whether in-house or outsourced, need to be fully aligned with lenders in order to maximise debt collections. Principals and servicers must have a mutual understanding of shifting situations and market conditions, in order to be able to adapt promptly and successfully to changing circumstances. Maximum recovery should mostly take precedent over speed. All members of a servicing entity, including asset managers and support staff, should be incentivised to always collect every last penny.

Motivation and incentivisation is a cornerstone of modern life, more so than ever before, as communication technology has increased public awareness and narrowed the information gulf with experts and leaders. Fully identifying and understanding the key drivers between actions and incentives is critical to commercial success in most businesses. This is complex and challenging generally, but more so for distressed debt, where incentivisation drivers may change during the life of loan portfolio work-outs as business gradually diminishes and winds down.

Incentivising asset managers

There is no point in paying asset managers high basic salaries that are not performance-linked. If this occurs, there is no incentive to either monetise in a timely manner or achieve top dollar. Indeed, there is every motivation to stretch the job out as long as possible, irrespective of results. Servicer payment should also be structured in a way that avoids the risk of liquidating too hastily at fire-sale prices. Asset manager compensation must clearly and obviously reward highest recovery, primarily, and quickest recovery secondly.

The problem then facing the successful asset manager is that if they are not prepared to move jurisdictions, they will have a short career with uncertain job prospects at the end of the monetisation process. This has similarities with the careers of professional sportspeople, which also tend to be short with uncertainty afterwards. The obvious and most workable solution to this issue is to pay significantly above market, performance-linked compensation packages, higher than is available elsewhere in the banking world. *Golden handshakes*, payable after a given period of time, can also help retain staff, but do not contribute towards motivating ongoing, high, collection performance.

Salary caps in accordance with grades or experience kill incentivisation for asset managers to maximise collections. Compensation can be a major stumbling block for government owned or sponsored entities, where pay scales are benchmarked or compared with other civil servants, and is a further reason why government entities may struggle to recruit sufficient quality that would enable them to maximise NPL performance.

Aligning risk and reward

Outsourced servicing contracts are often structured on a *cost plus* remuneration basis. This means that all the overheads of the entity are covered and, in addition, the servicer is paid a fee based on all monthly collections. This is weak alignment. Before we even consider aligning risk and reward, we need to be clear on what exactly is meant by *cost*.

Cost for one party may have a completely different worth for the other. Take the case of end of year bonuses – the servicer may want to give asset managers good bonuses, in order to reward their efforts in setting up a new platform, whilst the investor may feel that they are still in negative cash flow territory and does not want to increase costs further until their investment turns positive.

Servicer base costs are best linked to a mutually agreed *loan valuation level*. Servicers only add value once collections exceed loan valuation level. If loan valuation is acceptable for recovery then servicers are not needed and collections could be handled by lawyers. Alignment is optimised if servicers' cost of overhead is linked to loan valuation level, whereby they only receive incentive fees if collection exceeds this level. Increasing collection fees proportionally above this level ensures that the servicer is fully aligned in maximising collections. Remunerating asset managers in parallel with this is also good alignment.

Choosing the wrong reward

Some investors try to incentivise servicers on an IRR-linked basis, as this aligns the servicer with investment risk. The problem with this approach is complication in calculation and confusion over objectives, which are multiplied if there are several servicers and many asset managers involved in one investment. Incentivisation at the investor levels risks reducing individual asset manager commissions to the mean asset management entity level, whereby the better performers are paid the same as the weaker performers.

Servicing and investing involve different mind-sets. Investors make returns on money. Asset managers squeeze the maximum amount from reluctant borrowers and are best remunerated on an individual basis, relative to their own collection performance. Compensating two such vastly different approaches to performance in the same way when they have such different metrics makes no sense. Investors who pass this issue off as a servicer problem are fooling themselves. Computing and keeping track of IRRs on an ongoing basis at the company or group level distracts the asset managers from maximising collection at the loan level. This is a case of avoiding confusion, maintaining focus on collections and keeping it simple.

Summary

Except for dedicated international loan servicers, distressed debt is an atypical business model. It is intrinsically different to the majority of other businesses or industries. The normal commercial approach is to create a profitable business that grows in the expectation of increasing returns every year: shareholders and employees usually take a long-term view of the future; owners and managers are able to adjust operational strategies and redirect resources in order to continually improve efficiency and performance;

companies can constantly upgrade and develop new models. Repeat business is fundamental and enables them to eradicate mistakes or errors in the production process over time.

High volumes of distressed debt, on the other hand, only appear every once in a while. There is no time for dress rehearsals or improving the model over time and it is soon forgotten, once markets rebound. The concept of creating an entity that performs at the highest level of performance and efficiency for a limited period, and which is then dismantled and shut-down, is enormously challenging.

Striking the right balance between committing sufficient resources and investment in the knowledge that this will need to be reversed in the near future is the basis upon which all successful work-out platforms are predicated. A significant amount of resource wastage is inevitable and, like any removable or temporary structure, if the proper foundations are not completed the structure above will lack strength and probably underperform. You get out what you put in. Top performance can only ever be produced from strong foundations, robust structures and not cutting corners on the basis that the required resources are only temporary.

PART II

DISTRESSED DEBT SOLUTIONS

In Part I the distressed debt problem was examined and explained. Now, in Part II, the focus moves to providing solutions to these problems. The five solutions we will look at are:

1. Structure
2. Preparation and planning
3. Asset management
4. Borrowers
5. Collateral

These solutions are taken one at a time and dealt with in the coming chapters.

3. STRUCTURE SOLUTIONS

3.1 Response to crisis

Brand building

Capital efficiency and good customer service has been the key to success in the traditional brand-building banking model. Brand building is dynamic and best achieved by strictly adhering to processes and procedures carefully gauged from sensible risk and business formulae. A strong brand, benefiting from high loan growth, in favourable market conditions, creates the right foundations for a peak bank growth expansion rate. This method of operation works best in positive market conditions, where borrowers are comfortable borrowing more and more money to purchase assets that they believe will have a higher value tomorrow.

Since the 1990s, there has been a fundamental shift in banking away from earning spread income from loan assets held on balance sheet. Instead of a loan portfolio being part of a bank's assets, the portfolio was spun off and sold to investors with the bank earning origination fees. Portfolio quality was judged by historic collection, repayment or default rates. This technical approach was useful for making accurate cash flow predictions, but was a deceptive measure of true portfolio quality and risk. Future probability was driven by past performance which can work well up to an extent, provided any changes in underlying market conditions are gradual. Unexpected events, or major shocks to the system, can completely sideline this approach to quality control.

When crisis strikes

Once outlier results occur, the risk of the credit processing system completely breaking down is extremely high. When this occurs, the loan portfolio plummets in value and the bank is suddenly confronted with vast numbers of loan contracts that no longer perform. Distribution models become irrelevant. Brand, established processes and procedures are immaterial. The existing credit staff have no experience for what they are now confronted with and the bank has very limited infrastructure to manage their dilemma. It is now in crisis mode, holding portfolios of loan assets that are extremely difficult to monetise, that are only liquid at forced-sale values. On top of this, real estate markets have crashed, so the quality of their performing loan book is also eroding and there is a high risk of many more loans turning delinquent.

This is a time for accurate evaluation and carefully considered action. The US Federal Reserve has identified three core factors that they believe always contribute to bank failures:

1. Poor asset quality
2. Poor risk management
3. Passive bank management

Three parallel factors also contribute to a bank's recovery performance and speed of revival:

1. The bank needs to fully understand and accurately assess the market for all assets it is holding as security for loans. They need to know which market sectors will deteriorate furthest and which will likely recover first. Past credit evaluation is insufficient and probably wrong. Markets fundamentally change after downturn; the same may behave completely differently in rising, flat or falling markets. Accuracy of judgement is therefore critical.

2. The bank needs to fully understand its portfolio and its borrowers, what their true financial capability is and what they will likely do next. For complicated structured securities, this can be especially challenging. If the bank knows precious little about its borrowers, this is a major handicap.

3. Bank management actively making the correct calls will have an enormous impact upon the outcome. Poor judgement will make a bad situation worse.

Properly understanding what you hold, what is happening to it and what to do next is fundamental to any commercial situation and distressed debt is no different to everything else. Common sense prevails, but is of no use if you do not fully understand what you have and what you are really dealing with.

Possible courses of action

The specific method of dealing with distressed debt can only be decided on a case-by-case basis for each financial institution. There is no generic right or wrong course of action to be chosen. However, making the wrong decision, or flawed execution, can be extremely costly. Meanwhile, the pressure to act escalates exponentially if markets continue to slide, or if conditions risk further erosion.

When confronted with the need to resolve large quantities of non-performing loans, banks have a number of options:

1. Do nothing. Just respond to events as they occur, within existing structures.
2. Transfer responsibility for NPL work-out to a new specialist internal division.
3. Transfer the loans into a new special purpose vehicle (SPV), isolated from the banks main operations and balance sheet.
4. Make an immediate sale of loans to independent third parties.
5. Attempt a sale of loans at some time in the future.

Which action for dealing with distressed debt is best?

The decision to choose one of these options depends on the need for new capital, the cost, the investor and market appeal, all balanced against ongoing contagion risk and the market risk of long-term exposure. Loan work-outs are complex and time consuming, with different resources to the marketing-risk analysis performing loan model. Figure 3.1 illustrates the implications of these different approaches.

In most cases, doing nothing about non-performing loans is not a realistic option. There are always exceptions though. If a market recovery is V-shaped and the rebound occurs quickly, a bank having already sold its assets at immediate post-crash fire-sale levels would likely have given away substantial free upside to a happy buyer. A rising tide raises all boats; knowledge, timing and experience are key.

We always come back to the importance of fully understanding the underlying market conditions underpinning the credit business and what will happen next. If an institution had absolutely no idea that a major correction was imminent, what chance do they have of reasonably predicting market recovery? If this is the case, action is required to remedy such shortcomings, in order to ensure past mistakes are not repeated in the future.

Figure 3.1 – implications of different NPL resolution approaches

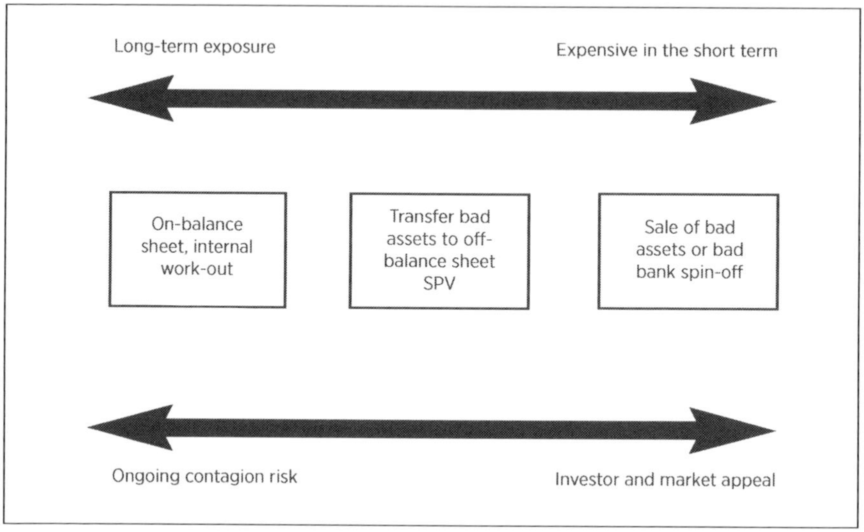

Continuing to hold assets, either on balance sheet or within a new vehicle is, superficially, the easiest short-term choice for a bank to make. It could however also turn out to be more costly than other options if their resolution plan is deficient or if market conditions deteriorate significantly further.

The critical issue is to understand and evaluate is whether time spent on work-outs pays off in the form of enhanced recoveries, or merely detracts from the lender's ability to originate new profitable business. This is an extremely difficult decision to make and it may have an enormous influence on the future of the institution for many years to come.

Wholesale disposal

The justification for banks selling off their loan books outright depends on prevailing market conditions, future prospects, and political and reputational considerations. After past downturns, rationale for wholesale disposal has included the following:

- Ratings, market, analyst and investor perception of the institution.

- Refocusing resources to concentrate on core profit-generating business.
- Balance sheet clean-up, sometimes after take-over or consolidation.
- Cash income generation.

Some of the different types of disposal or clean-up options that have been tried by financial institutions include:

1. *Outright sale*
2. *Outright sale* with future revenue sharing mechanism
3. *Outright sale* with future profit participation
4. *Structured sale* with servicing transferred to buyer
5. *No sale*, with outsourced servicing

These options have varying influence on the seller's business in terms of cash-flow, ongoing resource commitment and balance sheet impact, as shown in Table 3.1.

Table 3.1 – varying influence of different loan book dispoal options

Option	Immediate cash injection	Future cash revenue	Ongoing resource liability	Impact on balance sheet
Type 1: Outright sale	Maximum	None	None	Cleaned
Type 2: Outright sale, revenue sharing	Significant	Significant	Limited	Cleaned
Type 3: Outright sale, profit participation	Significant	Uncertain	Limited	Cleaned
Type 4: Structured sale	Limited	Significant	Limited	Reducing
Type 5: Outsourced servicing	None	Significant	Limited	No benefit

Expanding on the data in Table 3.1:

- Type 1, **outright sale**, is the cleanest and simplest option providing immediate cash revenue, with no future commitment and a completely clean balance sheet.
- Type 2, **outright sale with future revenue sharing mechanism**, provides less cash upfront in return for future upside, which may be particularly

beneficial in the event of an early market rebound. This type of transaction may require some future resource commitment, dependant upon the terms of future revenue sharing.

- Type 3, **outright sale with future profit participation**, tends to be less certain in terms of future upside. The additional complexity of determining profits with another party is not easy, and needs extremely careful determination of transactional terms.
- Type 4, **structured sale with servicing transferred to buyer**, is most useful when a seller has no need for immediate cash, but would like to transfer ownership and work-out resource commitment and responsibility to a third party, thereby enabling them to focus on core profit generating activities.
- Type 5, **no sale, with outsourced servicing**, has similar resource benefits to Type 4, but will likely require greatest management commitment, given its direct ongoing impact on the balance sheet.

Servicing continuity

Timing is the key to a successful loan book sale. However, once a lender has made the decision to sell their loan book, it is human nature to pay less attention to it. Servicing continuity is bound to suffer. A common, recurring feature after buying a portfolio is to discover a number of commercial borrowers, frustrated by delay and a lack of action, eagerly waiting to talk to the new owner of the debt. For residential portfolios, it is not unusual to find an armada of smaller borrowers camping out at your door, or waiting by the telephone for you to call them, so they can pay off their loan principal and accrued interest in full!

In 1999, at Lehman Brothers we wanted to be the first NPL portfolio buyer in a new South-East Asian jurisdiction. The biggest problem was that property prices were still clearly falling. However, no one wanted to openly admit to it. For the selling bank, it was of course bad for business. The local press was in complete denial, still claiming that 1997 had bypassed their country. We just made sure that we projected the real estate valuations forwards correctly and used a high discount rate. The bank valuations were wrong, at least double where they should have been. We bid 30 cents on the dollar, but the seller was expecting 60 cents and rejected our bid. Nine months later, they came back to us to accept our bid. We re-checked our numbers and resubmitted at 20 cents on the dollar. By now, the selling bank just viewed us as vultures and the relationship ended. Timing is all; two years later, they sold to a private equity fund at 15 cents on the dollar.

Whether a loan book or portfolio is sold to a third party, or transferred between departments within an in institution, it is critical to preserve continuity whereby the appropriate servicing resource is put in place as quickly as possible in order to protect legal positions, maintain enforcement of court proceedings, interface with borrowers and manage assets.

If the decision is made to continue holding distressed assets and work them out, substantial resources need to be mobilised. In order to take control of the situation, retraining or recruiting new staff with new skill sets is a first priority. This is not easy. Instead of credit officers, banks now desperately need emergency staff: financial doctors, engineers, police and firemen with specialist work-out skills. New tools and strategies are required that the bank is not resourced for, in addition to new expertise.

> Uncovering high-quality third-party servicers in new jurisdictions can be harder than finding deals. In Brazil we successfully bid for a new portfolio and appointed an untried local servicer who had what appeared to be a good track record. The result was sub-standard and we had no immediately available effective plan B. We ended up squandering legal claims and losing enormous leverage over borrowers that cost us a big chunk of our investment. After that experience we decided that, even in remote jurisdictions, unless there was a proven special servicer there that we already knew and trusted, it was better to set up your own servicing entity from scratch. Otherwise, it is better not to buy.

Changing attitudes

Banker mentality and culture is conservative. If the same approach is applied to resolutions, it guarantees that collection will be conservative too. A shift from banker mentality to the mindset of a speculative investor will positively impact collections but, in practice, this is difficult to engineer. Banks' overriding collection principles are fear of mistakes and minimisation of loss, which is in stark contrast to the most successful debt collectors, who are creative, adaptable and highly entrepreneurial, and see distressed debt as an opportunity to excel by achieving the highest possible collections.

Managing defaulted borrowers effectively is an extremely challenging and complex role that requires practice and training to perfect. For bank officers, the concept of customer service needs to be replaced by strategic borrower pressure. Changing from a passive, helpful service mindset to a smart, streetwise can-do mentality is not easy, and rarely is proper specialist work-out training or education provided, to undertake this effectively. Once default is considered unavoidable and irrevocable, most bank work-out divisions immediately focus on tough, impersonal, inflexible bargaining. If this fails, as mostly it does, legal execution is their favoured method of debt resolution.

The established models for resolving loans

The three established models for resolving loans are:

1. Internal work-out department
2. Bad bank
3. Special servicer

These are each reviewed individually in the following three sections.

3.2 Internal work-out

Internal work-out is the simplest and easiest short-term solution to managing distressed debts. It is usually structured as a new standalone work-out department within the existing bank structure, but detached from former credit divisions. Practically, it is best operated with separation in terms of personnel and management from credit. A critical decision therefore involves conflict; whether the same credit officers that have dealt with borrowers historically should deal with them in a distressed situation.

In terms of banking operations, internal work-out divisions avoid the need to reconfigure new IT, custodian or collection systems. Given the reduction in credit origination that will likely have occurred, work-out staff can usually operate from the vacant space previously occupied by credit personnel, which keeps building-occupational costs and additional expenditure down to a minimum.

The staffing problem

Motivating staff after a market crash can be an issue. In the immediate aftermath, the normal credit processes will have ground to a halt. Staff will have lots of time on their hands with very little to do and will be preoccupied with keeping their jobs. Most banks recruit aggressively during a boom market, and it is common sense that after the downturn they will likely have to downsize and shed staff. In the event of downsizing, most entities work on the principle of last in, first out, in order to minimise redundancy payments.

Most staff are very sensitive to this issue and where staff are represented by unions this can be particularly challenging. The usual soft solution is to transfer credit staff to the new NPL servicing division in order to avoid widespread redundancy. Some staff wrongly then view transfer as a step down. Others just see it as an emergency stop-gap until a better job opportunity comes along. Few recognise it as a positive, retraining opportunity that improves, expands and develops their core professional skill set.

Most importantly, credit staff are not conditioned, qualified or trained to be effective within a work-out situation. As a result, there is a high risk that the bank will end up with demotivated, poorly equipped staff that are only there because they have little other choice. Fulfilling a working function under the premise that *you are lucky to have a job* is demotivating, can be counterproductive and is unlikely to achieve the best work-out results.

Issues within work-out divisions in previous crises

After previous crises, a range of potentially difficult issues have been seen to occur with bank in-house work-out divisions. These may include:

1. **Job security**: staff transferred out of the mainstream bank may feel insecure and focus primarily on keeping their jobs at all costs. They may overcompensate by overstating collection potential within the work-out unit, in order to increase their perceived value in the short-term. This can create unreasonable collection expectations for the institution.
2. **Diminishing future prospects** may make staff over-protective and lead them to try to spin the job out as long as possible, rather than selling assets early and being made redundant.
3. For similar reasons, staff may try to **resist or discourage institutions from selling off loan portfolios** to third parties, by discrediting third-party bidders' pricing levels.
4. **Staff resistance to change**: a normal credit situation is a win-win situation for the bank and customer. The customer receives a loan and the bank makes money from them. NPLs are a zero-sum game where banks stand a high risk of losing out further. This can make some staff overly-inflexible towards defaulted borrowers. Alternatively, it can go the opposite way and some staff may favour borrowers, believing themselves to have been treated badly by the institution, feeling demotivated, and seeing resolution as an opportunity to get even.

5. In-house work-out staff, transferred from a credit division, may be more **entrenched around the accuracy of previous records**. Any deviation from what went before may be viewed as some form of implied criticism of their own past performance. Some officers can be extraordinarily sensitive to this issue. It may also breed intransigence that prevents work-out staff exploring new alternatives for resolution with borrowers.

6. **Inexperience of the commercial world** outside their institution or industry, and a shortage of suitable external training resources, may limit the effectiveness of collection staff in work-out.

7. **Working hours**: institutional staff are accustomed to working fixed hours, in accordance with stipulated terms and conditions. Changing working patterns and times is not easy. Dealing effectively with distressed debt demands more verbal communication with borrowers, either by telephone or in person. If the borrower is a corporation, this is not a problem, but if they are individuals, optimum communication is more likely to occur outside normal working hours, particularly evenings. Unless officers can adapt, this can limit their effectiveness and therefore that of the work-out unit.

8. **Remuneration**: institutional credit staff are compensated in accordance with industry-wide established terms and conditions. These may have large fixed components, with limited ability to adjust according to performance. NPL revenues are very different to credit revenues. Credit revenues are constant as long as a loan is making payments. They are generally fixed, with limited volatility, so credit institutions can operate profitably with a consistent overhead, which includes a high fixed component to staff remuneration. NPL collection is the opposite. Collections are extremely volatile; sometimes money is made and

> Dealing or negotiating with bank internal work-out departments for the purchase of loan books is usually a fruitless exercise. As a potential buyer of NPLs, you know that the deal won't go anywhere once the board of the selling bank sets up a meeting with their in-house work-out division to clarify why the bid-ask spread is so wide on your offer. The work-out unit come to protect their jobs and the CEO thinks he is the umpire; they may, for example, make claims that a home was sold down the road from your collateral well above your appraisal level and they have already received and rejected an offer for the loan way above what you are proposing to pay for it! This happens everywhere from Manila to Frankfurt, throughout Asia, the Middle East and Western Europe.

sometimes it is lost. High fixed overheads are incompatible with this business model. Changing remuneration packages significantly can be very difficult for staff transferred within the bank. For NPL work-out, this can result in serious misalignment between the objective of the work-out unit and the way its staff are compensated.

8. **Reputational issues**: where the work-out unit evicts debtors and the press somehow turns creditor's rightful legal actions into negative, potentially damaging headlines for the institution.

Which staff to transfer and how to manage them

An extremely difficult decision for internal work-out departments is which staff to transfer from other divisions of the bank. Some people will consider transfer as a sign that their institution views them negatively. Some may feel devalued, or even victimised, and may adopt a Gulag mentality that is not conducive to effective work.

Does the institution tell people they will be transferred back in from the cold if they perform well, or if market conditions change? Also, what standard of staff does the bank transfer? Does it transfer its better or worse performing individuals? Clearly, the quality of individuals transferred will impact collection results; weak staff will deliver poor collections. Does transferring better qualified staff in order to improve collections also mean that they will adopt a Gulag mentality and leave their job for the lure of the competition as soon as they can?

3.3 Bad banks

A bad bank is a separate legal entity from the mother banking institution; loans are transferred to it for work-out. It has its own management and personnel. It can operate from its own premises with its own brand, which can be completely unrelated to the mother institution.

Unlike commercial good banks, bad banks do not need to choose operational locations in competitive, high profile, retail locations. They do not need to be on the high street or within the most prestigious office locations. The key locational factor is ease of ability to communicate and meet with borrowers, which spawns its own specific geographical, transport, logistical and access issues.

The origin of the bad bank idea

The idea of a bad bank was first pioneered by Mellon Bank in 1988 in the USA. The bad bank had three purposes:

1. To clean up the bank balance sheet and restore market confidence.
2. To insulate mainstream profit-generating operations from contagion.
3. To clearly divide responsibility for good and bad bank operations.

This concept has been successfully implemented on many occasions since then, in recognition of the fact that as long as bad assets are mixed with good, investors and market analysts are uncertain about banks' financial health and performance. This may impair the ability of banks to borrow, lend, trade and raise capital.

The key to the success of bad banks is:

1. To see a clear transfer of risk from the good bank to the bad bank.
2. To see efficient NPL resolution, including a recycling of assets into productive or profitable use, at market price.

The quicker this can occur, the better, though this needs to be balanced against the need to maximise recoveries and minimise losses.

Different business approaches to good and bad banks

In order to set up and operate a successful bad bank, a new business approach is required. Assessing a good bank involves looking at:

- Quality, type and diversification of assets.
- Quality and relevant track record of management.
- Additional capital available for augmentation.
- Resilience to changing market conditions.
- Anticipated growth rate and strategy.
- Future market prospects.

A bad bank has its own parallel but different attributes:

- Quality, experience and motivation of asset managers.
- Quality and relevant track record of management.

- Additional capital available for alternative resolution strategies.
- Sufficient capital to withstand marked deterioration in market conditions.
- Anticipated wind-down rate and strategy.
- Future market prospects.

The business of banking is built upon the premise that over 90% of borrowers will pay their debts in full and on time. Distressed debt has the opposite dynamics. Collections are inevitably delayed and the lender is always scrambling to be compensated or paid. The borrower is usually stressed and at some point runs the risk of walking away or being forced into bankruptcy.

Given this fundamental difference between good and bad banks, dealing productively with distressed debts is best handled with detachment from the original credit process and lending decision. A fresh, unbiased approach is beneficial and, logically, this is best achieved by loan sale, or at least loan servicing transfer to another group or entity. Table 3.2 summarises the differences between a good bank and a bad bank.

Table 3.2 – summary of the differences between a good bank and a bad bank

Good bank	Bad bank
Market driven	Crisis driven
Highly competitive	No competition for new business
Extremely price sensitive	Maximum-price philosophy
Customer focused	Collections focused
Borrower relations critical	Borrower may be adversarial
Repeat business targeted	One-time transaction
Recommendations	No recommendations
Good reputation critical	Tough reputation critical
Expensive, appealing image	Glossy image counterproductive
Continuous brand building	Negative, bad brand image
Prime offices/retail	Secondary offices better value for money
Smart and polished	Aggressive and streetwise
Slick training programmes	Limited preparation
Glossy recruitment-drives	Emergency recruitment campaigns

When a good bank sets up a new bad bank, the only thing they share is ownership of the banking entities, the underlying assets and receivables. Otherwise, they have very little in common. Good banking and bad banking are very different businesses and do not add value to one another. Operationally, it makes limited sense to merge or run them together.

Operating a bad bank

> One of my more uncomfortable experiences occurred in Thailand. A borrower was accompanied to the meeting by a police general who, as soon as he sat down, unholstered his gun and placed it on the desk between us. He said nothing and just stared at me throughout. The meeting was very brief and nothing was progressed. The first priority was changing security arrangements in the office immediately afterwards. The borrower may have thought they were pressuring us to accept a lower price. The reality was that we marked the price upwards once we knew how important the loan was to them.

In the same way that banks spend considerable resources on appearance and impression, in order to appeal to their target audience, so bad banks need to consider their visual image carefully too. Over-affluent office fit-out may alienate borrowers who want to agree a resolution. Given that debtors will likely believe they have fallen on hard times, they may take offence and react negatively if they perceive that the lender has too much money and is not invested in their burden of loss.

In addition to operational issues, the critical factor in terms of office location and design is often staff retention. Given the career prospects within a bad bank may be relatively short term, it is important to optimise staff working conditions. Retaining bad bank staff is tough enough without creating additional working environment handicaps. Balancing all this out is challenging.

Collection officer presentation and image to borrowers is a basic requirement for successful recoveries. Borrowers will expect to meet with capable, professional, well-presented asset managers. As in any field of commerce, people associate price to presentation, and would likely expect to pay less to a grubby, badly presented debt collector.

Similar to the way that a bank can transfer staff over to an in-house work-out division, so it can transfer the same staff over to a new bad bank entity. The big advantage here is the ability to write new employment contracts, with terms and conditions that are better aligned to the business of debt collection, especially compensation structures. The downside is that the Gulag mentality may be exacerbated. Transferred staff may feel even more removed from their former employer, the good bank. They may suffer from demotivation, a loss of prestige, or even embarrassment within their peer group, once they no longer work for a prestigious banking brand.

This transfer issue is an absolutely critical support, retraining and orientation issue for newly established bad bank staff transferred from the good bank. It must be urgently addressed in order to optimise staff performance.

3.4 Special servicers

The third work-out alternative for resolving NPLs is to outsource them to a third-party loan servicer. A loan servicer can be a public or private entity that collects, monitors and reports loan payments. Most are independent from banks and are paid on a fee basis that relates to collection levels. They also handle property management, taxes, insurance, borrower communication and payment remittal. The key to successful servicer outsourcing is close alignment with the lender's objectives.

The four main types of loan servicer

Loan servicers can function as **master servicer**, **primary servicer**, **sub-servicer** or **special servicer**.

- A **master servicer** has responsibility for overall loan/bond oversight, reporting and compliance.
- A **primary servicer** has the same responsibilities as a master servicer together with responsibility for hands-on loan operations and collections.
- A **sub-servicer** is a separate entity to the master servicer, undertaking the same operational and collection servicing functions, and reporting to the master servicer.
- A **special servicer's** role is to maximise recovery and minimise loss from distressed debt obligations. A special servicer restructures loans, forecloses on defaulted loans, disposes of collateral and refunds the proceeds to lenders. Special servicers perform the same services as a bad bank, but work in an outsourced capacity from the lending institution. Bad banks and special servicers are sometimes called the undertakers of the credit world.

Most servicing entities can act as master, primary or special servicer. In addition, many independent servicers provide stand-by or back-up servicing facilities where they can step in and take over other parties' responsibilities at short notice, or provide parallel or virtual support packages.

> Appropriate special servicer incentivisation is critical. At Lehman we tried using an IRR servicer incentivisation formula in Eastern Europe. The servicers could never relate to the scheme and could never work out how to calculate where we were at any given time during the life of the investment. They were also paid a base fee plus collection fee. Operationally, their asset managers just focused on collections. They never tried to claim the incentivisation fee and after a while no one even bothered to talk about it further.

The distressed debt servicing industry

Formalisation of the distressed debt servicing industry occurred during the wake of the US Savings and Loans Crisis of 1989. Investors, in need of special servicer resources independent of the established banking sector, set up their own work-out entities. From the USA, this expertise was exported to Japan and developed considerably throughout Asia after the 1997 Asian Crisis, and from it spread to Europe and South America. The growth of structured finance products within the last decade has added substantially to the expansion of independent servicers.

Distressed debt is now a global financial sector industry, comprising multi-disciplinary professional advisers, specialist contractors, private and publicly listed investors, rated and non-rated asset-managers, loan servicers and debt collectors. Banks, institutions and investors can choose, if they wish, to outsource all or part of their servicing operations to a number of experienced, independent or attached servicers. Independent servicers have the advantage of full impartiality, whilst attached servicers are often part of bigger institutions that may be prepared to commit additional investment to distressed assets under their servicing control, in order to boost work-out collections and increase their revenues. Given their focus and specialisation, operational and performance standards within independent servicers should logically be expected to be higher than within bank in-house work out units.

The advantages of using a third-party servicer

The great advantage of using a third-party servicer is that they are already established and ready to go. They will also possess experience and a track record in undertaking collections. In addition to proven competence, they will also operate their own specialist software, which is specifically designed to manage work-out effectively and optimise distressed debt collections. As a third-party independent, they also remove reputational risk for the lender associated with possible bad press from collections. Special servicers may also be prepared to recruit former credit staff from their banking client, which may soften any negative redundancy fall-out for the bank.

Special servicers have come under criticism since 2008, in relation to resolving structured securities, where junior bondholders have been wiped out upon realisation. This may occur where the fee structure has incentivised the servicer to prioritise liquidation and does not allow enough time to fully explore loss mitigation. Ownership of the securities compounds this issue because it is spread over so many bondholders. Apart from the securities debate, and the fact that these were never envisaged with major downturn in mind, it highlights two issues: firstly, effective special servicing demands clear direction from the lender or loan owner. Secondly, aligned incentivisation is critical, with flexibility to adjust to changing conditions. If these are properly addressed, special servicing is an extremely efficient method of NPL work-out.

Using a third-party servicer also improves optionality, in terms of whether and when to sell off an NPL portfolio, or not. A fundamental issue for banks is to both avoid a fire sale loss by selling off NPLs early whilst also avoiding market reputation risk, which may occur if bad loans are retained in-house. The optimum model should therefore seek to provide flexibility, whilst preserving the opportunity to maximise return on NPL monetisation, resource allocation and future upside. NPLs need to be clearly removed off balance sheet as soon as possible, in order to avoid reputational and contagion risks, but how can this be achieved without a third-party sale?

Establishing a subsidiary bad bank NPL servicing entity

The most effective approach that best addresses all these objectives may therefore be to establish a new subsidiary, bad bank NPL servicing entity, and transfer loans and security into it. This is similar to a bad bank, but loan servicing should be undertaken by an independent third-party servicer outsource. The new NPL holding entity should be set up in a way that then facilitates its easy ownership transfer, sale or monetisation in the future.

The servicing structure and operations must be constituted and operated in a way that makes it easy for potential investors or buyers to analyse, price and ultimately take over all or part of the loan portfolio, together with the existing servicer contract, if they wish. Financial institutions that are unsure as to which work-out approach to follow may find it best to consider positioning themselves in the middle in this way, whereby they still have 100% control, but maximise future investor appeal and optimise ease of speedy disposition.

Accurately reconciling historic loan payments, records and reports is extremely difficult to facilitate without errors in the middle of a highly-pressured sales disposal transaction, so these issues are best resolved in advance, at the same time as loans are transferred over to the new work-out entity.

Executives and asset managers within the new servicing entity need to be incentivised to sell as quickly as possible at the highest price, both at the loan and asset level, or work-out entity level. In this way, assets or loans can be monetised on an individual basis until the time is right to sell off the entity. Alternatively, in the event that market conditions are unfavourable, or if other events dictate, the good bank also has the flexibility to hold the work-out entity indefinitely. In order to maximise both day-to-day work-out performance and future sale price level, in the event that the work-out entity is spun off, it should have:

- A separate stand-alone management and organisation.
- A separate independent IT and records system.
- An isolated client cash-management system.
- An isolated client documentary and custodian system.

All these factors facilitate the ability for new investor to take over the bad bank seamlessly. They also minimise drag on good bank resources in terms of management and monitoring, which are maybe better used fully focusing on core, good bank, profit-generating activities.

Which loan resolution method is best?

Amongst the three recognised models for resolving loans – internal work-out department, establishing a new bad bank, or outsourced special servicer – there is no generic right or wrong answer for choosing a particular method. Each institution should make its own decision, based on its own individual resources and needs. The benefits or disadvantages of each approach are summarised in Table 3.3.

Table 3.3 – summary of the benefits and disadvantages of the three models for loan resolution

Characteristic	Internal work-out	Bad bank	Special servicer
Cost	Cheapest	More expensive	More expensive
Ease of set-up	Easier	Hardest	Easiest
Ongoing management	High	Medium	Low
Work-out incentivisation	Lowest	Higher	Highest
Experience	Low	Low	High
Bank liability for redundancies	Low	Low	High
Third-party NPL investor or buyer appeal	More complicated	Straightforward	Optimum
Ease of bad bank spin off	Not applicable	Straightforward	Optimum
Market appeal & P.R.	Weak	Strong	Strongest

Efficient handover on sale of portfolio or transfer of servicing

Efficient handover, either upon sale of a portfolio or upon transfer of servicing to another entity, is fundamental. This involves not only transfer of loans, security, files and valuable documents, but communication with borrowers. The selling institution has legal obligations to advise borrowers of material change, that they are required to comply with. As much as possible, in a sale situation, the buyer should seek to work with the seller in managing this communication process, in order to gain maximum future servicing advantage.

Upon transfer, the new servicing entity will need to advise borrowers of the following:

- An introduction to the new owner or servicer.
- Clarification of contact details for both the servicer and the borrower.

- Clarification of the servicer's contact personnel.
- Clarification of loan payment and collection logistics.
- An invitation to meet.

The new servicing entity should confirm this information to borrowers, both in writing and by telephone. This exercise is best carried out by a specially assembled, properly trained, short-term customer service task-force unit.

Some interesting lessons can be gleaned from the experiences of investors purchasing loan books and taking over loan servicing from sellers. In some jurisdictions, the idea of an international big hitter taking over loans induces a form of psychological terror amongst local borrowers. In other cases, local debtors may conversely feel so confident of their situation that the foreign investor is viewed as easy meat.

The point here is that when change occurs, whether it is loan sale, servicing transfer or just change of personnel, lenders or investors need to recognise the new circumstance and the threats or opportunities this creates. Fundamental to this is an understanding of the prevailing servicing relationship dynamics between borrowers and the former lender or work-out entity. Generally, institutions and investors do not spend enough time on this issue; it is important to put effort into turning the specific circumstances to their future collection advantage, even using PR and publicity when appropriate.

3.5 Selling off loan books

The ten-step sales process

If a bank either chooses to sell, or has no option other than to sell off its loan book on a wholesale basis, it will need to go through a ten-step sales process:

1. Making choice of loans to be sold.
2. Giving executive approval for the proposed sale.
3. **Advertising notice of the sale and connecting with potential bidders.**
4. **Selecting bidders.**
5. **Bidders undertaking due diligence.**
6. **Bidders submitting their best price and entering final negotiations.**

7. **Selecting the winning bid and issuing a sales and purchase contract.**
8. **The winning bidder obtaining executive consent to proceed.**
9. **Payment transfers and the transaction closes.**
10. Loans and collateral are transferred to the buyer.

Dependant upon whether the transaction is a larger, first time sale, or a smaller replicated transaction, the public part of the bidding process for a portfolio, **items 3 to 9 above**, usually takes between three to six months. This timeframe excludes any allowance for the selling institution's approval process, choosing loans to be sold and preparing marketing and bidder information packs. It also excludes any allowance for handover of receivables, or transfer of legal positions after closing.

If these parts of the process at the front and rear ends are factored in, larger transactions could take up to 12 months in total, from beginning to end. Sellers attempting to drive through faster processes in order to achieve the earliest sale run the risk of not giving buyers enough time to maximise their bids, thereby failing to achieve the highest price.

The issues that drive NPL sales transactions

NPL sales transactions are usually driven by the following primary issues:

- The experience and history of the seller in NPL disposals.
- Seller type: whether a nationalised, publicly owned or privately owned institution.
- The size and type of portfolio to be sold.
- The timing of the sale relative to market conditions and recovery.
- Whether the bidders are domestic or international.
- Specific jurisdictional and regulatory issues.

Forward-thinking preparation is one of the most critical elements in creating certainty with bidders. Selling institutions may need to plan in advance for the possibility that the highest bid they receive for a portfolio is below book value. This would involve the need for additional capital to be raised in order to cover the shortfall, thereby causing additional unanticipated delay.

It is possible that if the selling institution ends up with an unexpected capital void, some bidders might be prepared to provide a quick-fix solution by purchasing equity as part of an overall package deal. However, approaching a transaction in this way would limit the number of bidders, add unnecessary complication and might lead to weaker bids.

Deciding what assets to sell

Once an institution elects to sell a portfolio, the first decision that needs to be made is the choice of assets to be sold. Each situation is unique, but the primary consideration will probably be based on performing or non-performing assets and strategic or non-strategic assets.

Figure 3.2 – selecting which assets to dispose of

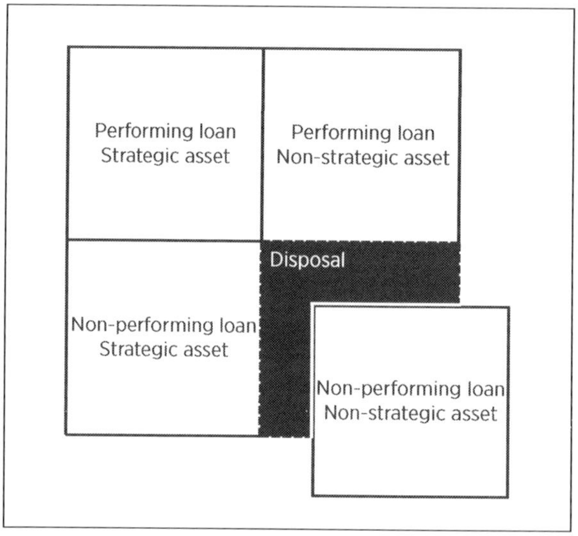

Non-performing, non-strategic assets are the obvious disposal target. Other non-strategic, performing loans that should be considered include assets that have a high risk of future default and assets that may have substantial mark-to-market risk. Strategic assets that are susceptible to unfair outside pressure, or loans with reputational issues, are prime candidates. Other considerations might include the complexity of assets, how difficult they might be to collect on, or dealing with the risk of ratings downgrades.

If the purpose of sale is to raise cash, the choice of assets needs to be sufficiently forward-looking in terms of the seller's future capital and funding constraints. If the purpose of sale is to clean up the balance sheet and loan book, this is best achieved at one time with a single sales campaign. Having a number of sales disposal campaigns runs the risk of the market believing the first campaign to have been unsuccessful and thereby undermining balance sheet confidence.

After a financial crisis, it is difficult to segregate bad assets more than once without weakening the credibility of retained assets. Average price cosmetics – that is average price per loan achieved upon sale – can in principle be improved by including performing, sub-performing loans and NPLs together for sale. This will come at a cost though, as any performing loans included will almost certainly be discounted at a similar rate to NPLs.

Tranching of assets

When determining which assets to select, the seller will also need to consider the tranching or grouping of loan types from a buyer's perspective. The servicing resource required for different loan classes varies considerably.

For example, servicing credit card receivables is completely different to servicing, say, corporate loans or collateralised loan obligations. As a result, the buyer may not want certain loan asset types and is only bidding because they are included with assets that they want to buy. Tranching different loan classes together therefore runs the risk of the buyer discounting down unwanted classes to option value, or even zero, and flipping them to a third party, or another bidder, for a quick profit immediately after closing.

Generally, the best selling price is achieved by separating different loan classes into different tranches, to be sold individually. If potential buyers are interested in multiple loan classes, they can bid on additional tranches. This needs to be balanced with size and anticipated purchase price though. If tranches are too small, they may run the risk of falling below the bidders' opportunity cost or minimum capital deployed threshold.

Deciding when to sell

Most institutions conduct NPL portfolio sales at a time that most benefits their annual financial results. This is frequently timed to coincide with the end of their financial year. One of the risks here is the likelihood of a competing institution also looking to sell at the same time. In any given market place there are usually only a small number of bidders who will pay top price. If they are distracted by competing sales campaigns they may not give sufficient consideration to a particular transaction, which will almost certainly result in a lower bid.

Also, some bidders may choose to bid on one portfolio only, in order to avoid concentration risk, and may end up ignoring a transaction that otherwise they would have competed on. Institutions therefore need to be clear on their NPL disposal timing priorities.

Choosing the optimum cut-off date for selling a portfolio is critically important, in terms of maximising seller revenue. The cut-off date is the day upon which loan cash flow will ultimately transfer to the potential buyer and is the date upon which they base the underwriting for their bid. This needs to be considered strategically in order to maximise sale proceeds. For larger loan balances, cut-off is best correlated in terms of borrower payment dates, anticipated cash flow and risk of future repayment shortfall or default. Sellers should retain the flexibility to add or remove loans during the sale process, in accordance with changing circumstances.

Quality of information

Institutions should also give early consideration on how best to advise borrowers and the market about the loan sale process. Selling a loan portfolio is sometimes a great advertisement for motivating delinquent borrowers. It is not unusual for some borrowers to fast-track payment of their loan under threat of sale, which can lead to unexpected collection windfalls between cut off and closing for the benefit of the buyer, dependant upon the terms of the transaction.

> In 2001 Lehman agreed to buy the NPL book of a bank in the Philippines. After the deal was announced worried borrowers rushed in to pay off their loans. The collections were so high the selling bank changed its mind and decided not to sell to us.

On the negative side for portfolio buyers, the selling bank might accept a pay-off for a particular loan below the bidder's underwriting calculation, which will result in a lower than anticipated collection. Both buyers and sellers therefore need to be absolutely clear on the terms of transactional documentation.

Quality of information, transparency and data integrity is fundamental to maximising sales proceeds. Any uncertainty or doubt on the bidder side will be discounted. Missing or inaccurate information will likely be marked to zero. If bidders can access loan officers it can help fill in gaps that can generally result in greater confidence and higher bids.

Inspection of physical loan files usually improves buyer confidence. Most institutions are unable or reluctant to provide bidders with access to borrowers, guarantors or property collateral, which generally has a negative impact upon bid levels.

> Chinese government sponsored AMCs were established to buy NPLs from banks to sell to investors. They paid far too much for the loans to the selling banks though. As a result, they can never sell on at realistic prices which has led to a fundamental lack of international confidence in the Chinese NPL market and, by association, the banking sector.

Buyer confidence

Strong buyer and bidder confidence also makes a critical contribution to maximising the sales price. Apart from market considerations, confidence can be influenced by a number of factors, including:

1. **The overall quality of the sales process**: seller knowledge and confidence.
2. **Transparency**: perceived openness and fairness towards bidders.
3. **Seller execution certainty**: is this a valuation exercise or a real commitment to sell?
4. **Reserve price**: does the seller have realistic market expectations?

Confident bidders will take the time and trouble on, and will commit expenditure to, transactions that they consider have a realistic chance of closing on a competitive basis. Sellers with a bad track record in executing transactions undermine buyer confidence which will likely result in reduced interest and lower bid levels.

> We would expect to have visually inspected at least 80% of properties by collateral value within a portfolio. Sellers discourage inspections, so we have to become expert at taking covert photographs from cars, checking into hotels under alias, visiting factory shops, making office job applications or getting lost in commercial buildings.

Controlling a bidding process

NPL sales results in the past show that the best price is achieved by sellers retaining flexibility according to changing circumstance and events, whilst extending the process to the widest possible market; i.e. having the greatest competition. A private sale with one other party is limiting and allows the bidder to take a safety-first, conservative view, minimising their pricing risk. It is better to extend competition through either phased or unphased tender, or auction to a limited number of participants, with competition maximised by opening up the process to any party who passes the seller's bidding criteria. *Phased* refers to the process of having repeated bidding rounds whereby lowest bidders are dropped from the next round of bidding.

The key to maximising bids is to preserve greatest control over the bid process at all times and always encourage bidders to go the extra yard on price. There is no doubt that, in many cases, the excitement and desire to beat the competition pushes bidders higher. Consistently maintaining the strongest negotiating position, with the ability to interact with bidders to negotiate up bid levels, benefits the seller. This is best achieved with a sale by open tender, followed by a seller option for a subsequent private, limited auction amongst the top bidders. Figure 3.3 illustrates how competitive bids can be maximised.

Figure 3.3 – maximising competitive NPL bids

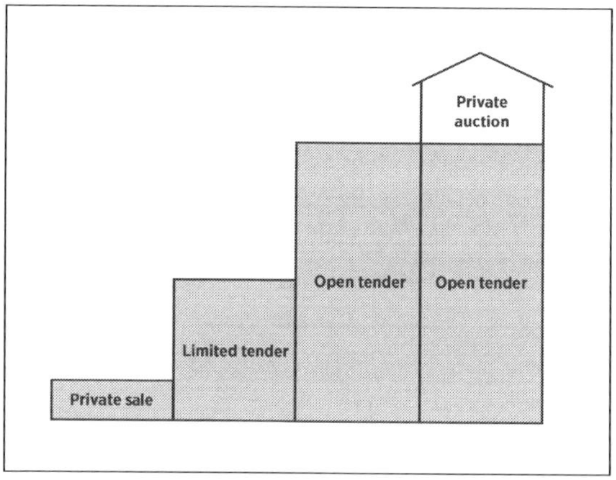

Using third-party sales advisers

Selling institutions may elect to sell their own NPLs or alternatively choose to employ third-party sales advisers. In terms of access to buyers, third-party consultants will have better buyer network contacts, be more experienced in selling NPLs and therefore can advise a seller from a potential buyer's perspective. Specialist consultancies will understandably be much closer to the NPL wholesale market than institutions. Placing a third party between buyer and seller also improves flexibility and strengthens the seller's bargaining position. This flexibility is lost if an institution decides to deal face to face with buyers.

A recurring problem within financial institutions is the risk of internal politics derailing NPL sale transactions. Internal work-out departments are often the least motivated to sell loans and may be conflicted given that the staff within may become redundant in the event of a loan book being sold.

Sometimes, sellers provide bidders with copies of property valuation reports. These are usually inaccurate, but can help explain bid-ask disparities. The accuracy of collateral valuation reports supplied by third-party advisers is generally significantly higher than those supplied by sellers.

The downside of using third-party sales consultants is fees. However, provided a consultant has suitable track record and experience, a selling institution should expect to receive greater than the costs of fees through equivalent sales price increase.

Qualifying bidders

Experienced third-party consultants will also know which investors are likely to pay the highest price for a portfolio and will be able to prequalify bidders. The normal method of qualifying bidders is through the payment of bidder qualification fees, which generally cuts out parties that are not serious. However, if these fees are perceived as overly-expensive it reflects badly on the seller and undermines execution certainty. *If sellers are unrealistic on qualification fees, what chance will there be of realism with the ultimate selling price?* Traditionally, market levels for these fees have been in the $10,000 to 50,000 range. Reasonable bidder qualification fees should reflect the cost of connecting with potential bidders and the production of an information memorandum.

Most of the big international accounting firms now have experienced, dedicated NPL groups that can provide advisory services to both institutions and investors covering most jurisdictions in the world.

Information memorandum

A preliminary information memorandum should clarify:

- Timeline, sales structure, bidding method, validity, seller disposal considerations, due diligence process and next steps.

It should include a description of loans as at the cut-off date in terms of:

- Outstanding principal balance (OPB), default interest, capitalised interest (if any).

- Number of loans, number of borrower groups, types of loans, loan age/maturity, performing/NPL, secured/unsecured/first lien.
- Currencies, geographical location, structured credits/derivatives (if any), commercial operating/non-operating/industry type.
- Unusual credit types, legal proceedings, bankruptcy. These should be stratified and segmented for easy overall analysis.
- If real estate valuations are included, it should be stated whether these were undertaken by the seller or independently, together with their date.
- Current loan servicing arrangements.

Providing bidders with data and granting enough time

Bidders need to be granted sufficient time and be provided with data of the best possible quality in order to maximise their bids. In recent times, electronic or virtual data rooms have been preferred to physical data rooms, though electronic data increases the needs for seller representations and warranties. If a physical data room is used, it must suit bidder numbers together with their consultant's needs, with easy access to data for all parties.

Legal ramifications

Representations and warranties made to buyers will have an impact upon the likely bid amounts. Drafting sale and purchase agreements as early as possible improves the certainty of execution. Bidders cannot finalise negotiations until they have had a chance to inspect transactional documentation, so the sooner this is expedited, the sooner the risk of bidders renegotiating terms is removed.

Also on the legal side, the logistics of loan, security and document transfer upon completion of the transaction need to be prepared for and agreed with the buyer. The winning bidder will likely use a different entity for their bid and legal closing. This, together with the need to obtain internal consents between bid and closing, including credit, treasury, funding, market risk, regulatory, product control, legal, tax, currency and letters of credit, is a further reason why larger complicated NPL transactions usually take longer than expected to close.

Before finalising a bid, a buyer will usually want to have completed diligence and fully understood at least 80%, by outstanding principal balance, of the portfolio for sale. Highest bidders usually employ the best third-party accountants, lawyers and appraisers. A competent potential buyer will also need to clarify future servicing resources before bidding. Bid price is effectively the net present value of future cash flow. In simple terms, future cash flow is determined by loan according to real estate or other collateral, mortgage recovery, plus other collections less costs.

Disparity in NPL bid-ask spreads

Buyers will almost certainly disagree with sellers' collateral valuations. Additional discrepancies may occur with non-operating corporates. Some commercial real estate may only have value to the existing operator whilst buildings, machinery, etc., may have limited value to other users. Buyers may attribute zero enterprise value to corporate NPLs. Bidders may discount operating company audit reports if they are not undertaken by large international accountants, and may also tend to discount information for non-listed private companies and for guarantors if not fully collateralised. Figure 3.4 shows how the bank seller and investor arrive at a different collateral valuation.

Figure 3.4 – how the bank seller and investor arrive at a different collateral valation

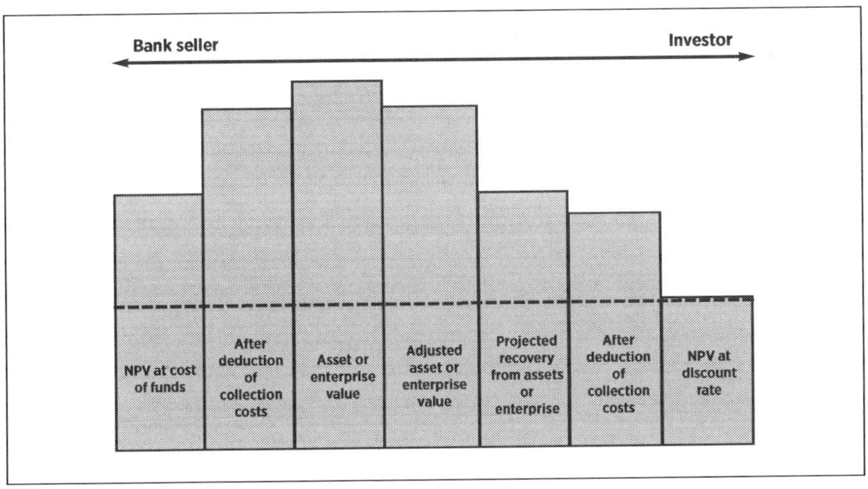

The buyer's pricing process starts by analysing the asset values or enterprise values that secure each loan. Then they assume a recovery rate against the loan in the future. They allocate costs against collecting a particular loan. The balance can be present valued back by between 15% and as much as 25%. In this way, the typical buyer discounts the cash flows twice – assuming very low recovery rates and then making doubly sure to protect their investment by assuming very high discount rates. In the event that real estate appraisals are discounted too, the cash flow can effectively be discounted three times. The final bid number is then adjusted by applying a variety of timing sensitivity scenarios, subject to the final risk-weighted discount rate, applied to the future cash flow.

Maximising portfolio sales

NPL portfolio sales are maximised by creating competitive auctions, with both local and international investors, and structuring the sale to retain upside. Proceeds are also maximised by reducing the discounts, often attributed by investors, as a result of poor data, confused bidding rules, weak selling conditions in sales documentation, or poor portfolio construction.

> International NPL investors should typically expect to close one-in-ten transactions. One-third of opportunities will likely be immediately rejected, so diligence will only be undertaken on the remaining two-thirds. With competent due diligence, accurate underwriting, liquidity and a good idea of what they are doing they should expect to close one in five deals that diligence is undertaken on.

Finally, retaining discipline in achieving target prices and utilising experienced advisors avoids potential losses in sale proceeds. If advisers can, as a minimum, eradicate either disparity in asset values or recovery rates, their fees are usually more than covered.

NPL books are a complicated and relatively illiquid commodity. As a result, selling NPL portfolios almost always takes longer than expected. Shaping agreement between the different perspectives of buyers and sellers is challenging.

In the aftermath of the 2008 financial crisis, uncertainty and volatility has further divided the risk horizons of institutional sellers and speculative buyers, increasing disparity in bid-ask spreads. As a result, straightforward wholesale cash transactions acceptable to both buyer and seller may not be easy to achieve in prevailing market conditions.

Fashions change and technology evolves. Banks looking to sell portfolios in the foreseeable future will probably need to structure transactions in ways that are much more sensitive to the core financial objectives of both parties, in order to close a transaction that maximises proceeds.

4. PREPARATION AND PLANNING SOLUTIONS

4.1 Core concepts and components

Working practice in the traditional credit-analysis distribution model used by banks focuses on good customer relationships and efficiency. The skill sets inherent to the profitable execution of this model are mostly superfluous when a bank is overwhelmed with NPLs. A whole range of additional skill sets are required that existing bank resources do not include.

New tools like foreclosure, restructuring, refinancing, revitalisation, bespoke litigation, information gathering, intelligence, engagement and negotiation skills suddenly come to the fore. Credit analysis experience alone is insufficiently broad compared with the wide range of skills required for successful debt collection.

The purpose of this chapter is to identify, list and relate the resources, attributes and skill sets that provide the foundation for effectively operating asset management platforms. Figure 4.1 summarises these resources, attributes and skill sets.

Figure 4.1 – the core asset management concepts and components

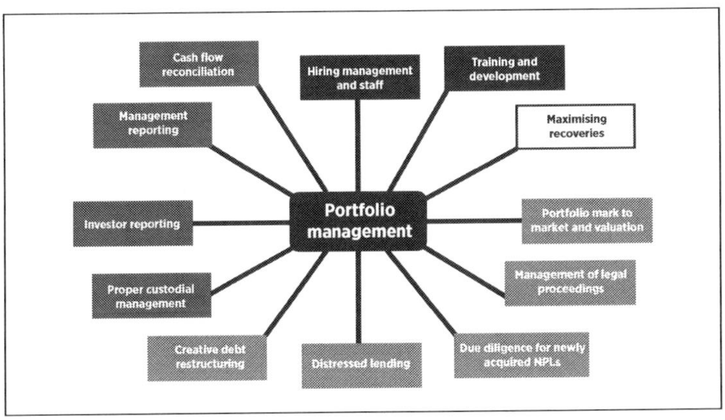

Structural and operational considerations

When establishing a servicing entity, the basic issues that need to be considered fall into two categories: *structural* and *operational* considerations. Each asset management case and portfolio is unique, but structural considerations might include, for example:

- Specific jurisdictional issues
- Local laws
- Regulatory control
- Shareholding and ownership structure
- Tax efficiency
- Legal system and issues
- Working capital, cash flow and dividends
- Cash management system
- Securitisation and rating agencies
- Ease of sale of entity/disintegrative ability
- Appeal, transparency and value of entity to third-party investors

Operational considerations might, for example, include:

- Size and type of portfolio to be managed
- Age and loan size distribution
- Location and geography
- Labour skill set availability and recruitment potential
- Staff compensation, incentivisation and training
- Staff security
- Custodian, document security and access
- Cash management and collection account processes
- IT and telecoms
- Reporting, quality control
- Audit and compliance
- Effectiveness of legal enforcement in jurisdiction
- Need for special teams

Core operational responsibilities and skill sets

Organisational requirements may vary case by case. Generally, the five principal organisational areas are:

1. Credit and financial analysis
2. Data analysis, processing and communication
3. Legal analysis and legal actions
4. Loan administration
5. Real estate valuation, ownership and disposition

The core resources and responsibilities essential to the organisation include the following:

Asset management

- Business plans
- Collections
- Debtor financial analysis
- Default management
- Default reporting
- Loss mitigation
- Research and information gathering
- Work-outs interaction and negotiation

Customer relations

- Contact detail verification
- Customer Q&A
- Default management
- Loss mitigation
- Messages and communication
- Occupancy/vacancy confirmation
- Skip tracing (keeping track of migrating borrowers)

Legal

- Assignment
- Bankruptcy
- Document tracking
- File room
- Forbearance
- Foreclosure
- Put-backs
- Registration
- Repayment plans.
- Releases
- Securitisation

Lender/loan stakeholder relations

- Billing/collections
- Cash management
- Cash reconciliation
- Metrics and oversight
- Stakeholder management reporting
- Stakeholder accounting

Process management

- Accounting
- Asset and asset manager monitoring
- Escrow analysis
- Loan watch-lists
- Payoffs
- Resolution and action approvals
- Surveillance and intelligence reporting

- Taxes and insurance
- Third party oversight

Real estate

- Acquisitions
- Appraisals
- Broker opinions
- Consultancy management
- Due diligence
- Pricing
- Property inspections
- Property management
- Property marketing
- Operating budget analysis
- Owned real estate and other assets
- Sales broking

Sales and acquisitions (if appropriate)

- Acquisitions
- Contract negotiation
- Credit review
- Data verification
- Deal modelling
- Due diligence
- Loan transfer
- Loan set-up
- Pipeline management
- Underwriting
- Upload and analysis

Core characteristics

Core traits of asset-management entities should include, as a minimum, the following:

Customer service

- Highly efficient and capable of managing portfolio diversity and volume.
- Excellent internal controls, policies and procedures resulting in superior service.

Employees

- Experienced executives/business unit management teams.
- Stable employee base with controlled turnover.
- Appropriate compensation and incentivisation programmes for all employees.
- Motivated, high quality workforce.

Process and controls

- Fully documented and updated policies and procedures available online to all staff.
- Strong adherence to appropriate asset management practices.
- Strong risk management.
- Clear, accurate and timely reporting capability.
- Well developed disaster recovery and business continuity plans.

Stability

- The overall stability of the corporate entity.
- Financial wherewithal of third parties.

Technology

- Automated state of the art fully disintegrative programs and support.
- Focus on using tech solutions to improve workflow, processes and service.

- Minimal manual manipulation of loan data.
- Automated decision support system.

Training

- Formal and effective training programmes.
- Comprehensive training programmes for all new employees.
- Ongoing training for all employees.
- Global standard trainers.

Office layout

The core structure can be divided between front office and back office functions and activities as follows:

Front end

- Asset administration:
    - Cash management
    - Change Management
    - Custodial
    - Legal – litigation, bankruptcy, foreclosure
    - NPL asset management
    - Acquisitions.
    - Action plan/business plan
    - Asset appraisal and analysis
    - Reporting/performance metrics
    - Work-outs, borrower interaction, negotiation
- Process administration:
    - Investment metrics and reporting
    - Loan/borrower management and communication
    - New loan set-up

- Real estate/hard asset management:
    - Acquisitions
    - Marketing
    - Pricing
    - Property management
    - Property specific work-out
    - Valuation

Back office

- Corporate:
    - Contracts, licensing and registration
    - Control of corporate documentation
    - Internal audit
    - Regulatory compliance
- Finance:
    - Budget
    - Cash management/disbursements
    - Collections/ cash reconciliation
    - Fee calculation
    - Financial statement production
    - Payroll
    - Tax/insurance management
- Human resource/administration:
    - Office management, purchasing
    - Staffing, employment rules
- Information technology:
    - Change management
    - Development/oversight/implementation

- Disaster recovery.
- IT procurement.
- Security, permissions and control.

Given the wide range of skills required, organisation of this process creates it own challenges. Special consideration needs to be given to group structure, teamwork and communication flow. Open-plan office layouts generally facilitate better management, monitoring and control of work-out units.

Security

The risk from hostile borrowers needs to be counteracted by high-quality security and careful configuration of meeting rooms where asset managers come into contact with borrowers. Video monitoring and recording borrower meetings benefits security and loan case records. In some situations, a physical security guard presence may be necessary.

Cash

Asset managers must never be put into a position whereby they have to touch cash. Collection accounts are very easy to set up with banks that have nationwide branch and ATM networks. If borrowers appear at offices with cash, they should be directed or accompanied to the nearest bank branch that has an agreed collection facility. Borrowers also need to be informed in advance of the time constraints this imposes, in the event they may wish to make cash settlements in accordance with contractual deadlines.

> Panic stations arise when a borrower comes rushing into the office with cash outside banking hours, just before a legal deadline. If there is any likelihood of this occurring, asset managers need to pre-warn them. Missing a deadline because the banks are shut is bad planning and you cannot turn away the cash. When this happened to us, we ended up with the money in our safe overnight. In the absence of a cashier, the collection was signed off by the CEO and the finance director, with approval from head office.

Investors purchasing portfolios where cash collections are likely to occur need to consider not only how they will service the portfolio, but how they will manage collections and plan accordingly. The seller bank may be able to provide collection services, provided they have sufficiently widespread distribution and their charges are competitive.

4.2 Resources for different loan types

The distressed debt collection business typically falls into three types of loan category. Each one has its own unique resource blend requirement. Loan types can be broadly categorised as follows:

1. System-driven collections for credit cards, small retail loans and leasing.
2. Management-driven collections for residential mortgage loans.
3. Management intensive collections for corporates, bonds and larger property collateralised loans.

Technical knowledge, such as financial, legal and property expertise is fundamental to most loan categories. One size does *not* fit all though and different loan categories require different skill-set mixes. Getting the balance right is the key to collection performance. Core skill components may also vary across different types of servicer and within different jurisdictions. Figure 4.2 illustrates the balance of systems and asset manager skill needed for different loan types.

Figure 4.2 – balance of systems and asset manager skill set by loan type

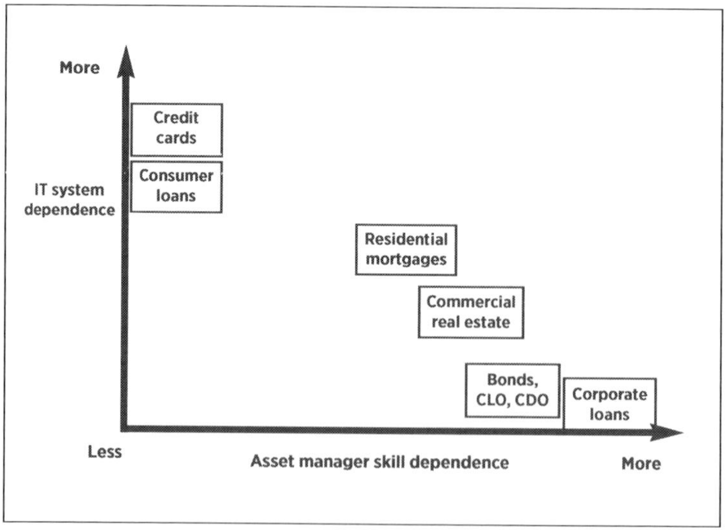

Typically, the larger the loan, the more challenging it will be to maximise collections. Smaller loans are more IT dependant; bigger loans are more relationship dependant. Similarly, when bidding for loan portfolios, credit card underwriting, for example, is more statistical, whilst larger loans demand accurate personal judgment.

Credit cards and consumer loans

Credit cards and consumer loans are generally small and unsecured. Extremely high volumes of loans or other receivables demand state of the art information technology records and communication systems. Transfer of ownership, particularly, involves intricate loan boarding and data input facilities that necessitate extreme accuracy.

The value of small loans is age driven – the older the loan, the lower its recovery potential. Efficient communication with the borrower is therefore critical to the collection process. Servicers generally operate from a call centre with hundreds of work stations, which have the ability to generate literally millions of bills and follow up letters on a daily basis. Good telesales facilities are therefore paramount.

Servicers can, in cases, employ debt collectors who operate from fleets of cars with mobile communication. Some servicers may also operate from a group of regional offices, in order to facilitate easy access to borrowers or debtors.

Residential mortgage loans

Residential mortgage loans are usually serviced in high volume. They also demand state of the art information technology records and communication systems. Servicing residential loans is predominantly process driven. Loans are categorised according to

> The key to optimising monetisation of big residential portfolios is ready provisioning of finance. Most people want to keep their homes and will gladly refinance their way out of the problem, which usually results in good collections near or at par.
>
> After 1997 in South East Asia, there was an acute liquidity shortage, so we bought a defunct finance company in order to obtain a lending licence and set up a new pioneering online residential lending facility. The new online initiative didn't do very well because it coincided with the local banking sector suddenly rebounding phoenix-style from the ashes of recession.
>
> An aggressive home loan local price war ensued. Loan to value offered by local banks started out at 80%, quickly rising to 90% and ultimately 100%. This was fantastic for us and the disappointment we suffered with online lending was more than compensated for by a boom in our portfolio collections. The local mortgage price war enabled us to resolve loans at levels significantly above par.

whether they are performing, restructured or at a particular point within the execution or negotiation process.

Asset managers tend to operate within teams that are specialist in one particular function. The collection process for an individual loan will therefore likely be passed through a number of different teams. Credit bidding may occur frequently, in which case servicers generally need a specialist property management and brokerage facility, either acting themselves or outsourced.

Servicers will generally also need a strong legal division capable of speed and volume. Borrowers rarely use professional advisors and negotiations are normally not overly complicated. The collateral is frequently a borrower's own home, so often they see greater asset value than any other party and will therefore pay more to keep the property.

The key to maximising collections is high volume procedural efficiency, and a great deal of management time is spent in monitoring ratios and percentages at different points in the resolution process.

Corporate, larger and more complicated loans

Corporate, larger and more complex loans demand top flight asset management skills, backed up by robust technology systems. Each loan and borrower is unique and requires individual, specialist attention on a case-by-case basis. Unlike small or medium-sized loans, where different skill sets are practiced by different teams, larger loans demand that asset managers are well versed in all disciplines. Resolving small loans requires close-knit, individual-discipline teams to complement one another; larger loans need their asset managers to be a jack of all trades.

> Purchasing a commercial loans portfolio in a new jurisdiction after a market crash can open the door to an *Aladdin's cave* of new opportunity. Firstly, it presents a seat at the local institutional creditors' club table. Once you own a part of a company's debt, you usually gain ready access to them and accurately pricing their risk becomes much easier.
>
> Afterwards, the same corporations' debts start to reappear every time you look at a new loan portfolio. Economies of scale and collateral arbitrage then give you a huge advantage every time you bid for a new piece of the debt, and increase your rate of return on everything you have bought. Occasionally you may gain overall control of the debt. Financing your investment out with a little profit on top, leaving you with an equity piece of a performing restructured corporation for free, is great business.

A detailed business plan, including a projected recovery strategy, is the starting point for each loan, which may adjust and vary according to circumstances. Larger loans normally take the longest to resolve, but may also have the best potential returns, sometimes with the capacity to generate huge windfall recoveries.

IT systems for all loan categories

For all loan categories, distressed debt asset management platforms need to be supported by high quality specialised IT systems and smart telephone systems. Distressed debt IT systems are very different to the traditional good bank IT system model and need to include subjects such as:

- Asset manager tracking.
- Business plans, default management and loan amendments.
- Detailed work-out status.
- Intelligence, litigation and foreclosure.
- Online access to valuable documents.
- Property level management and valuation details.
- Specialist analytics, metrics, surveillance and reporting systems.

Failure to implement the right IT system support will result in less efficiency, diminished performance and lower collections. Errors in loan-boarding onto a system, either for a new IT resource, or for a newly acquired portfolio, can be extremely costly, and mistakes can potentially take years to unravel.

Good information technology systems abound and can be readily purchased off the shelf, or can be adapted for a user's specific needs. A number of third-party servicers market their own proven custom-built, web-based systems that are packaged together with their services, or can be licensed independently.

Top flight personal skills are much more difficult to acquire than IT systems and cannot be readily found in abundance through normal recruitment channels. In most cases, personal skills represent the difference that makes the top performing bad banks and special servicers stand out.

4.3 Preparing the groundwork for resolutions

Compiling information, completing current situation assessments, adding new data, writing realistic, projected business plans and devising collection strategy are the foundations upon which each loan is processed for work-out. The word *projected* is important here, as plans and strategy may change as a result of new information or facts coming to light from outside events, investigations, or during borrower discussions.

Understanding all the angles

> When training a special servicer unit in Poland from a legal background, the asset managers were shocked to think that they could look at a loan from anything other than their own legal perspective. After they tried alternative approaches, their collection performance improved dramatically.

A common criticism of business plans is that, in many cases, they only view the loan and collection potential from the lender's perspective. Legally, of course, this may be correct, but unless the loan is viewed from every potential angle, opportunities to improve the lender's negotiating position may be missed. Many asset managers have never considered looking at a loan from any other viewpoint than their own. Before completing strategy or business plans, or commencing engagement or negotiations, it is therefore extremely important that the following are also fully understood:

- Value of assets to lender
- Value of assets to borrower
- Value of assets to any third party guarantors
- Value of assets to other third parties

These positions may also be constantly moving and adjusting, according to changing circumstances.

> **Requiring asset managers to compile detailed business plans ensures that they have studied all documentation in sufficient detail and have accurately reviewed past loan history. Asset managers should constantly challenge the original bank lender assumptions, such as legal actions and decisions, or asset valuation. Business plans originated by borrowers will always tilt resolution strategy in their favour, and may omit or gloss over facts that might give an advantage to the lender.**

The business plan

What should go into the business plan

A typical business plan should comprise a summary with subsequent detailed sections, such as the following:

Business plan summary

- Vital statistics of loan
- Vital statistics of borrower
- Vital statistics of guarantor(s)
- Borrower interaction summary
- Guarantor interaction summary
- Loan numbers by currency
- Collection projection summary and source
- Resolution strategy and opinion:
    - Source of value
    - Litigation strategy
- Strategy components:
    - Guarantors
    - Borrowers operations
    - Legal issues
    - Exit strategy
    - Collateral and security position
    - Administrative and general issues
- Collection cash flow summary

Detailed sections

- Detailed collection projection.
- Execution summary
- Real estate

  - Mortgages
  - Lien table
- Guarantor payments/pay-off
- Company payments/pay-off
- Other legal cases
- Debt summary, interest, total claim
- Loan detail and history
- Protocol schedule/payment plans
- Borrower operations:
  - Detail borrower personal connections
  - Intelligence/ surveillance summary
- Data summary breakdown
- Servicer Action and meeting log
- Other borrower obligations:
  - For example, unfunded letter of credit, export issues
- Collateral detail and valuation summary

Building an understanding of the borrower and obtaining further information

Much of the information that goes into the business plan is known at the loan valuation stage, when loans are acquired or underwritten. However, the key to a successful business plan is to build a deeper understanding of the borrower and other relevant parties, together with the addition of new or unknown information from outside the respective loan file.

When servicing a loan portfolio, the logical place to start is with the biggest loans and then work down to the smallest. For cases that are well collateralised, the focus of research is usually on the assets. For poorly collateralised loans, research focus shifts to the borrower, in order to try and uncover additional unknown information, from which additional collection advantage can be gained. This might, for example, include intelligence gathering by private investigators, or forensic analysis of past legal cases, or the loan history.

It is dangerous with well-collateralised cases, especially where the borrower comes forward to negotiate early, to not spend sufficient time and resources researching additional information about the borrower. This extra research might lead to further, previously obscure, collection opportunities.

Loan servicing planning begins at the diligence stage, even though you are unsure that you will win the portfolio. Sometimes, you get loan resolution assumptions wrong, in which case you need to allow for such a possibility by retaining flexibility in your strategic approach to servicing. In Turkey, for example, at Lehman we thought that much of our original portfolio would provide high-yield restructuring opportunities involving debt on big brand corporate loans. During diligence, we had also spotted that real estate markets were rising. After we won the bid and started servicing, we ended up with no high-yield restructurings. Our servicing constituted a collateral play, based on the real estate markets going up by 100% in the first year. In spite of this, we still doubled our original underwriting target.

Collection targets

Collection targets should be assigned based on each business plan. Targets should be range bound, in order to allow flexibility according to circumstances. The lower number should be the minimum possible collection amount. The top end of the range needs to be based on realistic scenarios, but should also constitute a significant challenge to asset managers. This gives them the opportunity to excel. Targets will also require periodic adjustment in accordance with changing market conditions and events.

Allocation of loan cases among asset managers

An important factor in maximising collections is optimum allocation of loan cases amongst asset managers within a work-out unit. This can be done by dividing up portfolios on a simple numerical or value basis, irrespective of loan detail. Alternatively, allocation can be determined by different types of anticipated resolution path; for example, execution cases to one asset manager, restructuring cases to another.

The other way to allocate is by matching asset managers to borrowers in accordance with experience and ability. This would mean that the biggest and most difficult loans and borrowers would, in theory, be allocated to the most experienced and talented managers. With this approach, top asset managers would probably end up handling a small number of high value cases, whilst junior managers would be handling higher volumes of easier to resolve, lower value cases. Figure 4.3 provides a summary illustration of which groups are the toughest and easiest borrowers to deal with.

Figure 4.3 – illustration of the toughest borrowers

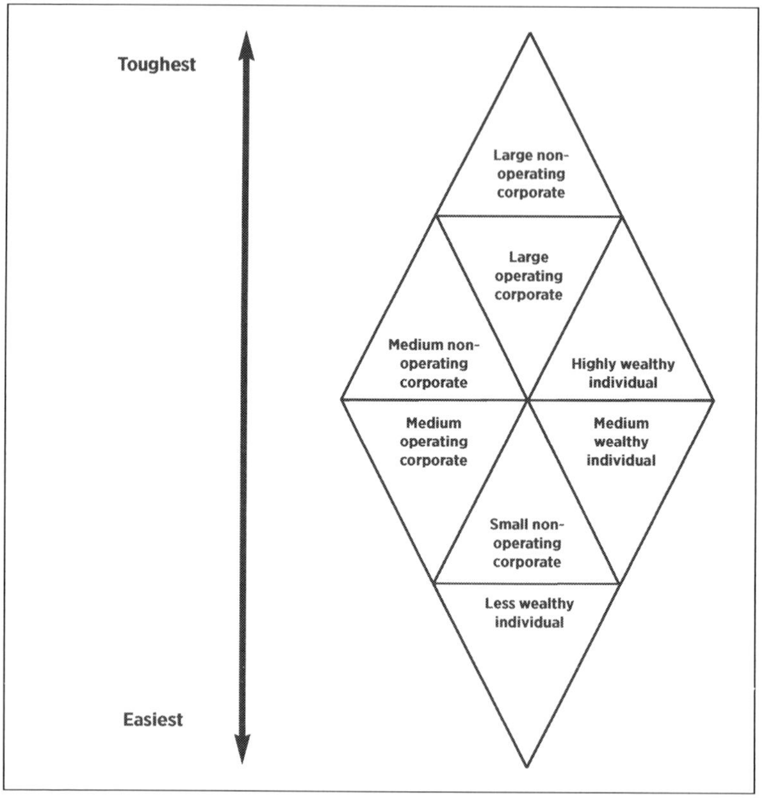

Note on Figure 4.3: non-operating *is meant in the functioning, not the strictly legal sense. E.g. In a falling bear market, most real estate developers are effectively non-operating, irrespective of their legal position.*

The solution to optimum allocation is generally driven by loan or portfolio type. It may also be influenced by particular social factors, or customs in some jurisdictions. For the smallest loans, where asset manager interaction with borrowers is less essential, either a numerical division or allocation by resolution type can work effectively. For the largest loans, with more challenging borrowers, cases are best assigned to asset managers in accordance with experience and track record.

Matching relevant experience and interpersonal skills produces best results; in jurisdictions where social hierarchy is important, there is no alternative to allocating according to status and interpersonal skills. Allocating larger loans by anticipated resolution path tends to water down personal influence and makes collections more process and procedurally driven, which limits collection opportunity.

> In jurisdictions where there is a strong social hierarchy system, asking questions or disagreeing with someone from a higher standing is taboo. Borrowers from the highest social strata would always expect to meet the servicing CEO.

Whichever method of allocation is chosen, switching cases where progress has been slow amongst asset managers can improve results. For larger loans, where personalities matter most, a change of personnel can change things drastically. Asset managers within a work-out unit therefore need to understand that no discredit or failure is inferred if a particular borrower case is transferred to a colleague.

> **Acquiring real estate**
>
> **In the event that real estate collateral is either acquired through credit bidding or voluntarily transferred, it is best handled by property professionals rather than asset managers. The decision to credit bid or accept property in settlement should be made by asset managers. Subsequent property management and asset realisation should be transferred, where possible, to a dedicated, properly trained and experienced REO (real estate owned) unit.**

4.4 Optimising collection distribution

Typically, resolution distribution follows a similar pattern each time. The primary servicing focus tends to be on the largest loans first, gradually working down to smallest loans last. Lenders or portfolio purchasers then tend to add a minimum notional profit, or return margin, on top of their purchase price or book value, in order to determine an asking price for each loan. Resolution generally starts with the simplest cases and then tends to work down in the following order:

1. Borrowers contacting the servicer to resolve early
2. Easier, well-collateralised resolutions
3. Toughest, poorly collateralised resolutions at the end

Loan resolution principles

The principles for loan resolution agreement are likely to be multi-dimensional. The lender will likely view another party's proposal from a number of angles. These might include those shown in Table 4.1.

Table 4.1 – typical principles used by lenders to weigh up whether to execute a loan resolution agreement

Principle	Execute	Do not execute
Liquidity	Cash flows in.	Significant outflow of cash.
Price	Top negotiated price.	Negotiated price is below target.
P & L	P&L gain.	P&L loss.
NPV (at hurdle)	NPV positive.	NPV strongly negative.
Market risk	Increasing market risk.	Reducing market risk.
Credit risk	Reduces risk.	Increases risk.
Operational risk	Eliminates complexity.	Increases risk.

The critical importance of flexibility

The type of approach to resolution shown in Table 4.1 is only a theoretical guide. A multi-dimensional approach of this type can usually work well as long as there is overriding commercial judgment that allows flexibility on the part of the lender. The key word is *flexibility*. In distressed debt resolution nothing should ever be set in stone. Deviation from previously tabled business plans often occurs and collection strategies and tactics constantly adjust to changing circumstances.

Optionality and uncertainty in the minds of borrowers and buyers encourages them to try to do a deal with the asset manager. This creates additional opportunity, opens up new resolution avenues and thereby increases seller options. More options usually lead to higher collections.

Conversely, where there is no flexibility, borrowers and buyers are discouraged from trying to do a deal. Where public accountability or a need for transparency requires full disclosure of transactions or resolution formulae, borrowers and buyers are both discouraged from negotiating and demotivated to act quickly, often preferring a wait and see attitude. This limits seller options and less options usually lead to lower collections.

Collection leakage risk

When investors buy loan portfolios, medium and larger loans are usually valued individually, subject to a risk-adjusted portfolio discount rate, which equates to future profit per loan. Once the servicing process commences, notional asking prices are determined, usually with a uniform profit margin added to the respective loan value. The servicer will then try to maximise profit by bargaining, but will also want to be seen to be commercial and ready to deal. There is usually also some pressure to *score an early goal*, in order to reassure investors that their investment was a good decision.

At this point, portfolio investors now stand the highest risk of suffering collection leakage. Early collections often tend to be made by trial and error, as asset managers familiarise themselves with the portfolio. As a result, servicing kick-off is the best time for borrowers to do deals that benefit them most, and when sellers are most at risk to underselling higher margin loans.

The lesson here is not to be pressured into making early resolutions at the outset. Servicers should retain their discipline and resolve when they are fully prepared and ready. Borrowers or buyers who pressure servicers for early resolutions will generally pay significantly more. Keen and eager buyers usually have money and believe they can do a better deal with the new owner of the debt. The new owner needs to recognise this vulnerability and ensure they are not being manipulated into selling too cheaply.

Investor pressure to achieve early collections can usually be counteracted by sharing with them high borrower offers that have been rejected, in anticipation of larger numbers. Negotiating early deals with eager borrowers is commercially appealing, but needs very careful consideration.

Collateral quality and collection targets

Setting uniform loan collection targets may not be the best way to maximise collections. It is relatively straightforward to achieve high target collections on the better collateralised, easier resolved cases, but extremely difficult to do the same on the poorly collateralised, tougher cases. The easy collection, good collateral cases will also likely be resolved first.

Figure 4.4 illustrates the relationship between collateral quality and ease of collection. Loans on the top right of the chart will tend to be determined first and those on the bottom left last.

Figure 4.4 – the relationship between collateral quality and ease of collection

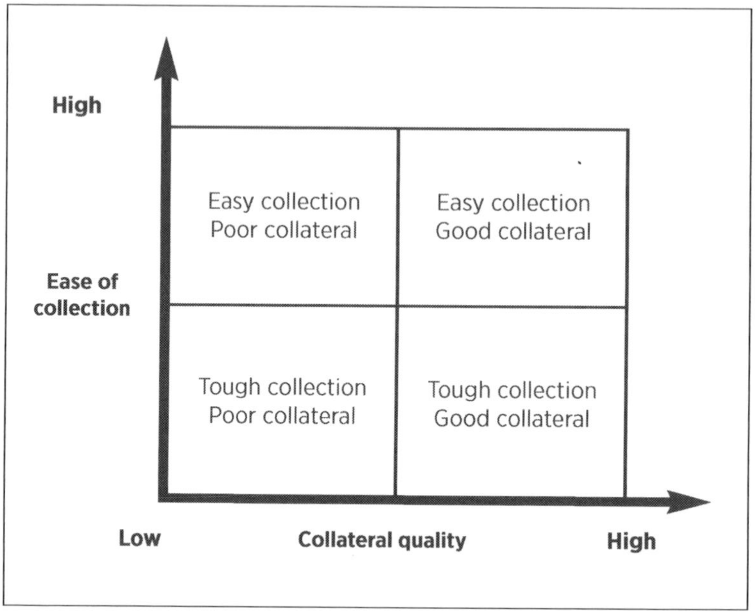

Collection target strategy may therefore be improved by skewing collection targets from the top right towards the bottom left of Figure 4.4, so the easy collection, good collateral cases have a much higher hurdle rate than the hardest loans. Instead of, say, a uniform target of 40% return on acquisition price across a portfolio, this could be adjusted amongst loans in accordance with how challenging they are to resolve, as shown in Table 4.3.

Table 4.3 – adjusting collection targets according to loan resolution difficulty

Category	Collection target
Easy collection, good collateral	50% to 100%
Easy collection, poor collateral	30% to 50%
Tough collection, good collateral	30% to 50%
Tough collection, poor collateral	10% to 30%

Passing the parcel to step up collections

A distressed loan trade is a one-off transaction. Collection can only be made once and there is no repeat business. It is therefore critical to squeeze out every last penny, by every means possible. A further tactic to help extract the absolute maximum occurs when an asset manager negotiates a satisfactory resolution amount with a borrower. This is known in the business as *pass the parcel.*

Once agreement is reached, the transaction is passed up to a higher authority for approval. The higher authority then rejects the deal and asks for a little more. This strategy could in theory be repeated a number of times, in order to gradually step collections up by small amounts, as high as possible.

Recovery times for small loans versus large loans

Borrower motivation to resolve early often depends on the importance of their collateral to them, or other commercial pressures. Smaller, simpler loans with less sophisticated borrowers can often be resolved early at high levels relative to loan principal. Smaller loans become increasingly difficult to resolve at high levels as time passes, as the risk of borrowers walking away, or being unable to be located, rises.

Big, complex commercial loans are generally the opposite. Early resolution offers from borrowers that seem attractive sometimes mean the asset manager has missed something, or is not in possession of all the facts. Generally, maximising recovery for larger loans takes time.

Collection distribution

An ideal collection distribution pattern for an NPL portfolio, in terms of collections as a percentage of Unpaid Principle Balance (UPB), might appear as shown in Figure 4.5

Starting off with first collections in excess of UPB is not only important for the market and other interested parties, but sets the right tone for following collections and facilitates any future potential hedging exercises. In the event that the portfolio is held in a bad bank, where the good bank wants to sell off the bad bank, sale may best be undertaken during the period of the portfolio lifetime where collections are closest to principal.

Figure 4.5 – ideal collection distribution for an NPL portfolio

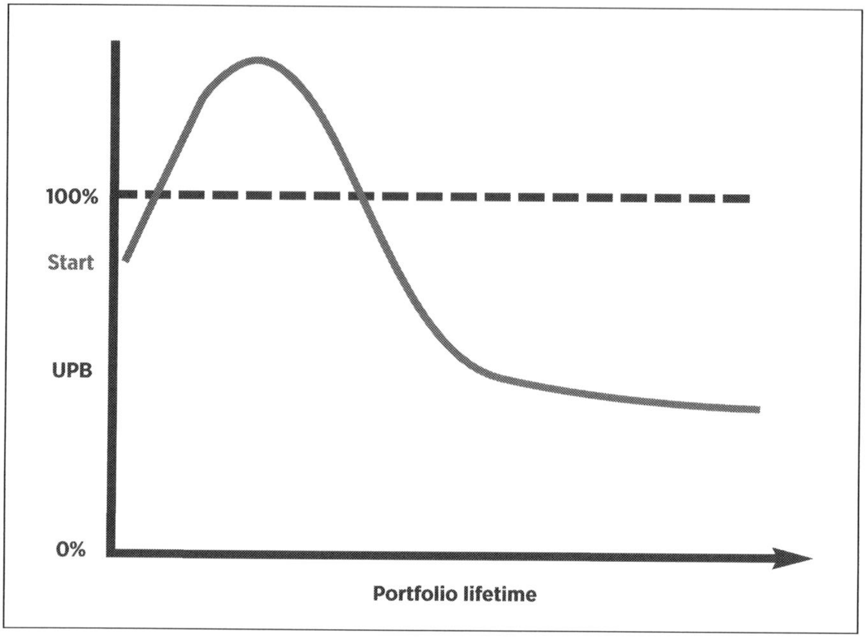

Pareto's Law that 80% of the best collections will be made from 20% of a loan portfolio also applies to NPLs. These loans should be identified as early as possible and allocated to the most able asset managers. Servicer CEOs should focus on monitoring these loans specifically.

5. ASSET MANAGEMENT SOLUTIONS

5.1 Skill sets for distressed asset managers

One of the primary sources of performance variability in servicing is asset managers. This is logical, given that this is where the primary interface with the borrower mostly occurs. As in any field of finance, dedication, application, good support and training are core ingredients for successful asset managers. Motivation and practice are also fundamental. Some bank credit officers fail to transition because they are unable to adapt to the challenge of learning and practicing new skill sets. Generally, the wider the range of previous finance related experience, the better new recruits perform.

The multi-disciplinary skill sets required by asset managers

To perform competently at the highest level, particularly with larger and more complicated loans, asset managers need to be able to put into practice a multi-disciplinary skill set of core professional competencies. These fall into three broad categories of technical knowledge:

1. Finance
2. Legal
3. Real estate

1. Finance

- Cash flows
- Corporate operations
- Company accounts
- Credit agreements
- Hedging

- Returns and sensitivity analysis
- Structured products: CDOs, CLOs, CMBS, RMBS
- Use of spreadsheets
- Writing business plans

2. Legal

- Bankruptcy law
- Commercial law
- Conveyancing
- Managing intelligence agents
- Managing lawyers
- Mortgages, pledges and attachments
- Threat, use and timing of legal challenge

3. Real estate

- Ability to assimilate accurate local market knowledge
- Appraisals
- Auctions
- Broking
- Credit bidding
- Good powers of observation, for site visits
- Investment
- Property management
- Real estate development
- Understanding market value drivers

For individuals to be able to practice such a wide range of skills competently is extremely challenging and few manage to achieve the highest level. Shared skill set functions amongst different asset managers runs the risk of unbalanced resolution strategies driven by the relative strength of different personalities and not by the merits of a specific resolution case. Except for smaller loans, passing cases amongst different departments without overall directional control from a single asset manager that understands each technical core competency will result in weaker strategies and potential collection leakage.

Buying the largest corporate loans and monetising them successfully is the ultimate servicing challenge and demands the highest levels of skill, performance and execution. Corporate debt can take many forms from secured commercial mortgages to senior and subordinated bonds, to equipment leasing loans. These may be fully performing, sub-performing or non-performing. Some may be convertible to equity.

Pricing is driven by estimating future performance and valuation of the company. The arbitrage is usually buying the debt at a discount and being refinanced out somewhere between par and your investment basis. Sometimes you may earn a lot more than par, especially if some of the debt converts to equity that appreciates in value as the company's operational performance improves. The risk is of course that you may lose money or even end up with nothing.

The typical sweet spot is investing up to $5 million and earning somewhere between $5 and 15 million two to three years later. One of our greatest successes occurred with a South Korean electronics company where we invested $43 million in debt and earned close to $168 million over four years, representing a $125 million profit on the deal.

Additional personal skills

In addition to technical skills, good business sense, commercial engagement, a positive can do attitude and negotiating skills are paramount.

Commercial common sense also dictates that asset managers need to be able to maximise collections, both at loan level, and through control of costs and expenses.

Identifying with other people, their psychology and perception also helps speed up personal interaction and improves understanding. Assuming that everybody else views the world the same as you is misleading and wastes precious time. The ability of asset managers to see a borrower's differing point of view helps resolve distressed debt more quickly, efficiently and successfully.

People are not always rational in commercial situations and are mostly under informed. To the general public, base pricing or valuation is not empirical; it is a constructive, context-dependant process that is further warped by personal emotions. If accurate pricing were the only yard-stick, hotel mini-bars, as an example, would not exist as we know them. People tend to pay more according to their ability to pay, rather than the merits of intrinsic value.

Asset managers exist to maximise collections in any way possible, and a borrower's willingness and ability to pay should therefore be exploited to the full.

Some of the more disappointing newly recruited asset managers at Lehman were bank credit officers who couldn't adapt. Many of these had terrific technical skills but could not develop their own interpersonal skills sufficiently. Generally, the wider the range of finance related experience, the better new asset management recruits performed. Former bank credit officers, who also had other relevant commercial experience, often came out on top.

The best advice to a newly recruited asset manager might be to treat every new NPL encountered like a foul up! Original bank information should never be trusted at face value. Everything should be independently tested. Thinking like a financial doctor, or a financial detective, is likely to be more productive than thinking like a banker. Fully understanding the current situation, even when not wholly supplied with the facts, is critical for deciding which strategy is likely to provide the best foundation for work-out.

Past crises in various jurisdictions have shown that, with ongoing coaching and good training, a bank credit officer can, on average, make the transition over to becoming a competent distressed asset manager after 12 months of full-time practice.

Comparing the skills of bank loan officers and debt asset managers

The procedures that are followed

Bank loan officers follow strict process and procedurally-driven, limited product lines, whilst distressed debt asset managers have an enormously more complicated job, with many more options and decisions to choose and execute. Usually there is no set strategy for asset managers; strategies may change mid-stream, and a number of different strategies may be running concurrently.

Typical distressed servicing actions could, for example, include the following:

- **Accelerated recovery**: refinancing and forfeiting close-out costs.
- **Asset sale**: third-party sale, usually completed at a discount.
- **Credit enhancement**: additional collateral for restructuring.
- **Discounted capital pay off**: early repayment for high risk cases.

- **Foreclosure and execution**: the last resort, but note other creditors rights.
- **Hedging**: currency hedging, swaps, CDS and derivative contracts.
- **Passive run-down**: credit paying down to (delayed) maturity.
- **Restructuring**: credit intensive and difficult to avoid future default.
- **Structured sale**: synthetic sale, where the lender retains a future interest.
- **Securitisation**: effective where there is certainty of cash flow.

A different working environment

Distressed asset management has other key differences compared with a bank credit officer's role. At its core, bank loan officers operate within a calculated risk environment with expectation of certainty, whilst distressed debt asset managers operate within an environment of uncertainty with variable outcomes, dependant on their actions. Bank loan officers usually approach borrowers with enthusiasm and openness, whilst distressed debt asset managers engage borrowers with caution, knowing that the resolution strategy they chose will likely influence the final collection amount.

The character of normal, good bank officers compared to that of NPL servicers

Character types of good bank credit, lending and transaction officers

At certain points within the credit process, the human factor comes into play. Within a normal functioning good bank credit/lending/transaction officers tend to fall into five distinct character types:

1. **Overly aggressive** – closing deals for the sake of achieving a closing, or to order, irrespective of the merits of the proposed transaction. They are probably highly competitive individuals and the purpose of closing the transaction is self-promotion. These optimistic characters are likely to be good communicators and highly motivated with a strong work ethic, but effectively risk gamblers. Market conditions are irrelevant and they may have limited or no market knowledge. Transactions closed by these characters will only ever work in a boom market and are likely the first to default in downturn.
2. **Experienced market player** – having excellent market knowledge and a good understanding of market conditions. These characters are critical to have around in difficult market conditions, or at the

beginning of a new market cycle and can produce solid, safe returns. However, their potential downside is that they may become prematurely risk averse as prices rise during the market cycle and thus prematurely pull back from new opportunity.

3. **Bureaucrats** – demonstrate outstanding attention to detail and will only approve or sponsor transactions that tick all the boxes. It is difficult to get them to change their position and they are therefore of limited benefit in competitive situations when an edge or something different is needed. They may have limited or no market knowledge and are unlikely to have any feel for changing market conditions. Their sensitivity to changing circumstances is like driving a car at 90mph towards a brick wall and not being aware of it until they run head-first into it. Some risk management and product control officers fall into this category.

4. **Conservative bureaucrats** – the same as the category above, but once they have ticked all the boxes they will knock off at least 10% as an additional safety margin. This makes them ineffective in difficult market conditions and of no benefit for institutions trying to build their business at the beginning of a market cycle. They would be most effective at the peak of the cycle prior to downturn, when their markdowns would mitigate later distressed losses. Distressed debt asset managers need to be careful not to fall into the trap of this kind of approach, in the event they become credit officers after market rebound, and credit returns to growth.

> Conservative bureaucrats are probably the worst characters because they are hard to spot and upper management often trust them. They can cause huge business damage and stifle franchise growth.

5. **Black balls** – they turn down almost everything, on the basis that nothing can then ever go wrong that they can be blamed for. A complete waste of time and hopefully quickly move on to find a new career. They would be at their most useful just before a market crash, but have usually long gone by then.

Distressed debt asset managers may fall into similar character patterns when they are working on NPL acquisitions or as investors on the buy side. Therefore, asset managers should try to understand which risk tendency they are likely to adopt in order to improve their own effectiveness.

Character types of asset managers involved in NPL resolution

Asset managers tend to fall into a parallel set of character types as far as NPL resolution is concerned:

1. **Overly aggressive** – again, closing deals for the sake of achieving a closing irrespective of the merits of the proposed transaction. They tend to focus primarily on speed and, as a result, leave money on the table and rarely maximise collections.
2. **Experienced market players** – again, having excellent market knowledge and a good understanding of market conditions. With patience and confidence, they usually make the best asset managers with the potential to achieve the highest collections.
3. **Bureaucrats** – again, outstanding attention to detail and will only approve or sponsor resolutions that tick all the boxes. Overly rigid and inflexible, they rarely maximise collections.

Investors and buyers of distressed debt usually tend to have asset managers falling in the first category, whilst bank work-out groups tend to employ asset managers in the third category. Best results are achieved by work-out entities with a concentration of asset managers in the second category.

5.2 Managing asset managers

More than ever, debt collection organisations now need expert individuals to develop talent and results from others under their direction, not by increasing controls upon them and not by monitoring them more closely. Rather, the key to progress and development is for managers and leaders to coach and train their subordinates to learn new skills that improve their collection performance. Developing, coaching and motivating people properly takes time, and there is a constant nagging risk, given the short-term cyclical nature of the distressed debt industry, that retraining efforts will be wasted if staff abruptly leave.

A combination of technical and personal skills

Becoming a top flight asset manager is not easy. Possession of both excellent technical knowledge and first class personal skill sets is fundamental. In order to reach the highest level of performance, asset managers need to have both of these. Technical knowledge without personal skills, or personal skills without technical knowledge, doesn't get there. Within the distressed debt industry, as with many other businesses, the technical skills are more straightforward – they can be picked up from books, universities, professional bodies and online. Practice and experience develop them.

Picking up personal skills necessary for effectively handling defaulted borrowers is much more difficult and is also more challenging to put into practice. Educational sources for personal skills are less structured than technical skills, which add to the learning challenge. As a result, technical skills tend to be prioritised over personal skills and education tends to be focused on technical knowledge. It has in the past been generally assumed that asset managers already have or will pick up the necessary personal skills as they go along.

Personal skills

Technical knowledge, as described in the last chapter, falls into three broad categories: finance, legal and real estate. Personal skills include:

- General commercial insight
- Communication ability
- Empathy
- Organisational ability
- Expertise in planning and executing strategy
- Engagement proficiency
- Powers of persuasion
- Strong negotiation skills

Asset managers can best help themselves by adopting the right approach and the correct attitude. Allied to sufficient desire and motivation, and with repeated practice, there is no reason why they cannot excel. Leaders can help their asset managers improve their performance by directing, encouraging, motivating and supporting them. Coaching and training is a core part of this process.

Leadership and good management

Three themes of leadership and group management

Books and courses abound on the subject of leadership and good management. Three basic themes tend to recur:

1. Work harder than your people.
2. Develop a good relationship with your staff.
3. Provide as much continuing education as possible.

The majority of managers tend to concentrate on the first theme because it is the easiest to control and implement personally, and gives most people a degree of self satisfaction. However, this theme probably has the least amount of impact on improving team collective performance.

Four phases of leadership and group management

Professional leadership mentors generally recognise at least four phases of group or team management emphasis. These are:

1. Instructing
2. Coaching
3. Reinforcing
4. Delegating

Management behaviour towards staff tends to be either directive or supportive, or a combination of both, dependant upon an employee's experience and ability. Coaching demands maximum directive and maximum supportive behaviour from managers. It is arguably the most time-consuming activity, but in asset management it is also the most fruitful in terms of debt collection productivity. Figure 5.1 shows the need for coaching at different phases of group management.

The asset management business requires enormous instructional focus at the beginning of the work-out process, given the need to orientate and train teams of people, most of whom have no experience for what they are now doing. The need for support and mentoring reduces as asset managers become more experienced, until the need to promote collection staff into management positions occurs. A danger with training, coaching and supporting is to consider the work-out process as only a temporary situation that does not justify full resource application and instead take human resource short-cuts.

Figure 5.1 – group management phases and the need for coaching

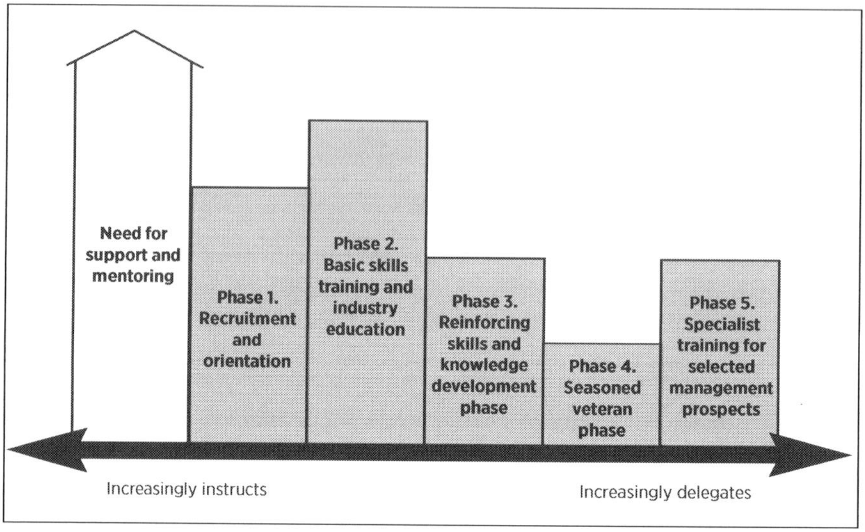

Understanding the subtle difference between coaching and training is important. Training tends to be more formalised and structured, and is usually focused on achieving specific knowledge goals. Coaching tends to be ongoing and perpetual – it can comprise just a few words or comments about an individual person's actions or performance. It can be used either to change what they are doing, or to reinforce a positive action. Both coaching and training should be considered as important motivational tools that are critical, not only for the advancement of staff, but for the personal development of managers too.

Assessing asset managers' training needs

Managers should be able to assess asset managers under their control and be able to identify for each individual, both for technical knowledge and personal skill sets:

- Character types in terms of approach to tasks
- Professional strengths and weaknesses
- Skill positives and negatives

- Gaps in knowledge
- Training needs

Finding gaps in knowledge should not be treated as a deficiency, but a coaching opportunity for both the manager and the subordinate. For each individual member of a team, evaluation, summarising and projection of their future educational needs, and then facilitating suitable training or educational resources to match, is the most effective way of improving both individual and team performance. Most asset managers are deficient in at least one technical area and need either support or coaching in areas of weakness.

Greatest upside in distressed debt resolutions is generally achieved through good negotiation. When assessing training needs, managers should therefore appreciate that maximum collections are more likely to flow from people skills rather than technical skills. As an example, legal execution is a process-driven resolution strategy with limited or no upside, so they should ration the time spent developing skills in this area in favour of more collection-productive disciplines.

Specialised trainers

Huge sums of money are tied up in distressed loan books, yet most banks choose to allocate little or no budget for training. This may be an extension of the *good money after bad* principle – there is a reluctance to put more money into training in an area that has already lost money – or could be because the concept of independent specialised trainers is relatively new in the distressed debt industry. It is obvious, however, that the ability to be able to hire independent trainers is a huge advantage for work-out entities, particularly at set-up when time and resources are at their most stretched.

Due to a general global shortage of training resources, at Lehman we ended up creating our own training programmes and doing it all ourselves.

The greatest risk with specialised outsourced training is that, unless training is subsequently reinforced and supported, asset managers will go back to old habits and forget what they have learned. Distressed debt work-out is complicated and extremely challenging. Effective outsourced training therefore usually demands a follow through programme and *train the trainer* courses for executive managers, in order to continue a more valuable long-term coaching programme.

Feedback from asset managers – most popular training areas

Training needs vary amongst different work-out organisations. Most motivated asset managers enjoy and appreciate learning new skill sets and approaches that increase productivity. In emerging markets or jurisdictions where they have no past experience of widescale distressed debt, technology transfer through training should be particularly cost effective.

In my experience,, asset managers generally tend to favour courses orientated towards improving collections. Typical favourites are the following subjects, ranked in order of popularity:

1. Negotiating skills
2. Overcoming objections
3. Managing borrowers
4. Effective business plans
5. NPL portfolio transactions
6. Real estate appraisal
7. Loan valuation techniques
8. Refinancing and restructuring
9. Legal skills
10. Finance and accounting skills
11. Procedural and compliance related issues

Encouraging integrity among staff

A recurring management issue, both for individual asset managers and servicing entities, is how to discourage disgruntled staff from negotiating deals on the side with borrowers. How do you stop demotivated asset managers putting money in their pockets at the lender's expense? How do you prevent a property manager renting out vacant units on the side?

Negotiating distressed transactions often involves compromise. They are all one-off transactions, with no repeat business occurring from which comparisons can be made. It is difficult to gain allegiance and loyalty from staff with limited employment horizons, especially if they are underpaid. These are ideal conditions for dishonesty to flourish.

So how do you prevent cheating occurring?

> There is a tendency to believe that deception is most likely to occur in jurisdictions with higher levels of corruption. I have seen first hand incidences in Thailand, South Korea, the Philippines and Turkey.
>
> However, it is equally likely to occur in mature markets. It occurred frequently in the UK in the early 1990s. Because there hadn't been a crash for 20 years in the West, people had forgotten what happened last time and there may be a tendency to think that cheating with debts wouldn't occur in the aftermath of the 2008 crisis!

The simple answer is, you cannot. Given the extraordinary nature and circumstances surrounding debt collection, it is inevitable that temptation will arise and will be succumbed to on occasion. Let's be clear; the vast majority of asset managers are clean and don't cheat, but such is the nature of the business that it will happen. Cheating tends to fall into two categories: accounting fraud or straightforward theft that leaves its own paper trail and will ultimately be revealed. Much more difficult to prove is collusion between asset manager and borrower. Often the only way to substantiate suspicions is to involve third-party investigators.

The following points may help:

- Don't make it easy for asset managers to cheat by underpaying them. Make sure they are fully and obviously compensated, motivated and aligned with the lender as best as possible in achieving the very highest collections.
- Make sure that asset managers acknowledge and sign up to a code of ethics stipulating policies on issues like gifts, and what they can and cannot do with borrowers, and procedures to follow under specific, difficult situations.
- Experienced asset managers, who consistently negotiate resolutions at the bottom end of their target collection range, demand special scrutiny.
- Borrower meetings should always have a minimum of two people in attendance. Personnel should be changed from time to time and borrowers should be switched between asset managers if suspicions are strong.
- Servicer reputation means nothing. Even the most respectable and trustworthy organisation may have no idea that fraud is occurring within their ranks.

- Check everything out! Attend meetings, re-run meeting videos and telephone records (for training purposes!) and undertake physical inspections. The more management gets involved, the harder it is for staff to act unilaterally.

When you check everything out, try and catch people doing it right, whereby the monitoring job is not viewed as negative surveillance, but as positive management interaction that provides encouragement and motivation.

If you do catch anybody cheating, make an example and throw the book at them.

5.3 Controlling the resolution process

Whoever controls the resolution process wins

When a new NPL asset management or work-out entity is established, first negotiated resolutions are critical for setting the collection tone with the market. Borrowers will be closely watching the resolution numbers in order to determine how easy it is to extract assets below market from the new work-out unit. Any form of perceived softness will be exploited by debtors or their associates.

It is also not unusual for larger defaulted borrowers to get together to set up their own action group that pools information about the asset management entity. This being the case, new entities may benefit from strategically choosing the order of first loan work-outs and considering how this will impact their reputation amongst interested observers. First numbers above outstanding principal balance also particularly benefit the lender in terms of scrutiny by auditors and potential investors.

> In Eastern Europe we foreclosed on a chocolate business. The workers from the factory were understandably dismayed and tried to attack our representatives at the court and threatened our offices. After beefing up our security, rather than be defensive we went on a publicity offensive and used the case to show the local market that we meant business and would not be deterred by scare tactics.

Allowing a borrower to drive or derail the recovery process will work primarily in the best interests of the borrower and not the asset managers. Debtors, promptly volunteering pay-offs, settlement or bankruptcy, or any other early self-modelled resolution, will almost certainly be trying to exercise an advantage, or be subject to time pressure. Such situations demand special scrutiny; changing the pace by slowing things down may swing the advantage back in the asset manager's favour.

At the beginning of the resolution process, the approach to work-out and timing will be influenced by the borrower. As a portfolio matures, other factors increasingly come into play, particularly servicer's actions.

The six positional categories of borrowers

Generally, borrowers take six positional stances when dealing with their debts:

1. Detached
2. In denial
3. Praying for time
4. Playing for time
5. Wants to deal, no cash
6. Wants to deal with cash

1. Detached

If a borrower has disappeared, cannot be contacted and shows total disinterest in the work-out process, the only option for the lender is legal process. This is the least dynamic resolution option and is best handled by outsourcing direct to lawyers.

2. In denial

> In 2009, I was introduced to an insolvent borrower in Europe, who was €500 million in debt. A month later, he contacted me again; I expected in order to progress our earlier meeting. Instead, to my surprise, he wanted to ask my advice about acquiring new debt in another jurisdiction, as a means of acquiring the underlying real estate. There is no point in wasting time with borrowers in denial like this.

If borrowers are in denial it is almost impossible to achieve any form of sensible negotiated agreement. Default is stressful and traumatic. It is not unusual for defaulted borrowers to go through a form of mental breakdown which neither they nor their associates may be aware of. This can make rational people unpredictable, forgetful and illogical. Asset managers need to be sensitive to this possibility and recognise that unless the borrower comes out of denial there is no point in wasting time negotiating with them.

Sometimes, a borrower can be brought back to the reality of their situation by the serving of legal notices or by commencing legal proceedings for possession of their assets. In other cases, borrowers may be unable to accept change, in which case recovery strategy will likely be hostile with an uncooperative borrower, leaving legal execution only as the most likely course of action.

3. Praying for time

This is the case of a borrower who understands the gravity of their condition, but can do nothing about improving or expediting it, and hopes that a white knight will appear in the future from nowhere to solve their problem. The optimum strategy for the asset manager is to get the borrower to accept and agree the reality of their situation. Through careful handling and good interpersonal skills, the asset manager may then be able to secure the co-operation of the borrower in order to speed up resolution proceedings. The asset manager may also be able to identify alternative commercial recovery options that increase collections, which stand a good chance of succeeding with borrower cooperation.

4. Playing for time

Playing for time is similar to praying for time, with the addition of borrower tales and sometimes elaborate supporting yarns, which are designed to give the impression that a solution is on the horizon. Phantom buyers, phantom refinancing facilities and a whole host of bad luck stories are normal. Once again, the optimum strategy for the asset manager is to make the borrower accept and agree the reality of the situation as soon as possible. However, borrowers that play games like this may not be inclined to work with the asset manager to

> In Turkey, a borrower used to come to meetings in a beat up old Audi. Afterwards he would drive to his local garage and swap back into his gleaming new black Mercedes. Attaching the Merc completely changed the negotiations. Chasing personal possessions, albeit limited in value, can carry enormous psychological weight. In another case, attaching and taking away the electrical goods in an elusive borrowers' mother's home incensed him, but brought him to the negotiating table the next day.

expedite things. They may always try to undermine progress and delay the process.

This situation highlights the importance of always following through on promised actions and on time. Borrowers need to understand that they will be well received if they behave honestly and fairly in a timely manner, and conversely will be rejected for subterfuge, irresponsibility, unreliability and broken promises.

5. Wants to do a deal, no cash

This is the situation where a borrower would like to execute a negotiated settlement on a loan, usually based around valuable assets, but has no cash or credit facilities to execute a deal. These instances need to be carefully considered on a case-by-case basis, as they represent an opportunity to secure the highest potential levels of collection. Usually a third party with cash is pivotal to an optimum solution, along with cooperation from the lender and good faith on behalf of the borrower. In order for the borrower to benefit, a transaction usually needs to be closed promptly, which also works in the lender's favour.

The need for speed also creates additional negotiating opportunity for the lender to squeeze out higher collections. For example, new joint ventures with solvent property developers can optimise collections where the lender puts in the land and possibly capital whilst the development partner develops out assets on a performance fee basis. The borrower can also benefit on a success-fee basis. Good market knowledge will help the lender decide, whether they will earn more by foreclosing early, or seeking ways to achieve potentially higher collections, in this type of way.

6. Wants to deal with cash

In theory, this is the easiest and quickest resolution situation. In practice, not. The sticking point is usually the negotiated amounts. Borrowers in this category tend to believe they are in a strong position and will negotiate accordingly. Dealing successfully with these types of situations therefore requires the strongest negotiating skills and sometimes demands the ultimate in nerves and brinkmanship.

What communication process to use

In normal everyday transactional situations, participants strike a balance between harrying or hounding the other party and letting them come back in their own time on commercial issues. They do this in order not to be seen to be too keen and thereby weakening their negotiating position. When dealing with distressed debt, the communication approach depends on the planned resolution strategy and the borrower's positional category.

At one end of the positional category range, *in denial*, borrowers will likely require constant and unremitting pressure and follow up in order to move things forward. At the other end of the scale, the normal commercial rules of engagement come into effect. When the defining moment in negotiations appears and you name your price, it is time to step back and wait for the other party to respond. Good control of verbal interaction, patience, the ability to listen and knowing when to respond in order not to weaken your position are basic skills for asset managers.

Resolution process milestones

In order to optimise both control and time management, asset managers also need to consider resolution process milestones and think about how this impacts their negotiating strength. Typically, milestones during the life of a loan work-out could include:

1. First engagement with a borrower.
2. Negotiated settlement with an obliging or cooperative borrower.
3. Instigation of legal proceedings against individuals or assets.
4. Advanced legal proceedings.
5. Execution and sale of assets.

The strength of lender's negotiating position through the resolution process typically might look like the undulating line shown in Figure 5.2.

As you can see in Figure 5.2, the strength of the lender's negotiating position adjusts up and down throughout the process. Generally, it starts out strongly on first engagement and gradually diminishes afterwards until commencement of legal proceedings. The shock of legal action spurs some borrowers into coming back to the negotiating table. From here on, negotiating strength diminishes until assets are on the brink of being sold to other parties. Clearly, negotiating with borrowers at times of peak strength should produce the best results for the lender.

Figure 5.2 – the strength of lender's negotiating position throughout the resolution process

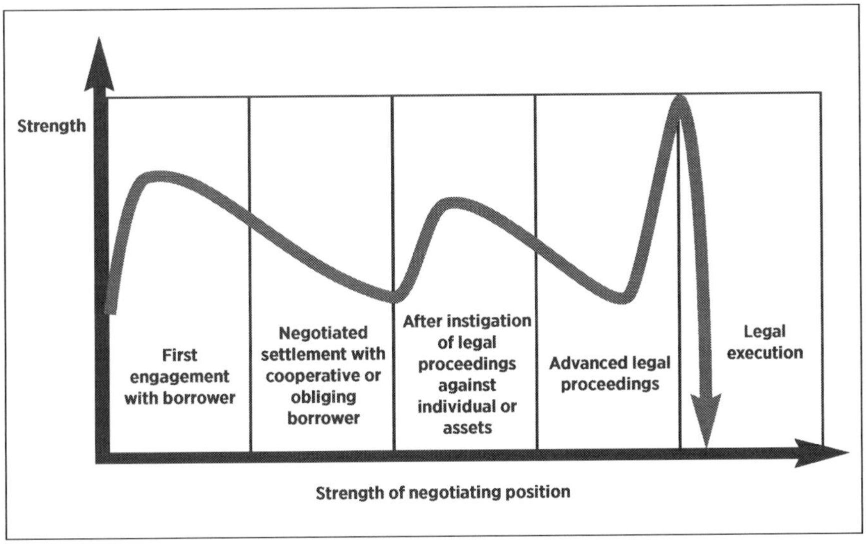

A combination of use of pressure, strong negotiating skills and a sense of timing are pivotal to executing most resolution strategies earliest. Clearly, there are exceptions. For example, at either end of the strategies range, passive loan pay down by installments at one end, or foreclosure and execution at the other, are strategies where asset managers have limited ability to influence time frame or collection amount. Some strategies in-between are variable – if for example a pay-off is financed by an institutional funder, the asset manager can do little to influence the amount of loan that is raised to fund the settlement.

Setting deadlines and monitoring progress

Where third parties are purchasing assets as part of a negotiated settlement, asset managers should impose strict achievable deadlines and monitor progress carefully. Sometimes this type of initiative may be just a delaying tactic by the borrower that needs to be flushed out as soon as possible. In such situations a degree of skepticism is healthy.

For this type of situation, or when selling on repossessed property, asset managers should only accept delays or grant extensions in the event that they have verified the true cause of hold-up with the third party responsible and find the explanation reasonable. Distressed borrowers and associates tend to be notoriously unreliable in terms of executing settlements on time, if at all. Giving the benefit of the doubt rarely works in the asset manager's favour, who should always be prepared to re-market a property at the first sign of hesitation.

Universal settlements

For larger, more complicated borrower loans or groups, it is best to settle globally at one time, including all loans and assets with the borrower, as leverage may be reduced if individual pieces of collateral are released. Global settlements avoid the risk of having the best assets cherry-picked by the borrower or their associates. Sometimes it may not be possible or practical to settle globally. If this occurs, it is almost certain that the best assets will be taken out first. This can be acceptable to a lender provided that the credit quality of the remaining pooled assets is bettered to compensate for the loss of the highest-quality assets.

Credit quality is determined by:

- Liquidity; the ease of sale of the remaining assets.
- The cash flow and debt service coverage of the remaining assets.
- The outstanding principal balance of the remaining assets.
- The value of remaining assets upon sale.
- Market conditions for sale of the remaining assets.

In the event of individual asset being released, the collateral-to-debt ratio should only ever swing in the lender's favour. This usually means that the best assets will need to be sold at significantly overinflated prices in

> Government AMCs can at times get cherry-picked by borrowers. Sometimes the AMCs have administrative difficulties because different banks have originated a number of loans with one borrower, or where different loans are linked by common personal guarantee only. Where AMCs have inflexible, transparent resolution formulae, pressure for high collections may drive them into resolving only the best collateralised loans in accordance with their high hurdle rates.
>
> The remaining loan dregs have limited or no collateral value. By resolving the better loans first though they lose all leverage over what is left. This ensures that their future collections will be paltry if they can collect anything at all.

order to compensate for the loss of credit quality in the remaining assets. The alternative approach, of releasing the best assets at market price, will ultimately make the asset manager's job harder, as they will likely be left with limited demand assets that are very difficult to sell and no leverage to pressure the borrower.

5.4 The asset manager toolkit

Whilst the asset manager core skill set is technically complicated, many of the tools of the trade used every day are straightforward and simple.

The basic tools of the asset manager

Basic tools include the following:

- Bankruptcy threat
- Foreclosure advice
- Intelligence gathering
- Legal attachments to assets
- Legal meetings
- Letters
- Litigation
- Meetings
- Phone calls

The actions asset managers can take include:

- Credit bidding
- New agreements
- Personal recourse
- Recourse to assets
- Recourse to guarantors
- Recourse to other parties
- Refinancing
- Revitalisation

Choosing the right tools according to circumstances at the right time is the key to maximising collections. This sounds simple, but in practice is challenging.

Flexibility to adjust tools during the process

In addition, circumstances and events may constantly shift, in which case asset managers need to retain the flexibility to change tools midstream. For example, threat of litigation, implementation of litigation or removal of legal action are three different actions that need to be carried out, increased, lowered or removed, according to developments and negotiation between asset manager and borrower.

In essence, an NPL is a lender-borrower relationship that has broken down. Like any other kind of relationship that involves people, it does not mean the relationship is irretrievable. Many borrowers would like to repair the relationship but lack the capacity to undertake this. Fundamental to repairing the relationship is the borrower demonstrating the utmost good faith, with the asset manager being able to exercise their judgment in deciding how much pressure to apply and what combination of strategies is best to pursue under the individual circumstances of each case.

Debt collectors that have insufficient flexibility to adjust mid-stream may find their options are limited, which makes it difficult to maximise collections. There is also a risk of some institutions, particularly government owned or sponsored entities, being overly litigatious, process driven and inflexible which narrows their options.

A performing loan going into default, and a borrower becoming a debtor,

A classic example of resolution inflexibility limiting collections was the Turkish government AMC, where litigation was their overriding collection strategy. We purchased a portfolio from them in 2005 whereby they retained upside collections as effectively our partner. Even though they had sold the portfolio to Lehman, retaining a degree of control was a critically important factor to them.

We managed to resolve loans that had caused collection difficulty for them through being more flexible and pursuing more creative strategies. I think this also pleased them because someone else was effectively making decisions that were difficult for them to make. They were one of the few institutions to sell NPLs that countenanced the event of the buyer going bankrupt. After the Lehman bankruptcy in 2008, they were ultimately able to claim a multi-million dollar bond and claw back the remaining portfolio for nothing, which overall was a fantastic deal for their government.

requires extreme adjustment. Managing change effectively has a significant impact upon this transition. Assisting borrowers in managing change generally speeds up the resolution process. In order to optimise use of their tool kit, asset managers need to understand the process of change and how this may be influencing borrowers.

Everybody has their own unique tolerance to change:

- One-third of people accept change without much problem.
- One-third of people have a minor reaction to change.
- One-third of people have a major reaction; a problem.

Extreme stress is a major impediment to accepting change. The majority of defaulting borrowers in practice have a problem to some degree of adjusting to change.

The four stages of change

Figure 5.3 – the four stages of change

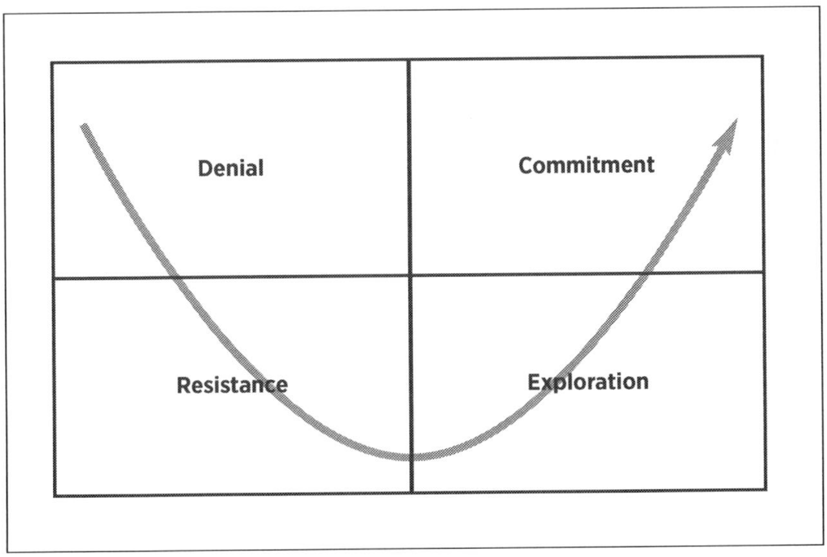

Everyone needs to go through the four stages shown in Figure 5.3 in order to successfully manage change. Asset managers therefore need to understand where borrowers are in this evolution. Borrowers frequently want to minimise or avoid the exploration stage, which usually means they are still in denial, and commitment is unlikely to be reached. The higher the arrow is in the chart in Figure 5.3, the greater the speed and ease of change. This means that resistance to the change process passes quicker and loss of productivity is minimised.

Self-assessment by asset managers

In situations where asset managers have been transferred out of a good bank into a bad bank or work-out unit, they may also need to assess themselves in terms of where they are in these four stages of change management evolution.

Making best use of the toolkit

In order to make the best use of their toolkit it is important for work-out units to employ the *best in class* service providers in all support functions, such as:

- Accounting
- Appraisals
- Investigations and intelligence
- Law
- Property management
- Real estate advisory
- Real estate brokerage

In areas such as law, it is important to identify different best in class operators for different functions. For example, the best bankruptcy lawyers may not be the best at foreclosure. Also on the legal side, managers should constantly try to improve collateral position through further attachment. This is a dynamic process that continually needs to be reviewed from all angles in regard to new information that comes to light.

> In Turkey we were losing every time we fought a bankruptcy case until we managed to convince the top bankruptcy lawyer to work for us. He effectively became our new servicer and subsequently negotiated some great settlements for us with the most difficult borrower groups.

Most effective use of the toolkit is achieved as a result of having the fullest possible knowledge of the loan and collateral details and the borrower. The phrase from the Chinese *Art of War* – "know thy enemy" – is particularly appropriate.

There is a clear and direct link between collection performance and knowledge. Figure 5.4 shows that if an asset manager knows everything there is to know about the respective borrower's case they will likely maximise collections and *win the battle*. Conversely, if they know very little, the borrower will likely win. Anything in between is effectively a stalemate with neither party triumphing.

Figure 5.4 – how greater understanding improves collections (inspired by Sun Tzu, *The Art of War*: knowing your enemy)

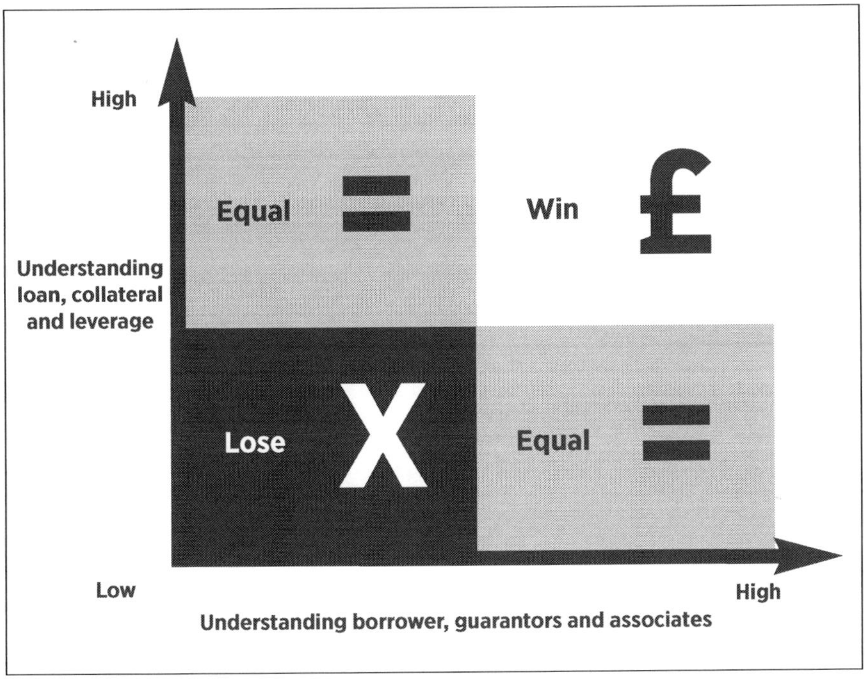

This throws up two important issues. Firstly, the need for the asset manager to engage, drive and actively manage negotiation with the borrower in order to stay in control. The second issue is time related. If insufficient time is spent on a particular case the asset manager may not know enough about the borrower, with the result that the manager will probably lose the battle. Critically, therefore, asset managers should never commence negotiations with a borrower until **they** have found out everything they need to know and are fully prepared.

Setting price expectation levels

Setting pricing expectation levels as soon as possible during the resolution process helps focus the borrower's mind at a suitably high level. *Setting the bar* correctly for pricing is a key skill.

Setting the bar for distressed debt is the opposite of the high jump or the pole vault in athletics, where jumpers set the bar and raise it thereafter. With distressed debt, once the bar is set, it will likely only be lowered through negotiation. Once a number is released, it is almost impossible to raise the bar afterwards unless new material facts come to light.

> Setting high price expectations with borrowers can sometimes cause shock, friction and unpleasantness. It may result in displays of aggression and anger, and it is quite common for them to storm out of meetings. Generally speaking, the greater the emotion shown at these times, the more the borrower cares. Most times, they eventually return to the negotiating table with revised higher offers.

Setting the bar is also known as *anchoring* or *priming* by price psychologists. The basic idea is that getting your number in first gives you an advantage over your opponent. The first number named within a negotiation silently shifts the other side's expectation upwards of what they will have to pay or accept. This simple rule may be the most important and easily applied finding of the psychology of price.

Having said this, the asset manager must be careful not to name a completely ridiculous figure which would destroy credibility. The asset manager must also be prepared to explain how the price is constructed. Successful anchoring is about is setting a high price capable of structured justification, but not expecting to achieve it.

The rarity of uncomplicated resolution

Other than smaller simple loans, or clear-cut foreclosure and liquidation processes, straightforward uncomplicated resolution is a rarity. The occasional situation where borrowers have the cash to pay out in full begs the question why they defaulted in the first instance. Given that most other resolution strategies involve people, transaction implementation is by nature uncertain and time delays are normal. Some situations may require performance from third parties such as brokers, financiers or intermediaries in order to close. Usually there is more than one third party involved, which compounds the problem of execution certainty.

Servicing entities should also have the flexibility to be able to step outside the box, e.g. purchase additional debt from other creditors, or take out junior liens where additional collateral or claims can improve their negotiating position and economics. **Maximisation of asset monetisation requires entrepreneurial approaches of this kind.**

Treating NPLs like gold

As NPLs are by definition distressed, it is sometimes normal human behaviour to consider them and the resolution process to be somehow tarnished or cheap. Such attitudes are misguided. The objective when dealing with NPLs is collections. NPLs can be particularly valuable because they generally present resolution opportunities from a number of uniquely different angles, including assets and/or individuals, which may ultimately far exceed original expectation.

An asset management entity, like many any other businesses, is limited in what it can do about reducing operational costs. A high proportion of cost is fixed and is difficult to decrease this substantially without reducing performance. Revenues can always be improved through craft and skill, and profits are always most influenced by maximising top line collection performance, as a result of choosing the right tools for the job.

5.5 Measuring asset manager performance

How asset managers can be assessed

Asset managers can be assessed and compared according to:

- Collection against set targets.
- Collection as a percentage of book value or purchase price.
- Collection as a percentage of loan principal.
- Collection net of cost of collection.
- Total collections.
- Total and average collections monthly, quarterly and annually.

The text book approach to loan valuation

Asset managers should also be assessed against individual loan valuations. The established text book approach for valuing loans is a three-step process:

Step 1 Gather and analyse loan information.

Step 2 Determine the most appropriate method of loan resolution and future cash flow collection.

Step 3 Complete the loan valuation calculation according to one of these scenarios:

- Non-operating borrower through monetisation of assets.
- Operating borrower through operational cash flow.
- Plus collection input from guarantors or others.

Step 1: The loan information is typically grouped and analysed under a number of different headings

Reference information

- Loan ID
- Commencement maturity
- Loan amount
- Interest rate
- Loan currency
- Loan status
- Collections
- Last payment
- Amortisation
- Current outstanding principal balance
- Default interest

Borrower information

- Name
- Address

- Borrower type
- Industry
- Operating or non-operating?
- Reputation
- Legal status
- Number of loans
- Secured
- Unsecured
- Non-cash obligations
- Total borrower obligation

Guarantor information (for each guarantor)

- Name
- Address
- Industry
- Operating?
- Legal status
- Total guarantor obligation

Collateral information

- Category
- Description location
- Size
- Mortgage information
- Senior loan?
- Lien position?
- Prior lien value
- Pledge information
- Cross-collateralisation
- Foreclosure status

Real estate appraisal

- Date
- Valuer
- Type
- Use
- Description
- Vacant/occupied?
- Current status
- Time to realisation
- Open market value
- Value in use
- Forced sale value

Lien analysis table

- List properties and open market values
- List all liens by rank
- Include cross-collateralisation
- Calculate recoverable mortgage amount

Legal information

- Borrower lawyer
- Bank lawyer
- Legal opinion
- Action type
- List litigation
- Current status
- Date of last court appearance

Step 2: Determine the most appropriate method of loan resolution and future cash flow collection

Once the gathered loan information is analysed and tabled, different methods of future cash flow collection are reviewed. Scenario analysis can then be undertaken case by case, based upon:

- Collections from company cash flow or additional equity.
- Collections from voluntary sale of assets.
- Collections through refinancing of assets.
- Collections from forced liquidation of assets.
- Attachment of additional assets.
- Any other sources of income.
- Voluntary collections from guarantors.
- Forced liquidation of guarantor's assets.

The scenario which determines the maximum NPV of the loan can then be identified.

Step 3: Loan valuation in accordance with chosen collection scenario

Figures 5.5a and 5.5b show two different typical loan valuation approaches for different collection scenarios.

Figure 5.5a – Scenario 1: Non-operating borrower – asset liquidation

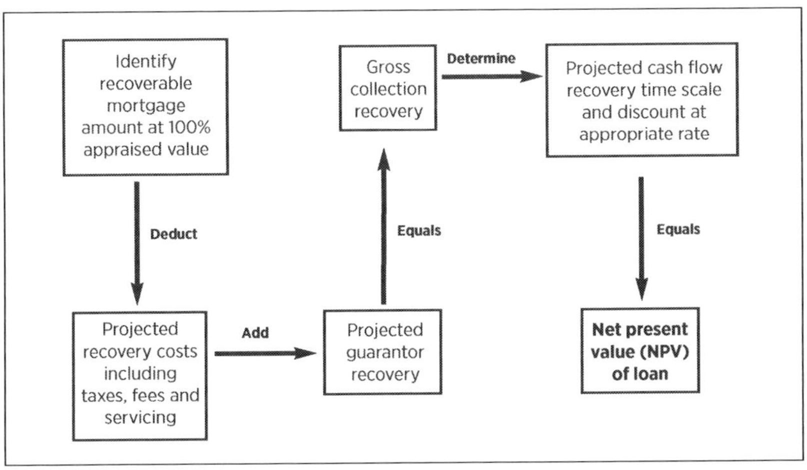

The starting point for the approach shown in Figure 5.5a is to identify the recoverable mortgage amount. What we mean by this is the lower of either the secured mortgage amount or the underlying property collateralising the loan. When a new loan is originated the amount of the loan principal will in most cases be significantly lower than the open market value of the underlying collateral and is the amount the lender would expect to collect in the event of default and liquidation of the asset.

After a market crash though, the underlying property value may fall considerably, even below the loan principal amount. If this is the case, the lender will only ever be able to collect the value of the collateral upon liquidation. As a result, when valuing secured NPLs, the starting point is the lower of either the loan or the current market value of the property supporting the loan. In some cases this can be more complicated where a number of different loans are secured by one property or properties in the ownership of one borrower. Additional complexity also occurs where different loans secured by one property are held by different lending institutions and have different security and payment priority in the event of liquidation.

Once we have identified the recoverable mortgage amount, we will deduct the collection costs including taxes, all fees and servicing expenses. If it is possible to identify additional supportable collections from guarantors, then this can be added to the projected recovery from the loan, again net of collection costs. These two numbers, the net recoverable mortgage amount plus the net revovery from guarantors (if any) totalled together are what we call the gross collection recovery.

We create a cash flow recovery projection based upon the information we hold. This cash flow is then discounted at an appropriate discount rate equivalent either to our cost of money or in accordance with our required investment hurdle rate. The result of this calculation is the net present value of the loan and equates to the text book value of the respective loan.

The starting point for the approach shown in Figure 5.5b is to identify the future anticipated cash flow emanating from the business operations of the borrower plus any other collection sources. This can be extremely complicated and time consuming to identify accurately, particularly when dealing with large commercial concerns.

Once we have identified cash flow emanating from the borrower we can determine the size of loan that can be serviced by the borrower including interest payments and some requied target amortisation, which also allows the borrower to maintain operations. This can be calculated in a number of ways, such as using multiples of EBITDA. We call this exercise loan sizing. A decision then needs to be made about whether this new loan size and payment terms are acceptable to the lender.

Figure 5.5b – Scenario 2: Operating borrower – repayment from cash flow

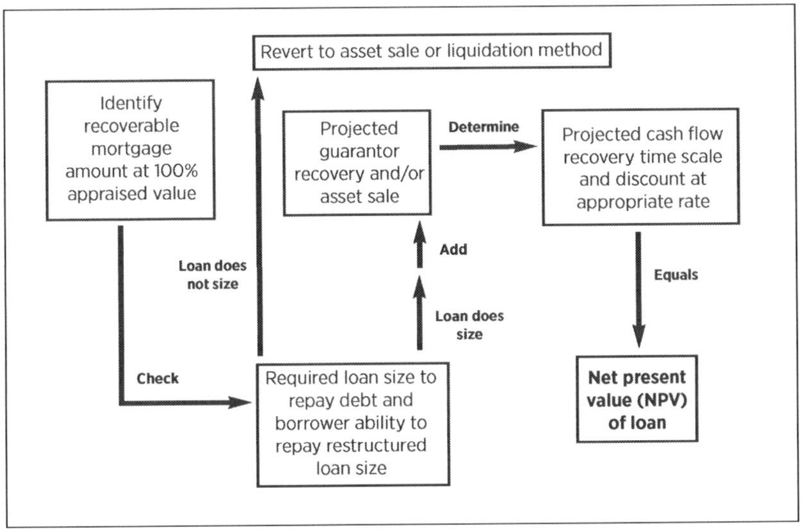

If this is the case, we will deduct the collection costs including taxes, all fees and servicing expenses. If it is possible to identify additional supportable collections from guarantors then this can be added to the projected recovery from the company cash flow, again net of collection costs. These two numbers, the net recoverable payments from cash flow plus the net revovery from guarantors (if any), totalled together are the gross collection recovery.

Once again, we then create a cash flow recovery projection based upon the information we hold. This cash flow is then discounted at an appropriate discount rate equivelant either to our cost of money or in accordance with our required investment hurdle rate. The result of this calculation is the net present value of the loan and equates to the text book value of the respective loan.

A problem occurs with this approach in the event that the loan sizing is insufficient to match the economic expectations of the lender, or if a higher collection can be realised through liquidation of collateral. If this occurs the loan valuation will then be calculated under the method shown in Figure 5.5a.

What is good for valuation may not be good enough for collections

The valuation approaches shown in Figures 5.5a and 5.5b could be called the classic valuation methods and they are the foundation level upon which NPL investors base their underwriting. This type of approach to valuation would satisfy public auditors and government asset management entities in terms of establishing a reasonable valuation determination.

However, whilst this rigid approach is appropriate for valuation, it is unacceptable for collections. If text book valuation level was acceptable for recovery it would be better to appoint lawyers as servicers and not have asset managers at all. In reality, collections should always exceed text book valuation level.

Asset managers only add value when their collections exceed loan valuation level.

It is therefore important that their collection performance should also be assessed against the text book valuation of the loan.

The difference between text book loan valuations and actual collections

Collections should always exceed valuation because valuation is an academic exercise based on numerical facts such as:

- Loans
- Assets
- Guarantees

Collection occurs in the real world, and also involves people such as:

- Borrowers
- Associates
- Guarantors
- Unknown third parties

People can be logical or illogical. Assets are usually logical. People and assets combined are frequently illogical. Borrower emotional attachment to assets is illogical, but frequently occurs. As far as asset managers are concerned, this can either be an obstruction or an opportunity.

> When training asset managers from an experienced special servicer unit in Germany, the room went stony silent when I informed them that they only added value when their collections exceeded loan valuation level. Their concerned faces told their own story. Breaking work-out units free from a process-driven text-book valuation mentality is enormously challenging but extremely profitable.

Collection includes human factors and emotions such as fear, uncertainty, greed, envy and pride. This is not empirical and can be unpredictable. Different personalities react differently to different situations and no two people are the same. Good asset managers therefore manipulate and capitalise upon the human factors to increase collections. Collection may also involve hidden factors or involve assumptions, which are not shown within loan files, or which are not in the public domain.

Collections of the top managers

Top asset managers have both the biggest net collections and the highest cents on the dollar collection amounts. Apart from first class technical knowledge, top debt collection performers are normally differentiated by their adaptability, empathy and communication skills. Adaptability is required to be able to adjust swiftly and seamlessly according to changing events and strategies. Empathy is essential to understanding borrowers' positions. Communication skills provide the opportunity to use this to their advantage.

Focus and time management of top managers

In terms of focus and time management three routine operational tendencies tend to recur with top-flight asset managers:

1. There is a clear concentration on collections.
2. There is no confusion between activity and achievement.
3. Administration and reporting is delegated to others.

Time allocation varies according to portfolio phase. Time management breakdown for a top-flight asset manager might typically be divided as shown in Figure 5.6.

Figure 5.6 – time management breakdown for a top-flight asset manager

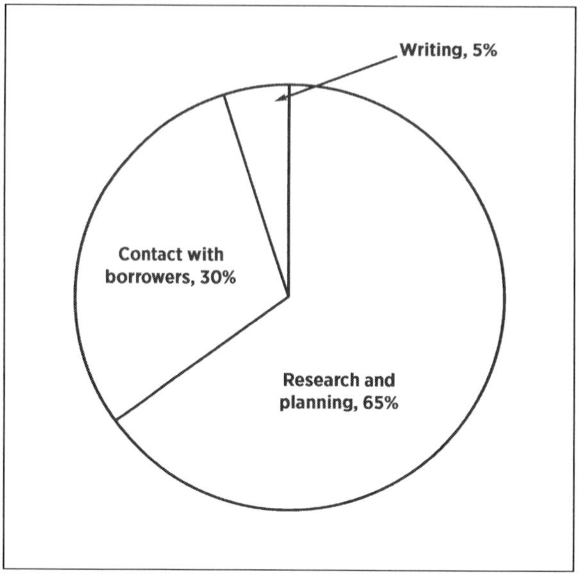

Top asset management performers also:

- Do not prioritise friendlier borrowers over more difficult people.
- Do not spend more time on favoured resolution methods.
- Do not put off what they don't like doing.

Case priorities for managers

Borrower case priorities are threefold:

1. Urgent with high collection potential.
2. Not urgent with high collection potential.
3. Urgent with low collection potential.

Cases that are not urgent with low collection potential tend to be ignored by the top performers, so a work-out unit is generally better served by allocating these to junior or subordinate staff.

Pareto's Law generally also applies to asset managers, with 80% of collections coming from 20% of borrower cases. Given that 80% of this occurs in 20% of their time, the business of collections is highly focused.

Figure 5.7 – Pareto's Law of collections

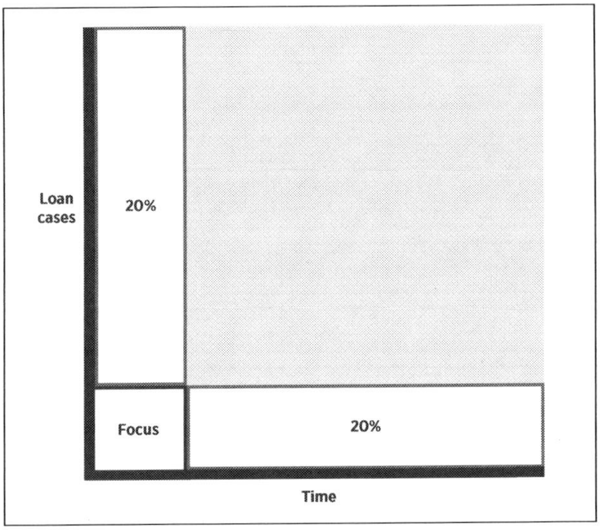

It is clearly apparaent fron the bottom left-hand corner of Figure 5.7 how tightly focused the business of collections is both in terms of which borrower case to focus upon and how much time asset managers should allocate to them.

6. BORROWER SOLUTIONS

6.1 Dealing with defaulted borrowers

Debt is emotive and personal; financial institutions are impersonal. People are sensitive to other people's emotions; institutions either don't acknowledge emotions or avoid them.

As a result, it is no surprise that banks struggle to deal effectively with defaulted borrowers and fail to optimise all potential opportunities. The depersonalised securitised lending era has raised even more barriers for defaulted borrowers and lenders to join together for mutual commercial advantage.

The easiest situation for a bank to deal with is for a defaulted borrower to walk away from their collateral so the institution can liquidate the security quickly and efficiently. This brings in cash within a predictable time frame, enables the institution to close the file and write off the loss. It also avoids the need to engage in difficult emotional discussions and negotiations and, above all, lose time making difficult choices. The only problem with this accomplishment is that it may not maximise collection from the loan.

Performing loans are a **business process**. Marketing, systems, controls and efficiency are the basis for optimum process. Unless the borrower chooses to walk away, defaulted loans are a **personal process**. Borrower attitude, expectations and personality are then the drivers for resolution pace.

Understanding borrowers

The importance of empathy

The key to understanding borrowers is empathy. Many people associate the word empathy with caring or feeling sorry for other people. This is not strictly true. Empathy is to feel the emotion. Sympathy is to feel *for* the emotion. A good definition of empathy for our purposes is: *identification with and understanding of another's situation, feelings, and motives.*

Astute asset managers view people like icebergs. What you see above the surface is a fraction of what is hidden below the surface. Unless you start to understand this, you will find it difficult to extract the maximum collection from borrowers. Figure 6.1 illustrates this situation – empathy is the key to unlocking other people's inner feelings.

Figure 6.1 – maximum collections come from the information that is most difficult to extract

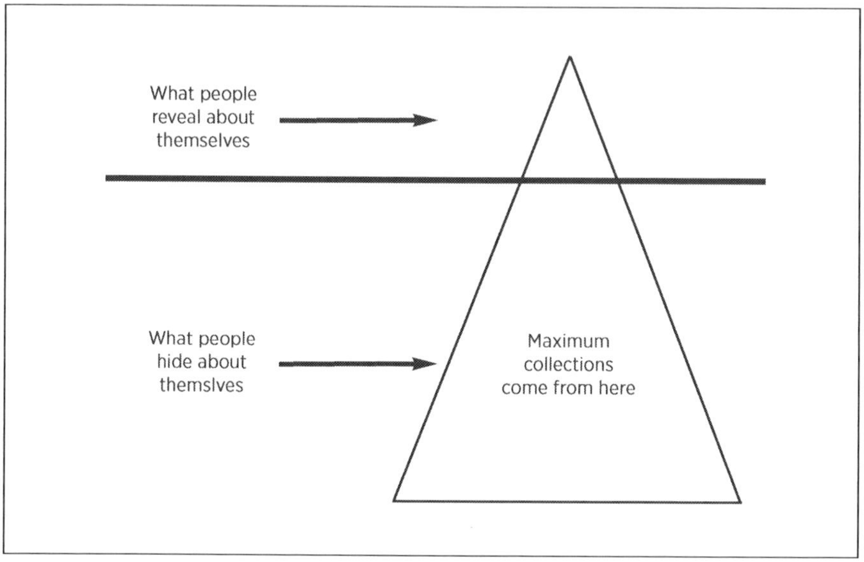

A change of borrower mindset

With a performing loan a borrower feels in control of the situation and is predictable. Upon default though, the mind-set of the borrower will almost certainly change. The first thing the borrower will feel will be loss of control and once this occurs they may become completely unpredictable.

Will they be helpful? Will they open up and work with you to optimise the situation, or will they work against you by being contrary, obstructive and hiding things?

A performing borrower feels respected, which encourages them to generally follow the moral high ground. A delinquent borrower may feel a loss of self-respect which may motivate some to abandon morality in favour of cheating, dishonesty and generally acting in an underhand manner.

People naturally limit what they are prepared to declare or reveal about themselves in unnatural or stressful situations. The starting point for dealing effectively with defaulted borrowers is to try and understand three things, in order to enter the resolution process in the strongest possible position:

1. As much hidden, *under the surface*, relevant information about the borrower as possible; the bulk of the submerged iceberg.
2. Whether the borrower has realistic expectations and their view of the likely resolution outcome.
3. The borrower's feelings and attitude towards the resolution process, the servicing entity and the asset manager.

NPL resolutions tend to fall into two broad categories; *liquidation solutions* or *creative solutions*. In both categories, negotiation with the borrower stands a good chance of coming into play. The most effective way of assessing a borrower in these situations is to regard them as an investor. The key in measuring them is to recognise the balance between their financial and emotional intelligence.

Financial decisions driven by emotion are usually bad decisions. The best investors are unemotional; the worst are driven by emotion. Emotional borrowers therefore tend to negotiate badly. Asset managers should always be looking to gain advantage from emotion and maybe take a lead from other industries. For example, undertakers have been renowned for over-selling to customers blinded by grief.

The borrower's approach to the resolution process

Hope springs eternal, especially with debt. The borrower's approach to the resolution process will generally be determined by their view of the likely outcome and what they stand to gain or lose by it. Their views on outcomes, from best to worst, may look something like the following:

	↑	
Winning strategy		**Win**
Workable plan		
Probable solution		
Possible solution		
Unlikely solution		
Hopeless		**Lose**
	↓	

Borrower attitudes are not fixed and may change with circumstances, or interaction with asset managers. These can range from:

Attitude	
Focused optimism	**Win** ↑
Shows deference	
Helpful	
Polite	
Nervous receptive	
Nervous volatile	
Nervous defensive	
Tentative uncertain	
Hostile	
Openly rude	
Resigned to fate	
Disinterested	**Lose** ↓

Clearly understanding where borrowers are in this process works in the asset manager's favour, in terms of prioritising potentially speedier cases and choosing the optimum resolution strategy.

Interaction with borrowers

There is a tendency in the new information age to believe that as technology progresses human interaction matters less. In the world of distressed debt this idea is counterproductive. In many cases, the difference between achieving good collections and the highest possible collections is driven by human interaction between the asset manager and borrower.

The most essential thing before meeting borrowers is to be fully prepared; both mentally and tactically. Always remember that you can choose your friends, you can choose where you want to live, you can choose a partner, but you cannot choose the borrowers you will deal with. **Therefore never take things personally.**

Borrowers' ideas of fairness

Most human beings are prejudiced by a sense of fairness. If they feel they have been treated unfairly by markets or circumstance or bad luck, some people expect to be compensated positively by the next person to make up for their misfortune. Some people believe that if a debt has been purchased at a discount, then it is only fair that the new buyer splits the upside 50/50 and does not profit from their bad luck.

Asset managers need to recognise this tendency and eradicate a borrower's sense of injustice or being picked upon as soon as possible in the resolution process. Borrowers must understand that debt resolution is not a personal vendetta against them. A loan is a legal obligation. Fairness is immaterial because business is business.

The start of the resolution process

Entering the resolution process with a defaulted borrower is a bit like playing blind poker with people you have never met before. You are unsure of what you will encounter at the table in terms of ability, character, attitude and what cards they hold. You want to find out as quickly as possible how strong a hand they are holding and what tactics they will employ. At the same time, you don't want to give away too much about the cards you are holding, in order to keep the other party uncertain of your position. The larger and more complex the loan or loans, the more significant this may be, and in situations where there has been a transfer of loans to new investors, a cautious opening approach is basic common sense.

The rules for meeting people are similar in every situation in life where individuals greet or are introduced to each other for the first time. People feel motivated to respond warmly to positive energy, exuded by a personable manner reinforced with a smile, a firm handshake and good appearance. Defaulted borrowers may display

> In Eastern Europe, the owner of a business empire in ruins had a fearsome reputation. At our first meeting, we didn't discuss his debts or possible resolution. He told me the story of his remarkable life and how he had come from nothing to having hundreds of millions of dollars in his current account. All he wanted was to be shown the same respect that he received at the height of his success. Humility costs nothing and I was glad to oblige.
>
> After a few cordial meetings, he ended up acting as the asset manager and advised me on how to best resolve his case. We avoided lengthy legal actions and unnecessary costs by establishing a good working relationship based on mutual respect which eventually led to a terrific collection result.

negative energy through hostility, aggression, tension, nervousness, fear and disappointment.

This is understandable and asset managers should not take negativity personally, react to it or be intimated by it. The key to overcoming this is to continue countering negative energy with a polite, positive-energy approach and a more successful, interpersonal process should ultimately follow.

Angry borrowers

It is to be expected that at some time asset managers will encounter angry people. Given the emotive nature of debt, this is inevitable. Defusing the situation is not difficult with practice. They should try the following process:

- **Listen and hear the borrower out.**
- **Never apologise nor tell them to calm down.**
- **Repeat and summarise the points that have made them angry.**
- **Making notes can help calm things down.**
- **Reassure them you understand, are in control of the situation and move on.**

Handled smoothly this can benefit you further down the resolution process, especially if the borrower thinks they owe you, because of their outburst.

Show respect without being soft

The attitude that asset managers display towards borrowers is also fundamental. Asset managers should show respect, value them as people and resepct their individual qualities, especially past successes, even if they do not like them. Some commercial borrowers may have lost more money than the average man could ever dream of earning in a lifetime. Acknowledgement of these types of things shows respect for past achievement, and it does not mean you are being soft with them. Building rapport with borrowers makes them feel that you understand their problems, in which case they will likely be much more co-operative.

Uncooperative borrowers can become more accommodating if handled correctly. In the event that legal pressure is applied to a borrower and they have a positive relationship with the asset manager, they may suddenly become more helpful when they see things moving against them. Conversely, if the relationship is bad, they may become more stubborn or even turn openly adversarial, where going against the asset manager becomes a crusade, and is more important than good commercial sense. Asset managers should communicate sensitively and clearly, be sincere and understanding, and not be concerned about using humour. Humour can make a serious issue less traumatic and ease tension, all of which helps the resolution process move forwards more smoothly.

Some debtors may generally try to make their position sound worse than it is in the hope they will drive a better bargain from the debt collector. The more borrowers do this, the more likely it may be that they have something to hide. Borrowers need to understand from the outset that sob stories and pleading poverty are counterproductive, gain nothing, slow down resolution and merely delay the day when they can get on with their lives again.

For most people, including defaulted borrowers, fear, uncertainty and greed are the greatest influences on decisions. Pride can be a driver or an obstacle, and for some debtors public humiliation is more important than cash. Borrowers should be constantly reminded that the opportunity cost of solving problems with you wastes their time. As a result, they are missing out making profits again from cheaper assets elsewhere in the recovery phase. The more entrepreneurial types of borrower are particularly sensitive to this issue.

> In most jurisdictions, owner occupiers are one of the softest asset management collection opportunities because of their emotional attachment to their home. Fear of loss is an extraordinarily strong driver with some of the biggest commercial occupiers too. In a number of jurisdictions, I have encountered the situation where a government AMC holds huge commercial loans secured by real estate that represents a fraction of the loan principal.
>
> The AMC doesn't evict them because it may lead to noticeable unemployment, they know they will only get a small part of their loan principal back and, every now and again, the borrower pays some interest. As a buyer of the loan, the first thing you do is evict them. After the shock of realising that you mean business has subsided, it is surprising how often additional cash or assets materialise in order to raise funds for a discounted pay-off.

The best approach to defaulted borrowers is to be direct, be appropriate, show a sense of urgency, take responsibility, remain calm and in control, and be willing to listen. Asset managers will almost certainly be confronted with frustration, anger, impatience, rudeness, stress and depression. This is all part of the job though, the same way as dentists have to endure patients with bad breath!

In the event that borrowers become adversarial or hostile, and the relationship irreparably breaks down, good relations with the borrower are a matter of professional courtesy, and not critical to maximising collection. At the other extreme, some smaller borrowers who are not well versed in commerce just want encouragement to make obvious, difficult decisions, or need help in choosing amongst an array of difficult options.

Negotiating

Negotiating is a core skill in debt collections, so it is very important that asset managers overcome any fear or reticence over negotiating. Generally, most people don't enjoy negotiating due to:

- A lack of understanding of the negotiating process.
- A misguided fear of conflict or combat.
- Fear of losing face.
- An irrational feeling of discomfort or stress.
- Not having received proper training in negotiations.

As a result, some asset managers completely sidestep negotiation, and revert to process and procedures, avoiding all interpersonal conflict, or pick a number, draw a line in the sand and stick to it. Failure to engage the borrower like this risks losing collection opportunity. Asset managers avoiding negotiation may also end up increasing the risk of further alienating the borrower, which can lead to lower or slower collections, or both.

Understanding what negotiation is

A good starting point is to understand what negotiation really is. A negotiation is the ongoing process through which two or more parties, whose positions are not necessarily consistent, work in an effort to reach an agreement. Some people think negotiation is something that occurs after both parties have tabled their position or request and cannot reach an agreement in any other way. Negotiation is not an isolated event; it is an ongoing process that starts the moment you first engage with the other party. Differing initial positions are often a misunderstood aspect of negotiation and those who focus only on the eventual outcome or decision, without spending time exploring, are less effective negotiators.

Successful negotiation generally includes fully understanding the other party's position or needs and following this through post-decision implementation. Negotiation finishes when communication permanently ceases or a transaction is closed.

Nobody negotiates within a vacuum. There are always two sides to a negotiation, but the best negotiators control both sides. Up front agreements are not negotiation. They sound great but in practice rarely close as one party invariably thinks it has lost and afterwards changes its mind.

Compromise

Compromise causes confusion about the negotiation process. Compromise is the most used and abused tactic in the negotiating process. It is usually a mathematical calculation splitting the two parties' numerical positions. The problem with compromise is that it may be a lose-lose situation when neither party believes there has been a successful outcome. Splitting the difference in this way may mean that one side is below their minimum threshold whilst the other is above their maximum threshold. The chances of subsequent deal breakdown is therefore very high, especially with NPLs.

Compromise is best used at the end of the negotiating process in order to shut smaller gaps in position, and should be tied to agreement and transaction closing. Compromising prematurely stands a high risk of failure.

The four phases of a transaction

There are four phases to any transaction, as shown in Figure 6.2.

Figure 6.2 – the four phases of a transaction

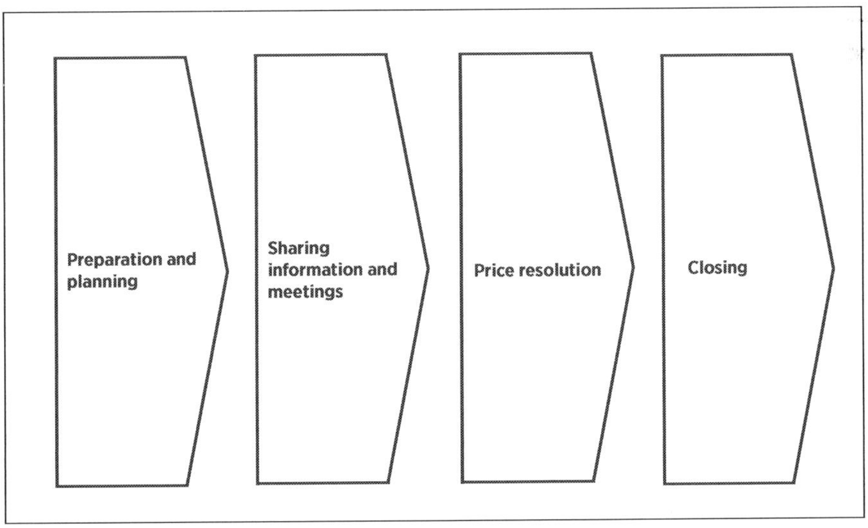

Asset managers need to understand exactly which phase of this process they are in and recognise transition through the phases. Maximising recovery occurs in the price resolution phase, but the foundation for creating the strongest negotiating position begins in the first stage. Once maximum price is negotiated, the transaction should immediately move to closing.

There are five approaches to price resolution:

1. **Auction sale**: in theory, achieving the best price.
2. **Sticker price**: no discounts.
3. **Sticker plus or minus**: where the counterparty has leverage, e.g. volume.
4. **Haggling**: getting the best price, irrespective of the counterparty's respect for you.
5. **Bargaining**: like haggling, but keeping the relationship with the counterparty on good terms.

In resolving distressed debt we are most focused on approaches 1 and 4. **Approach 1 – Auction sale** – occurs after repossession of collateral. Negotiation occurs in approaches 3 to 5, but in distressed debt resolution we are most concerned with approach 4 – **Haggling**.

In some other areas of business negotiating is considered to be a win-win situation. Not so with debt collection. In the distressed business, negotiation is a zero-sum game with no repeat orders. I win, you lose, or you win, I lose. Any loss of principal means the asset manager has lost. Win-win in distressed debt generally means the asset manager hasn't maximised collection.

Verbal persuasion

In most walks of life, the more verbally persuasive you are the more successful you will likely be, and debt collection is no different. Learning and developing persuasion skills are therefore extremely important. If you show flexibility and take an interest in the other party and their situation, you will have a greater chance of success.

Like all people in a value proposition situation, asset managers should try to link their value statements to, in this case, tangible material benefits that they have identified may influence the borrower. Sufficient empathy can soften what would otherwise seem to be too powerful an approach. Successful persuasion must be reasoned. The right approach is not to listen to what the other party says, ignore the points they make and then tell them what to do.

People can generally only be persuaded if:

1. They have considered all their options.
2. They have looked at and fully understand the advantages and disadvantages.
3, They can then select the most appropriate course of action according to the circumstances.
4. Objections have been overcome. Objections are a normal factor of commercial life and raising them demonstrates greater interest from the other party. They should not therefore be viewed as something negative. Neither should they be ignored or bypassed, or they will return again at a later stage. Once objections are overcome, closure may occur soon after.

Understanding people's views on gains and losses

Asset managers with an attitude of *no matter how much I am offered, I can probably collect 10% more*, will maximise collections. Despite their numerical nature, price decisions almost always have a strong intuitive component. A price is not the solution to a maths problem; it is a guess about what the other party will pay.

However, people may have opposite views about gains and losses. If a person is offered either $10,000 or, alternatively, an 80% chance of $11,000 with a 20% chance of nothing, they will generally chose the first option. In the reverse situation though, if they are being sued for $10,000 but have a 20% chance of winning at court with an 80% chance of losing $11,000, they may likely chose to go to court. Pain at loss is often a stronger emotion than joy of gain and asset managers need to recognise and be able to address this type of behavioural sophistication.

The factors that influence a party's position and stance

Where two competing or adversarial parties attempt to resolve a situation three factors influence their stance:

1. Power
2. Time
3. Information

With distressed debt, power is usually derived from cash, collateral, leverage, values, markets and legal position. Banks particularly tend to pay attention to power only and neglect the opportunities to use time and information to influence and manipulate the situation further in their favour. The best asset management involves slowing things down when a borrower is in a hurry to resolve and speeding things up when a borrower is dragging their feet in order to try and tilt the playing field their way. As in most fields of business, information asymmetry always benefits the holder of the information.

Psychologists are unanimous that in any form of dispute, conflict or negotiation there are two fundamentals at work:

1. Objective differences
2. Emotions and perceptions

Asset managers need to recognise the difference between objective differences and emotions, and not fall into the trap of being sidetracked into negotiating over trivial irrational issues.

Well-represented borrowers are the biggest challenge as competent advisers understand numbers and remove emotion from negotiations. This is not always the case though, as some third-party advisers can be a borrower liability.

Whichever method of negotiating is deployed, an understanding of the negotiating process and skills training will improve collection performance. Negotiation is probably the single most important personal skill set for asset managers, so they should take the trouble to improve their negotiating skills, whilst asset management entities should invest in the highest quality training resources in order to maximise performance in this critical area.

Rules of engagement when dealing with defaulted borrowers

The following represent some useful rules of engagement when dealing with defaulted borrowers:

- Each borrower case is a unique cocktail. Therefore, do not make broad assumptions.
- Check out all the facts during the first discussion. Information in the loan file, if any, may be misleading or incorrect. Listen carefully; borrowers frequently trip themselves up.

- Operationally, optimal servicing of distressed loans demands detachment from the original credit process and lending decision, i.e. a new approach to loan resolution. Therefore do not assume that what has happened previously is correct or appropriate.
- Asset managers are frequently handicapped from the outset as a result of a previous loan officer's expectation management, dealings, or personal relationship with a borrower. Usually this needs to be undone before a new process can begin, which uses up additional time.
- Always look for the **HAIR**: **H**idden **A**ssets **I**n **R**eserve. Many sophisticated borrowers will have moved or transferred assets away, in order to hide them from creditors. Unearthing a nominee is a gold mine to an asset manager. It is best to take the view that if no assets are found it means the asset manager hasn't found them, not that they don't exist.
- If intimidated by the borrower advise them that the threat is recorded and another asset manager can take over the case, so threats are pointless.
- If you are offered any form of personal inducement, advise the borrower that you consider this a down-payment to the company and it will be included within any proposed repayment plan. Then make a policy report to your superior.
- When portfolios have been traded at a discount to principal, confusion between operational strategy and loan economics is commonplace and potentially counterproductive.

  If loan sale pricing numbers have been published there is a tendency for borrowers to expect that resolution economics will also be adjusted in line with the new transaction price and the underlying loan balances therefore become irrelevant. This is completely wrong, so it is therefore critical that borrowers and the market at large understand that commercial reality is unchanged as soon as possible.

> In Thailand after 1997 we purchased a particular NPL portfolio at 17 cents on the dollar. The media and the market thought we had paid 30 cents on the dollar. After closing the deal, a number of borrowers offered us 50-60 cents on the dollar to resolve their particular loan, which they thought was an excellent return for us. For us, this was a great information gathering exercise. We of course declined their offers and eventually ended up averaging 125 cents on the dollar for collections for the portfolio.

- In this situation, where loan sale discounts are public knowledge some more entrepreneurial borrowers believe they have a divine right, driven by fairness, to split the difference between the purchase price and loan principal and buy their loan back at a deep discount. Some may be particularly aggressive in their stance, in which case they may need to be immediately corrected equally firmly.
- When portfolios are sold, buyers should beware of strategic defaulters. Strategic defaulters are borrowers who stop paying once a new owner takes over their loan in the belief that this will help them pressure the buyers so they can negotiate a lower resolution amount later. The best solution here for the new owner is to counteract with aggressive, hostile action which raises borrower concerns that they may now lose their assets to a third party.

The three most important goals when dealing with defaulted borrowers are:

1. **Maximum collections**
2. **Fastest collections**
3. **Most cost-efficient collections**

6.2 Refinancing and restructuring

When dealing with defaulted borrowers, extending additional credit, refinancing or restructuring is the ultimate credit decision and a huge challenge. Restructurings are extraordinarily time-consuming and work-out groups and asset managers may struggle to find the time to concentrate on understanding the problems and executing effectively. With a borrower having already gone into distress once, the odds of default recurring are very high. In theory, the high risk of this happening needs to be reflected in the cost of new credit, but the higher the credit cost, the greater the risk of repeat default.

The key to the success of this exercise is aligning the lender and the borrower, not just on payments, but in terms of motivation and desire to ensure loan payments are made. An overburdened or demotivated borrower has a high risk of walking away at any time, in which case the restructured loan is effectively an unpredictable put option back to the lender.

In normal market situations, refinancing or restructuring usually occurs for a variety of reasons. In principle there is an urgent need to adapt to changing market conditions in order to maintain or re-establish profitability. There is rarely a single causative factor; rather a series of events that need to be fully grasped in order to choose the correct solution. Making skilled judgements about the survival prospects, enterprise value, legal, management and restructuring process from outside a company, in order to reset an overly indebted balance sheet, is enormously difficult.

> One of the safest restructuring opportunities can be corporates who get into trouble because of foreign currency loans or failed currency hedging strategies. The chances of the underlying company still being stable and continuing to perform solidly after debt restructuring are good compared to other reasons for default.

In normal market conditions, restructuring may be needed for buy-outs, M&A, takeovers, distress or bankruptcy. After a crash, the combination of non-performance on debt plus market downturn can be especially challenging. The key is to fully understand the borrower's business and how it works. Full disclosure is critical and taking what borrowers say at face value is naïve.

Blaming default on over-leverage in a market downturn is simplistic. Casino borrowers will always be reckless gamblers and can rarely be trusted to act responsibly. Assessing a defaulted corporate borrower in downturn has its own unique quandaries:

- Is the core business still financially viable?
- How long will the downturn last?
- Can the borrower adapt to new market conditions?
- At what level will the borrower perform?

> **Corporates that try to make their accounts look bad in order to discourage their creditors can find this tactic backfires when they look for refinancing and need their accounts to look good.**

Cash flow is king

In order to extend new credit, the lender must be certain of future performance. Cash flow and how much can realistically flow to the lender is the key determinant. There must be significant cash flow and debt-service coverage benefit, otherwise restructuring is pointless. Risk avoidance or risk shifting is core and there must be an acceptably low risk of the lender's current position being impaired further.

Basing underwriting on industry turnaround stories is extremely risky. Generally, market or sectoral indicators are secondary to supportable cash-flow projections for the specific entity. As a guide, when restructuring distressed investors usually work on the principle of a maximum new loan facility equivalent to four times EBITDA (earnings before interest, taxes, depreciation and amortisation).

In the event that a restructured payment proposal is agreed, lenders should make a new protocol or loan agreement that clearly swings in the lender's favour, in the event that the borrower defaults again. This could include things such as:

- The provision of additional collateral.
- Springing liens that are created and perfected, in the event that the company fails to meet pre-agreed performance targets.
- In the event of default, all prior repayments will be credited to default interest, not principal.

Restructuring is not easy

> Companies experiencing disputes between major shareholders, or embroiled in internal personal disputes amongst owners and managers are generally best avoided for restructuring. You risk wasting all your time on the family dispute instead of focusing on the company.

Restructuring is never simple: there are many legal, ownership, financial and operational issues that must be overcome in a changing environment. Quick, efficient, communication and reporting to stakeholders is critical. In accomplishing its objectives, the lender must exert as much control as possible, without taking direct management responsibility. If a company is family owned and poor management is revealed as the core problem that needs to be resolved, this is usually terminal.

A new trend of chief restructuring officers is a reflection of the complication involved in restructuring. A third-party designated work-out advisory specialist is usually a minimum requirement. Such consultants need to be pre-approved by the lender and can be particularly helpful in solving lender's time allocation issues. Doing this as early as possible during the process helps ensure that both the lender and the borrower are not wasting their time.

The success of restructuring generally depends on difficult, emotionless, decisions being made by agile and flexible management teams. The best solution is usually a combination of sell-off and substantial cost-cutting with slimmed-down, profitable divisions retained. If casino borrowers are involved, they must be kept in a credit straightjacket. Cash management controls and lockboxes are common sense.

The key to maintaining or restoring credibility with the lender is to ensure there is a regular and timely information flow. Under normal circumstances, lenders need reports on a regular basis. In times of crisis, they need them continuously. The quicker a problem can be indentified or anticipated and communicated, the higher the probability of pulling through.

> I asked one of Turkey's most eminent economists why after their 2001 crash some owners of great product brands came out of it well and others didn't. The obvious answer was of course that the good operators survive and the weak perish. The problem is that the weak still tend to blame the crash and ignore their own failings. A great brand is not necessarily a great business. Lenders, when restructuring, should take note.

The ultimate challenge is to strike a balance between lender's protection and impairing the company's ability to execute a turnaround strategy by draining its funds, slowing cash flow and limiting freedom to operate. In a turnaround, business actions that are reasonable and maybe even essential for company survival may increase risk to unacceptable levels for lenders.

It is human nature for people running companies to want to blame their problems upon external factors. This being the case, they will likely believe that their business will recover once market conditions improve. Historically, this is only true in 10% of cases though, and the reality may be that management is the cause of the problem but are unable or unwilling to admit it.

Refinancing options are much more limited in the aftermath of crises or market crashes. In this event, existing lenders may feel greater pressure to go along with borrowers in marginal cases, given that downturns usually reduce the opportunity for new private equity cash injections. The danger they face though is that extending further credit or undertaking debt for equity swaps may just be putting off until tomorrow difficult decisions that need to be made today.

7. COLLATERAL SOLUTIONS

7.1 Credit bidding (REO)

In most jurisdictions, when assets are foreclosed upon and auctioned, the lender has the right to bid for those assets in competition with other market participants. Instead of bidding with cash, the lender or debt holder can bid up to the full amount of their secured debt claim in order to acquire those assets. In the event that the lender wanted to bid above their legal claim amount the balance would need to be paid in cash. If the successful bid amount falls below the lender's legal claim amount the debt is extinguished only up to the level of the bid and the borrower remains liable for the balance up to the legal claim amount. This practice is known as *credit bidding*.

Credit bidding can help prevent an asset being sold at auction for a price less than the creditor considers adequate. The big negative with auctioning repossessed properties is that the market at large knows the lender has to sell, which encourages bottom-fishing bargain hunting. The auction price may also be low because of commercial reasons, such as shortage of real demand for unusual properties, or poor promotion, or may be due to asset-related issues, like the need to evict difficult borrowers that are occupying the premises.

Credit bidding can also be used to give a creditor an opportunity to bid-up the auction price. It is particularly useful in jurisdictions where there may be negative issues associated with selling assets at court auction. Properties acquired in this way are often referred to as REO (real estate owned).

The difficulties of the credit bidding process

Credit bidding appears to be a straightforward process, but in practice is never as easy as it sounds and has three particular problems:

1. Extreme time pressure for accuracy when deciding how much to bid.

2. The types of property bid for may not be prime in which case making accurate predictions is at its most challenging with a wider potential margin for error.
3. Risk of moral hazard: a lower duty of care may occur, given cash does not have to be raised in order to make the purchase.

1. Time and accuracy pressures on bid pricing

The main difficulty with credit bidding is pricing. **The concept of investing in property by credit bidding with the understanding that the collateral will be sold on again shortly after auction demands extreme accuracy and is one of the most challenging real estate underwriting judgments facing professionals.** The typical investment horizon for property is usually somewhere between three and seven years, or even longer. This means that if investors get it wrong and pay too much for an asset they may have many years grace, during which time market prices can rise and bail-out a faulty buying decision.

Credit bidders, by comparison, may only have months to realise their investment, in which case they have to get the purchase price absolutely right if they want to show a return. In a falling market, inaccuracy can be disastrous and, in a worst case, ultimately lead to an embarrassing loss on the bid amount. Unlike investment fund managers that can hide for many years, credit bidding professionals can very quickly get found out.

Accurate due diligence and careful credit committee decisions are critical to getting credit bid calls right. Bidders need to recognise the particular time challenge posed by credit bidding and match their diligence accordingly. The key determinants that need to be fully summarised for the anticipated holding period of the property include:

- The rationale and objective of the credit bid
- The projected time period to disposition
- Key numbers, case background, business plan and description
- A comprehensive SWOT (strengths, weaknesses, opportunities, and threats) analysis of options
- Clarification of assumptions used, e.g. whether the property has been inspected internally, etc.
- Additional expenditure and cost of money for the anticipated hold period.

- A financial comparison of bidding against allowing the auction to prevail
- A credit bid upper limit recommendation

Assumptions are the key area to be highlighted in the above analysis as these are generally the areas of greatest uncertainty and the fulcrums upon which the pricing hinges.

This summary of key determinants should be supported by:

- Realistic property valuation
- Realistic property valuation in a worst case scenario
- Market conditions and movement within the real estate sector generally
- Localised market conditions
- Size of market/demand for specific property
- Market supply
- Average realisation time for the specific property in the current market
- Volatility of the local market and sector
- Market trend specific to the property
- Legal and transfer costs
- Marketing and promotional costs
- Property management and operational costs
- Property and mechanical engineering survey for tenanted properties
- Other ongoing payments and costs
- Unpaid liabilities specific to the property: contractors, juristic
- Core capex requirements
- Cosmetic capex expenditure need
- Property cash flow and risk of deterioration (if appropriate)
- Tenancy issues (if appropriate)

A core consideration above is full detail around the specific local market for the asset during the short period that it is proposed to hold it for.

Transition from lender to property owner

Moving position, from being a lender to a property owner, demands a complete new range of property ownership and management skills, all of which needs to be fully resourced, in order to make the correct decisions. In addition to having to deal with operational and potential tenancy issues, the credit bidder may well be confronted with the fact that the previous owner may have fallen short on issues like maintenance and capital expenditure. Indeed, given they have defaulted on loan payments, the chances of this occurring is high.

Evicted tenants may have caused damage to a property, either maliciously or in order to salvage resalable fixtures, so it is prudent to assume the worst. These factors all potentially impact salability, which should be allowed for. Good presentation and capital expenditure (capex) in particular will have a critical effect upon final sale realisation price and needs to be fully understood.

There are two types of capex in this situation:

1. **Core capex**: fundamental condition problems with the building requiring major expenditure, the costs of which will be deducted from the purchase price by the eventual buyer.

2. **Cosmetic capex**: smaller costs which, if spent, will improve the appearance of the building. This may attract more potential buyers and therefore should increase the final sale amount. The dangers here are that: the cost of improvement must be matched or exceeded by an increase in sale amount; additional building work will add to time and delay receipt of sale proceeds; and, the credit bidder will need to fund additional cash to pay for the improvements. These are difficult decisions to make, requiring careful consideration. Subordinating responsibility runs a high risk of paying out more money and delaying recovery, without leading to the benefit of increased sales revenues.

2. The types of property bid for

The second problem with credit bidding that frequently occurs is relative to the type of properties that go to auction. The best properties in the centre of the largest conurbations, where the need for space is highest, rarely get so far as public auction of any kind. Demand for the best properties ensures that they generally get sold or are resolved quickly. In the event that they ever go to auction, peak demand levels usually ensure that creditors can mostly achieve a good price without having to bid.

The relationship between super-prime properties and the most remote assets in terms of demand and supply and price is *not* a straight line such as the one shown in Figure 7.1.

Figure 7.1 – the relationship between super-prime properties and remote assets does not follow the pattern shown here, as you might expect

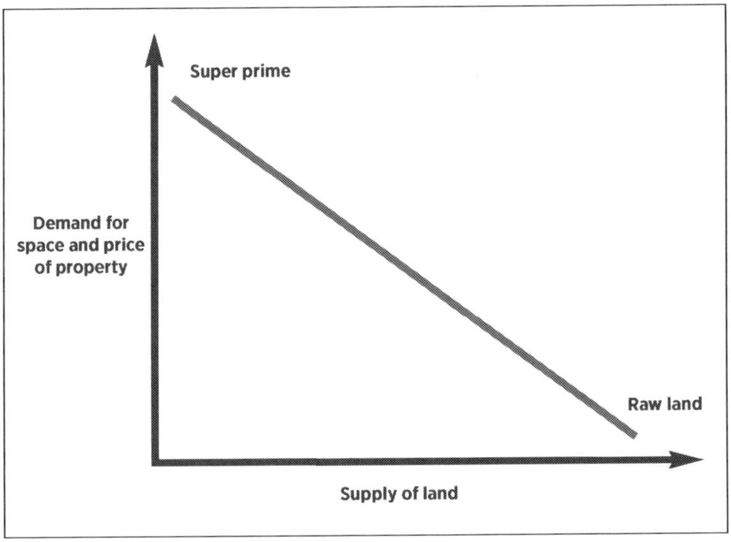

A more accurate relationship is a steep inverted curve as shown in Figure 7.2.

Figure 7.2 – an accurate depiction of the steep inverted curve relationship between super-prime properties and remote assets

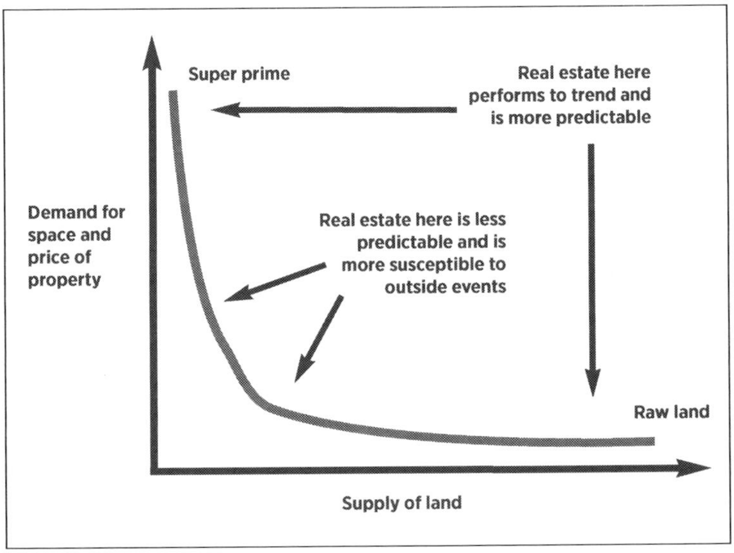

Most NPL properties, and particularly those that are auctioned, are more likely to appear in the middle segment of the curve in Figure 7.2, where demand is weaker and supply is greater. Consequently, demand and supply have a much more volatile relationship, with higher susceptibility to external events in the middle segment of the curve by comparison with the horizontal or vertical section of the curve.

The chances of making wrong assumptions, or conditions changing adversely, increase in the centre of the curve. Greater stability occurs at both ends of the curve, where demand and supply are respectively inelastic. Demand for prime central property is typically consistently strong, with limited ability to increase supply, so price movements occur more gradually. At the other end of the curve, the supply of raw land in some jurisdictions is virtually infinite, which also limits the speed of potential movement in pricing. Getting assumptions right is therefore much easier at the ends of the curve, given that the underlying conditions are less susceptible to demand/supply imbalances, or to pricing volatility.

3. The risk of moral hazard and a lower duty of care

The third potential problem with credit bidding is the lack of cash required at auction. Because payment is in kind and does not involve hard cash, bidders tend to be more relaxed about bidding and, if in doubt, are more prepared to take greater risks. Where this hazard frequently manifests itself is in the situation when the creditor takes possession of a property because an adversarial occupying borrower is trying to derail marketing, either to delay transfer, or to ensure the property sells under market.

The creditor may have to bid *blind*, or partly so, without the benefit of proper internal inspection or access to accurate facilities condition reports, or running expense information. This can seriously risk the profitability of a credit bid, when it turns out that either the property is in a lot worse condition than originally envisaged and accordingly sells at a lower price, or the profit is eaten up by unanticipated expenses. This is one of the risks of the game and a frequent reason for creditors failing to fulfil expectation by credit bidding.

If the property is purchased, it is critical that the creditor fully understands the market and the asset and is certain that they can sell it on for a reasonable profit after deduction of holding and opportunity costs.

Deciding the amount of the bid

> Credit bidding under claim amount and successfully selling on significantly above this level is great asset management.
>
> The overriding necessity to get the numbers 100% right is crystallised in joint venture collection situations with revenue sharing. In one portfolio in Southern Europe, for example, we had to revenue share with the government, which meant they took a top-slice of every penny we collected. A credit bid is in essence a collection, so when we won at auction we had to immediately pay out cash to the government, equivalent to their revenue share. This removed the moral hazard luxury of zero investment and clearly focused our minds on accuracy. The great benefit was of course that we didn't need to share the increased sale proceeds with our partner and could keep all the upside for ourselves.

In portfolio situations credit bidders, are generally not sufficiently selective. They tend to view the principle of credit bidding from a macro-position. This generally works well as long as market conditions remain buoyant. In volatile markets it is more difficult and if the market flattens out or falls, there is a very high risk of being left with a big inventory of properties that can only be sold at a loss.

The most accurate way of deciding the amount of credit bid is to back into a net bid amount, flowing from the realistic market price. After market price is determined, transaction costs and fees, other expenses, plus an allowance for profit, should be deducted, in order to expose a net bid price. This would then be the maximum bid amount tabled at auction. In the event that the property is purchased below this number, it should in theory create even greater profits for the lender.

What is a reasonable profit level?

The purpose of buying at auction is to take over assets that otherwise would be clearly sold under realistic market price or to increase collections where, for example, a property is purchased under the lender's claim amount and sold on above the claim amount. Whatever the rationale, it is therefore implicit that the property must be sold on for a profit. There is little point in buying an asset and then achieving no gain by selling for the same price. Creating additional work is pointless if nothing is gained.

An essential issue is therefore how much profit should be made in order to recompense the lender for the additional trouble and resource used in going through this process, which has taken up time that could have been used profitably elsewhere.

A reasonable minimum profit margin target for an individual property might be 10% of purchase price. Anything less than this and it is not really worth doing. When undertaking feasibilities, a 20% notional profit margin provides a contingency in the event that any of the base property assumptions are incorrect, which invariably they are. A 30% profit margin represents excellent business, reflects the risks involved, and clearly justifies the additional work that was needed.

The major potential legal or practical stumbling block with credit-bidding may stem from inter-creditor agreement caveats. Bidders need to be clear that transfer of the property does not constitute a breach of other lender's loan agreements. They also need to be aware of approval rights relating to management or operation of a particular property once it is taken over.

Banks are in the business of lending money, from which they derive income. Loans generate cash. Taking over properties does the opposite. Real estate generates costs in terms of property maintenance, management, insurances, taxes and running costs that would normally be paid by the borrower. Banks are not geared up to hold real estate, even less so in a volatile property market. Owning large portfolios of property is extremely risky and should be considered extremely carefully. The opportunity cost of holding real estate is high and needs to be reflected in commensurate returns.

7.2 Real estate valuation – making appraisals work

A recurring criticism of real estate appraisers is uncertainty of valuation output, driven by the variation of opinions that can be given by different appraisers on the same property. The challenge facing appraisers is that no two properties are identical; each one is unique. The chances of finding similar properties adjacent to one another, in similar condition, at the same time are almost impossible, the only exception being volume residential construction. This uniqueness dictates that uncertainty is unavoidable within property apparaisal. A valuer's job is to try and minimise uncertainty to the best of their ability given all the relevant facts and information at their disposal.

Property is a localised product, often transacted on a private basis. In real estate there are no exchanges or centralised trading platform like stock markets to determine market price. As a result, wildly fluctuating valuation numbers frequently occur that may undermine investment certainty.

One of the fundamental problems is that market value does not necessarily equate to price. For example, it doesn't take into account a special buyer with a unique perspective who might pay more for a particular property. (A property developer is an example of a special buyer.) Uncertainty is then compounded by the fact that valuation is historical, whereas price occurs in the present or the future. New concepts, products and regulations, such as zero carbon regulations implemented by governments, which positively impact future building running costs and thus should lead to these houses retaining higher residual values in the future, are currently adding complication to this already complex issue. Credit valuations are normally undertaken in positive market conditions. After correction, markets change and the fundamental basis of valuation alters, which can make earlier credit valuations appear extremely inaccurate.

Tolerance of valuation uncertainty tends to vary according to market conditions. In a rising market, inaccurate valuations escape attention and are generally immaterial. In a flat or falling market though, accurate valuation is pivotal to correct credit calls. If credit professionals were to apply the same rules for choosing an appraiser in a bear market as a boom market, results will disappoint. In a boom market, high volume, delivery and price are the main drivers. In a bear market, these priorities need to be changed. Table 7.1 illustrates the qualities that are sought in an appraiser in boom markets versus the qualities that are sought in bear markets.

Table 7.1 – priority ranking for financial institutions choosing an appraiser

Boom market		Bear market
Price/cost	1	Capability
Capacity	2	Knowledge
Reputation/experience	3	Reputation/experience
Knowledge	4	Capacity
Capability	5	Price/cost

The results of institution's appraiser choice have four outcomes in terms of cost and output:

1. High price, high uncertainty
2. Low price, high uncertainty
3. High price, low uncertainty
4. Low price, low uncertainty

In a boom market, a low price outcome is fine irrespective of quality of output; in a bear market, only low uncertainty output will work, irrespective of price.

Current market value is fine as a credit benchmark in normal market conditions. However, distressed investors base value upon future resolution timing discounted at an appropriate rate. The core issue is the need for an unequivocal hard number, upon which credit or debt resolution decisions can be based going forwards. If there is any doubt or valuation uncertainty, the final valuation number may be discounted.

The problem for the appraiser is that they may not be able to provide an unequivocal real estate valuation number for all seasons. The best way that asset managers can overcome this mismatch and avoid discounting unnecessarily is for them to try to bridge the uncertainty gap by better understanding the appraisal process.

Understanding the appraisal process

The following points are fundamental for asset managers to understand the appraisal process:

1. Timing and market movement
2. Scope of work and definition of valuation
3. Methods of valuation
4. Assumptions
5. Comparable properties
6. Property inspections
7. Valuation reports

1. Timing and market movement

Appraisers peg their valuation to a given, usually current, point in time. Appraisers will generally not project valuations forwards as this is considered to involve guesswork. In a rising market this is not a problem but in a falling market this is insufficient for good credit evaluation. Asset managers, therefore, either need appraisers to complete frequent updates, or must themselves take the current valuation and project numbers forwards with the addition of future trend lines of their choosing, in order to identify a reasonable range of values.

Figure 7.3 shows the difficulties of matching time to valuation. In this case, not only is realisation projected to occur 18 months into the future, but the original valuation is based on outdated comparable evidence. The result is a present-day *triple whammy* with the potential for extreme inaccuracy.

Figure 7.3 – the valuation *triple whammy*

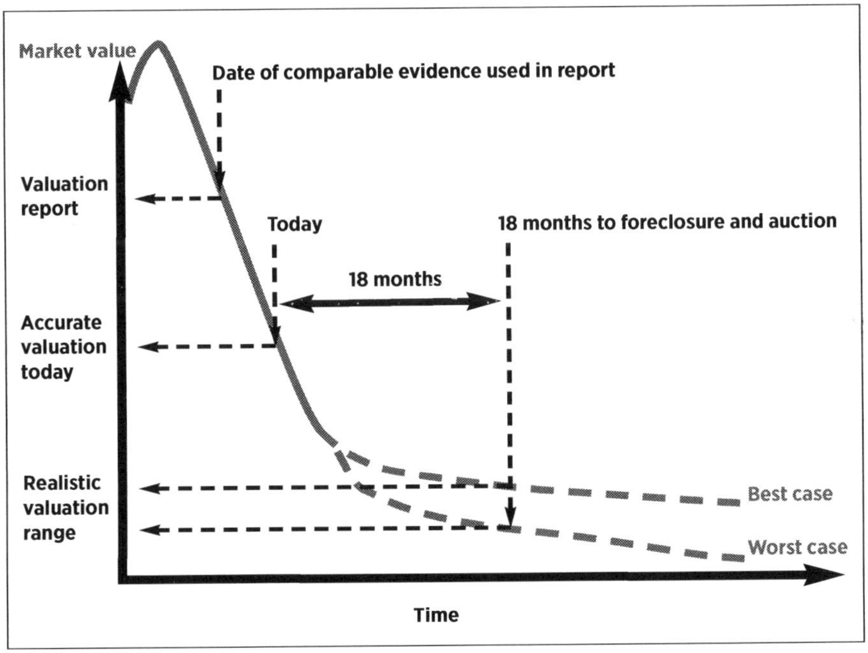

The key for the NPL professional is to be able to accurately project forward valuation level to the time when property sale realisation will likely occur. Ratings agencies make forward projections based on mathematical techniques that have fallen short during the past crisis though. It is therefore up to the valuation user to predict the future value trend and the chances of property condition upon which the valuation is based being sustained, using a mixture of mathematical formulae, property knowledge and commercial common sense.

2. Scope of work and definition of valuation

This needs to be carefully studied. It should clarify:

1. The client and intended users
2. The intended use of the report
3. A definition of value
4. Any hypothetical conditions or extraordinary assumptions
5. The date
6. A description of the subject property

Based on this, the appraiser should identify the methodology, extent of investigation and a reasoned conclusion for choice of method of valuation. The definition of value can vary with different valuation approaches, appraisers and within different jurisdictions. The scope should also clarify whether a highest and best use study of the property has been considered and is included.

> Some jurisdictions have their own unique way of assessing value. For example Germany has subtle differences from the rest of Europe. One of the Philippines' local appraisal institutes had its own unique definition of open market value that effectively overstated value when property prices were falling.

3. Methods of valuation

Some standard international approaches include:

- Comparable approach
- Cost approach
- Income capitalisation approach

The income approach can also be undertaken by other methods such as:

- Discounted cash flow
- Residual method

The **comparable approach** is based upon the principle of substitution. It assumes that a prudent individual would not pay more than the equivalent cost of a substitute property. This approach is only as good as the comparable data used in determining the substitute value. Special attention needs to be given to the comparable data used, its source, and its relative weighting, in order to determine how reliable the final number computation is.

The **cost approach** is based upon the theory of calculating land value by comparable approach and then adding on the depreciated value of any buildings and improvements. This is not a fully transaction-based approach, which limits its helpfulness. It is however beneficial when there are no alternatives, or for calculating replacement cost for building insurance purpose. It is also a useful benchmark for other approaches.

The **income approach** is generally used for commercial and investment properties. It can be accurate for income-producing properties provided sufficient market data exists for inputs. It works by capitalising an income stream into a value indication. It is determined by calculating net operating income less operating costs, excluding debt service, tax and depreciation, all capitalised at a market driven rate of yield. Rental rates are determined either through current rent roll or comparable market rental evidence. If comparable market evidence is used to determine rental value, then special attention also needs to be given to the comparable data used, its source, date and relative weighting in order to determine reliability.

Discounted cash flow is also used as a valuation method for commercial and investment properties. It is particularly useful for larger buildings and income-producing properties, where rental income fluctuates or occupancy is more volatile, such as hotels. It utilises a similar determination of NOI (net operating income) less operating costs and capital expenditure, plus a future lump sum reversion upon eventual sale, all discounted at an appropriate market driven rate. Similar to the income approach, rental rates are also determined either through the current rent roll or comparable market rental evidence.

The **residual method** is used for raw land or buildings where redevelopment is commercially viable. It is based on the expected price that a completed development will be sold for on the open market. The residual valuation remains after deduction of total expected development costs, including allowance for risk and profit. It includes more assumptions than any other valuation method which proportionally increases the risk of inaccuracy. In a bear market this method can be extraordinarily inaccurate.

The key to minimisation of uncertainty in appraisal methodology is for the valuer to demonstrate the valuation approach from a number of different methods and fully rationalise the reason for adopting a particular approach.

Mass appraisals: Mass appraisals including statistical models have gained acceptance in recent years, particularly for situations involving high volumes of litigation-driven compensation. These are limited by sudden changes in market conditions or extreme market volatility.

Value-in-use: Valuation users need to be clear to distinguish between open market value and value-in-use, where the value to the current user may differ from the open market. This is particularly relevant to bespoke commercial facilities such as manufacturing plants, for which there may be no other users for the current facility.

Banks in emerging markets especially tend to become confused between open market value and value in use. After periods of sustained economic growth and a boom in manufacturing, banks get into the habit of lending to corporates secured by production facilities. The reality is that many of these facilities are of such a particular size and design that there is no alternative user that would want to use them as is. Local appraisers will support the myth by undertaking valuation on a discounted replacement cost basis. In terms of true open market value, the facilities are worth scrap value only and the land may well be contaminated to the extent that it is not usable.

This is a huge problem for the lending bank, as they will have the loan marked against so-called collateral that costs tens or even hundreds of millions of dollars to construct, that in the event of borrower failure is effectively valueless. Coming to terms with the reality that a facility is extremely valuable one day to an important customer but is worthless the next is difficult. This type of situation was very common in Asia after 1997 and is obviously apparent in newly booming jurisdictions like China and India now.

4. Assumptions

The more assumptions there are within an appraisal, the greater the chance of inaccuracy and uncertainty. If assumptions are wrong, no matter how technically perfect the appraisal, the result will always be wrong. It is therefore critical to focus on and challenge the following assumptions:

- Assumptions on appraisal method
- Assumptions on valuation inputs
- Assumptions regarding comparable properties

- Local market appraisal customs or approaches

Professional appraisal organisations have tried to reduce and minimise the use of assumption but the unique nature of real estate makes assumption unavoidable.

It is critical to be clear to what extent assumptions used are based on hard evidence or knowledgeable guesswork and thereby gauge their future reliability. For example, if a commercial building is the only one of its kind in a town, occupancy could be extremely volatile. If the same building is in the central business district and represents a fraction of the stock, it will likely perform to trend.

Some other questions worth asking include:

- Are vacancy/rental/yield rates used in valuation backed up by hard market evidence?
- What is the specific market trend for all these factors and how is the trend proven?
- How much future competition is in the pipeline that will impact the chosen valuation inputs in the future?

The more questions asked, the clearer the basis for assumptions will become and therefore valuation reliability will be enhanced and uncertainty reduced.

5. Comparable properties

Comparables are used for sales transactions, rental levels, yields, discount rates, expenses and construction costs. Comparables need to be checked for property type, timing, locational metrics (geography and visibility) size and condition to assess true comparability. The date of transactions is key; more so in changing market conditions. The weighting of comparables against the subject property can be highly subjective with wide margins for error.

Appraisals frequently fall short on the number of and relevance of comparables which is the most frequent global criticism leveled at valuation reports. Uncertainty decreases in proportion to the number of relevant comparables included. A lack of comparables may bring into question the valuer's true local market knowledge. In a bear market less transactions tend to occur which makes finding accurate comparables even more difficult.

6. Property inspections

Ocular inspection of properties is critical to achieving accurate valuation numbers in difficult market conditions. Internal inspection is generally less essential given property condition is lower down the valuation priorities. A competent, knowledgeable valuer can often determine internal condition from external inspection. High standardisation and public listing of transactions provides an opportunity to check individual appraisals and benchmark portfolio appraisals, though this is less effective in volatile market conditions.

7. Valuation reports

Valuation reports should be clearly structured giving the reader a clear line of sight from the subject property through assumptions, approach and methodology to the final result. If this is done well, assumption weaknesses should be easy to spot. Appraisers tend to standardise commentaries through cut and paste techniques, which limit relevance to individual properties and can lead to commentary errors. Reports tend to follow pro-forma patterns, which provide only the minimum amount of essential information that the valuer needs to include.

Unless valuers are instructed on exactly what asset mangers want and how they want it structured, they will do it their way, which will prioritise their work flow efficiency rather than the client's specific requirements. Market commentaries are an extremely useful source of information, particularly in unknown jurisdictions. However, commentaries need to be quantified by numbers in order to be more effective. For example, "market has fallen by *x*% since *y*" is much more effective than the vague generic phrase, "the market has softened."

Sensitivity analysis

Sensitivity analysis, by adopting different circumstances with the main assumptions, is a useful way of determining best and worst-case scenarios. However, valuers and their professional bodies are usually against this idea, believing it to be confusing, and prefer to focus on an individual number. This is an ongoing debate amongst valuers, accountants and other professionals that may rage on for many years.

Forced sale values

Forced sale values are sometimes adopted by clients during extreme uncertainty when confronted with adverse market conditions or valuation vagueness. The concept of forced sale valuations or immediate liquidation value needs to be handled with caution. For some properties, short-term liquidation may not be a realistic option. If the property has higher value-in-use than open market value, or if it is practically illiquid, forced sale value may be virtually zero.

Replacement cost

Replacement cost is a useful benchmark for valuations undertaken by the comparable, income or discounted cash flow methods. In a falling market, investors generally feel comfortable buying as soon as property values fall to, or below, replacement cost. This principal tends to work as long as replacement cost is lower than open market value. If replacement cost is higher than valuation undertaken by the income or the discounted cash flow method, then replacement cost is usually irrelevant. Properties in this category are likely in the wrong use. In some jurisdictions, discounted replacement cost is overused by banks, which is a main contributor to mispriced loan books.

> In some emerging markets discounted replacement cost is the standard property valuation method adopted by banks and some have never heard of cash flow. Whilst this can lead to some ridiculous appraisal results for uses like manufacturing, conversely they can hopelessly undervalue assets like hotels and high-yielding commercial properties.

Value to an existing occupier

The value of a property to an existing occupier is generally higher than open market value, taking into account the costs involved in moving and fitting out an alternative or similar property. The occupier may also attribute some emotional value to a property, particularly in a residential situation. In this sense, existing occupiers have similarities with the concept of a special buyer.

Understand and communicate with the appraiser

Whilst no appraiser would ever admit to it, it is difficult for them to break free from price anchoring or priming influences on their results. Some valuers may also be pressured to provide more favourable valuations, as a result of their desire to secure high volume repeat business from some valuation users.

It is fundamental that asset managers understand exactly what a particular valuation means in order to increase their own effectiveness. Uncertainty in valuation will be minimised by the asset manager preparing the appraiser and having a mutual clear understanding of exact client needs. If the asset manager does this, and asks the right questions afterwards, there is no reason why accurate real estate valuations cannot be consistently achieved, even in the most difficult market conditions.

7.3 Property valuation benchmarking

What is benchmarking?

Property loans can be originated at different times by several loan offices in sundry locations within an institution. Market conditions and prices may vary with time. As a result, it is not easy to keep track of pricing correlation and sectoral concentration risk within a loan book. Institutions record loans numerically in chronological or in alphabetical order by borrower name. When an institution sells a portfolio, loans are generally listed one by one with overall analysis restricted to broad level segmentation around, location, property type and value. Given that a portfolio may comprise many thousand loans, obtaining sufficient level of understanding is especially challenging for potential buyers.

An individual, accurate property valuation is always useful for investors. However, the ability to isolate, analyse, equate and contrast a large number of different appraisals within a loan book or portfolio provides the investor with an extremely useful insight on consistency and overall accuracy of output. This, in turn, gives a better insight on the quality of a loan book as a whole. Concentration risk, for example, and how it is being treated by the seller, if at all, becomes immediately evident when otherwise it may get lost in the mass of detailed portfolio information supplied by the seller. Isolating and analysing only the property valuations within a portfolio is known as property valuation *benchmarking*.

Normally, at the loan origination stage, banks will query individual valuations with appraisers if they have concerns over the accuracy of the result. Once accepted by the bank though, the valuation number is recorded as the undisputed collateral value and there is no more debate. NPL investors , will go through a similar individual property valuation process as banks, but if they have any doubt they will discount the valuation number in their underwriting inputs. This can be subjective and overly-generalised though. Discounts of 10% to 20% are common and in unusual situations in unproven or sliding markets portfolio valuation numbers can be discounted by as much as 50% to 70%.

Portfolios may include hundreds or even thousands of different valuations, dependant upon size. These may be undertaken by a panel of valuers in different locations and sometimes not from the same company. In these situations, ensuring consistency and accuracy is critical in assessing accuracy for both lenders and NPL investors. Benchmarking is effectively extracting and listing specific valuation report outputs in a format so they can be readily compared. There is no generic right or wrong way of undertaking it and each portfolio may require its own specific analysis, in accordance with its formation.

The three aims of benchmarking

A benchmarking exercise increases confidence and removes uncertainty around valuation accuracy. Given the generic uncertainty around valuation, it is the construction equivalent of driving piles into shifting ground conditions. It has three aims:

1. To ensure consistency of appraiser output across the portfolio as a whole.
2. To test geographical, sectoral and locational consistency.
3. To provide a guide as to the overall reliability of the valuation results.

1. To ensure consistency of appraiser output across the portfolio as a whole

A price per square foot or metre, as appropriate for its respective market, is extracted from each individual property valuation. The results are then grouped together for comparison purposes into logical accumulations of similar locations. Comparing, for example, a city centre building with a rural property is pointless. Generally, at its most basic, there needs to be a clear division between urban and rural locations. Larger conurbations will likely require subdivision from central business district to suburbs. Land prices cannot be compared with buildings, and vice versa.

Property price per square metre or per square foot results should be grouped together in individual zones for comparison, ranged from highest value to lowest, as follows:

By geographical location: regionally, gradually focusing in to a more localised analysis. Logically, it should start with the capital city, followed by the national capital region, other cities, their hinterlands, and ultimately through less urbanised locations out to the rural extremities.

- By property sector, use or type.
- By sales and rentals.
- By method of valuation: comparable or capitalisation of income.
- It can be compared with previous bank valuations, if appropriate.
- It can be compared with sale price or book price, if appropriate.

In map format, choice of benchmarking zones might look something like the diagram shown in Figure 7.4.

Figure 7.4 – how benchmarking zones might look in map format

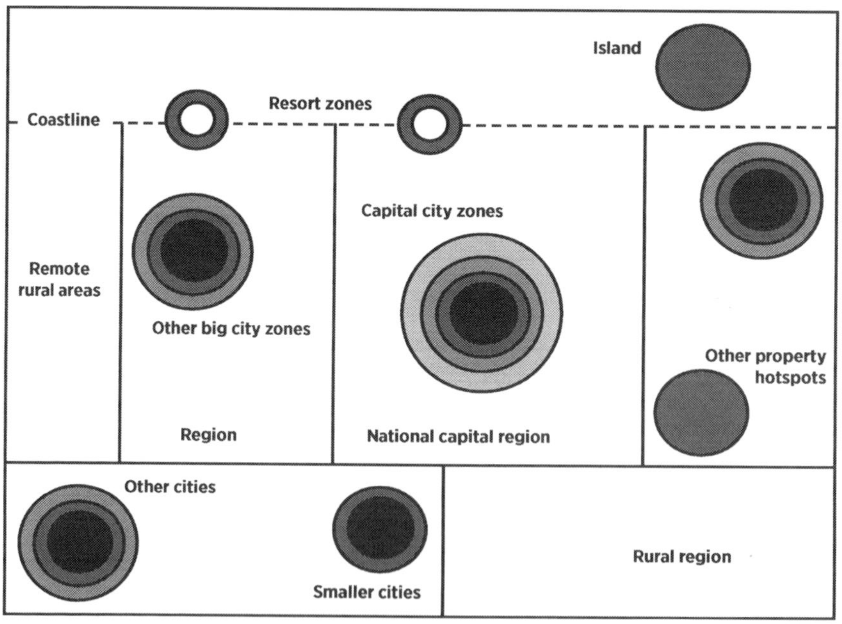

The example in Figure 7.4 shows a capital city divided into concentric rings where it would be expected that values would fall emanating out from the centre. Other high value zones are likely to occur close to mass transport hubs and within specific areas of other major cities or in the resort areas where demand for space is high. Values would be expected to tail off significantly into rural areas of the national capital region, and gradually step down further into other rural regions punctuated by individual higher value property hot spots. Lowest prices would be generally be expected in the most remote rural regions.

This type of breakdown will show whether, for example, some valuers are consistently lower in their output than others. It will also clarify whether consistent capitalisation or discount rates are being used. If the analysis is completed logically, and in sufficient detail, inconsistencies in the results of valuation that demand further attention will stand out. A solid benchmarking exercise can also highlight where valuers may be using the wrong valuation methodology.

2. To test geographical, sectoral and locational consistency

The first section of a benchmarking analysis should show a clear, logical, stepped, distribution downwards in weighted average price per square metre or foot, from super-prime to the most remote rural areas. If it doesn't, further investigation is required. The value curve should be steeply inverted at the top end and should follow a logical sequence, from central business districts through the suburbs, to ultimately flatten out with undeveloped and agricultural land.

> Property zones for valuation benchmarking need extremely careful consideration in order to provide the most effective analysis. Value compositions mostly follow travel, communication and facility patterns. Postal codes, for example, benefit the postal services; they are not there to clarify values and may indeed dislocate meaningful analysis. Government boundaries may be equally misleading.

Whilst in theory appraisers are supposed to be the experts, banks with large loan books may sometimes be in a better position to empirically determine the bigger picture. If you own thousands of secured mortgage loans within a specific market, this provides a great opportunity to understand what is going on in the market.

As a result of analysis like this, investors can grasp a better understanding of whether value discounting is appropriate in specific uses, sectors or locations, rather than a portfolio as a whole, if they have concerns over valuation output. In some cases a valuation benchmarking exercise can show that banks may have actually undervalued some properties or sectors which, in a competitive bidding situation, can be extremely advantageous.

3. To provide a guide as to the overall reliability of the valuation results

A parallel analysis of the number of sales comparables used in appraisals is a useful indicator of the overall reliability of valuation accuracy. As noted previously, shortage of comparable evidence is the most frequent criticism of appraisal output globally. The only true, fully effective valuation comparable is a **completed sale of a similar property**.

A benchmarking exercise can therefore be extended in order to determine the degree to which valuations have been based on empirical evidence, i.e. completed sales, or subjective assessment of what it is believed properties should sell for. If valuation output is based on the latter then an investor might be right to doubt the accuracy of the overall valuation output and either discount individual property values accordingly or increase the discount rate on future cash flow as a whole.

Prices of properties for sale, otherwise known as listing prices or asking prices, discounted by the appraiser, or information from internet research, are not empirical evidence of transaction prices. In these situations, greater human judgement is required, in which case there must be some doubt around the precision and reliability of output.

What is more, different appraisers will have different judgement based on their respective experiences. In the absence of hard sales, comparables and other data, it is common for a valuer to be influenced by previous valuations and transactional information for the subject property. For the comparables benchmarking exercise, therefore, only dated, hard, true sales transaction comparables should be incorporated.

The second section of a benchmarking exercise can therefore be used to compare and analyse completed transaction comparables, extracted from valuation reports, within the identical grouping parameters as valuations in the first section of the benchmarking analysis. Comparison should be made on a similar price per square foot or metre basis, and should cover both sales and rentals. The weighted average price for both property valuations in the first section and for comparables in the second section of the benchmarking analysis should clearly correlate with each other.

The two key determinants for evaluating comparables are:

1. **Date**. If comparables are historic, this will raise questions regarding the accuracy of valuation output. Time series comparison can also give an indicator as to the rate of price change within a given market.

2. **Number of comparables.** It is not unusual to find a situation where for, say, 1000 property valuation reports, there are only 10 or 20 actual completed sales transactions included amongst them all. The ratio of sales comparables against number of valuations is an indicator of the reliability of overall valuation output. If, therefore, the appraiser can only find 20 comparables across 1000 property valuations, this gives a sales comparable reliability ratio of 2% for valuation output.

Bank auditors, product control and risk managers, like bank officers, generally accept individual third-party valuation output without too much question. However, in terms of data analysis, if an individual valuation were a piece of fruit, a benchmarking exercise is like an orchard, providing colossal amounts of information by comparison. Professionals and investors that use such techniques will gain an advantage in gaining a more accurate picture of realistic collateral values.

> As an investor entering a new jurisdiction, a benchmarking analysis is always high and early on the agenda. It can quickly quantify demand disparity between, for example, the capital city, the national capital region and the rest of the country. This is very helpful in accurately risk weighting different types of collateral.
>
> In a number of Mediterranean jurisdictions in the middle of the past decade, it was plainly evident that the sun seeker second home market had distorted land prices by comparison with the domestic market. This is very helpful when trying to price risk accurately and identify what is the true concentration risk. Making inter-jurisdictional comparisons can, in some cases, give you a more accurate perspective than local players. On a number of occasions, we walked away from some jurisdictions, such as Greece, because the local property pricing patterns, revealed by benchmarking, made no sense.

7.4 Real estate development – credit blind spot

When property markets crash, many developers fail and a huge number of partially completed development sites are repossessed. Every real estate or finance professional knows that development is extremely risky, yet every time the cycle moves the wrong way there are always a number of high profile development casualties whose bank credit lines made no sense at all. The history of downturns is littered with financial institutions that have hopelessly misread the market and suffered the consequences as a result of a fundamental misunderstanding of development risk.

Assessing real estate developers

In addition to track record and financial criterion, it is helpful to study a development company's shareholding ownership and management when trying to understand and assess it. The core expertise and skill set of top management is a good guide to its strengths and weaknesses, and the way that the company will tend to approach development. Figure 7.5 shows the key expertise and skill sets of a development company.

Figure 7.5 – the key expertise and core skill sets in real estate development

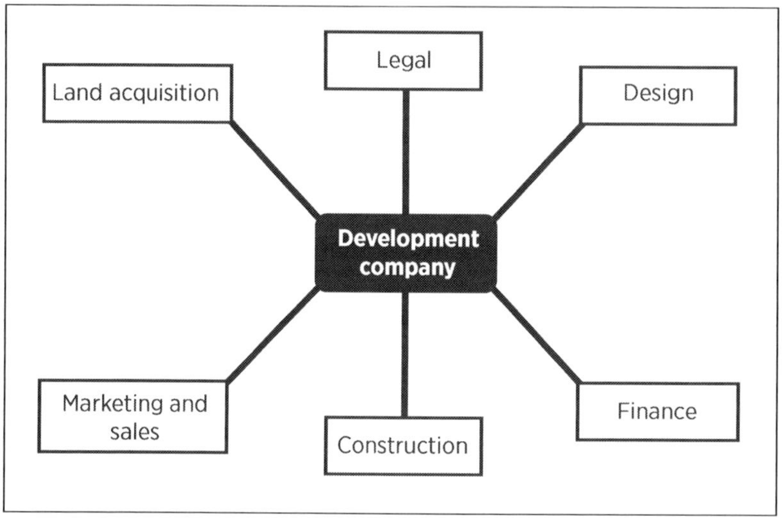

The ability of each core skill set or division's ability to influence profitability varies. For example, a top lawyer or finance officer could probably shave, say, 10% off the costs of their division without losing productivity. A top flight construction professional could probably influence bottom line performance by much more. Good marketing and design can add 5% onto top line revenue. By far the greatest influence, though, is land acquisition price, which has the capacity to influence profitability virtually infinitely.

If the relative ability of different skill sets to influence overall development profitability were ranked, it would look something like the following:

1. Land acquisition
2. Marketing and design
3. Construction

4. Finance
5. Legal

Greatest profits by far are generated by land planning gain or rising property values. Rising prices impact land values, value of construction in progress and finished unsold units. For some developers, rising property prices is their only profit. By comparison, construction and other divisions may frequently be run at cost and produce zero or marginal returns, especially in a boom market. If rising property prices are the developer's delight, rising costs are their nemesis. As long as rising costs are absorbed by rising property prices in a boom market, everything works well. If costs rise in a flat or falling market, everything breaks down.

The four catagories of real estate developers

Every developer is different and, in appraisal phraseology, each one is a special purchaser. They generally tend to fall into four categories:

1. **Land assemblers** are specialists at buying raw land cheaply and maximising planning gain. Sometimes this cheap land advantage is a disincentive to maximising efficiency in other parts of their organisation, in which case they would be better off trading land. A significant advantage is the ability to quickly divest land for profit under threat of adverse market conditions, given their ability to acquire below market price. In some jurisdictions, families or individuals become developers because they own a piece of prime land and want to retain all the value unlocked by development. Their success is usually dependant upon timing; in a boom market some can make money, but as soon as the market turns they generally have major problems.

2. **Contractors turned developers** are usually able to benefit from a construction cost advantage over developers from other categories. They generally have a good understanding of prices as a result of undertaking construction work for other parties. There is a risk that as the market becomes more competitive, they purchase land with a contractor's profit return only. Given this is normally lower than a developer's return, they can be left with a very slim contingency in the event the market turns.

3. **Marketeers** can usually achieve top dollar on sales revenue that gives them a significant competitive advantage, which enables them to pay more for land. Their latent weakness is usually on the cost side, given

they will have to pay market price for construction and land, which leaves them with minimal contingency in the event of downturn. If they are unable to purchase land, other than by competitive tender, this increases market risk dramatically.

4. **Leverage engineers** are expert at creating new holding structures and obtaining extremely high leverage from banks. For them, development is a numbers game and they are equally comfortable applying their skills to other industries. Unless they have a fundamental understanding of the market they usually appear in boom conditions only and lose interest or go bankrupt as soon as property prices stop rising.

Lending to developers

The optimum developer to lend to is one who specialises in cheap assembly and ownership of land. Conservatively run, low-leveraged developers are usually good credit. The issue facing banks is that there are relatively few developers in this category, and their supply diminishes further as property cycles grow and land prices rise. The worst category of developer to lend to is highly leveraged operators seeking an arbitrage opportunity in the differential between interest rates and the rate of market price increase. Risk for this type of developer is usually hopelessly mispriced, which encourages gambling with bank's money and is almost certain to guarantee failure when markets turn for the worst.

Public listing should only have a limited impact upon credit decisions. Public listing and development are rarely compatible, given the volatility of property cycles and the inability of property to generate consistently sustained shareholder returns. This weakness is overcome when a development company is part of a large conglomerate, whereby cash flow from other industries is available to subsidise property market downturn. Where developers and real estate companies are listed independently, book value usually equals net asset value minus debt, which again generally works back to land values. In some cases, developers may see public listing as a means of cashing out, after they have sold their most valuable land. Investors understand this, but banks sometimes seem not to.

The fundamental error that banks make is to treat developers like any other corporate customer, considering track record, ownership, accounts and past performance when making credit decisions. They do not spend enough time bottoming out volatility and, instead, focus only on overall trend. They rarely consider where land prices may be within the property cycle, look no further than third-party land valuations and lend more with time. Clearly, at the beginning of a new property cycle when land prices are lower, it is much easier for developers to make outsized returns. **Therefore banks should in theory lend more money to developers at the beginning of a property cycle and less as land prices rise. In practice they do the opposite, in which case it is only a matter of time before they lose their money.**

Many developers don't last beyond one property cycle

Figure 7.6 – risk and longevity indicators of developers

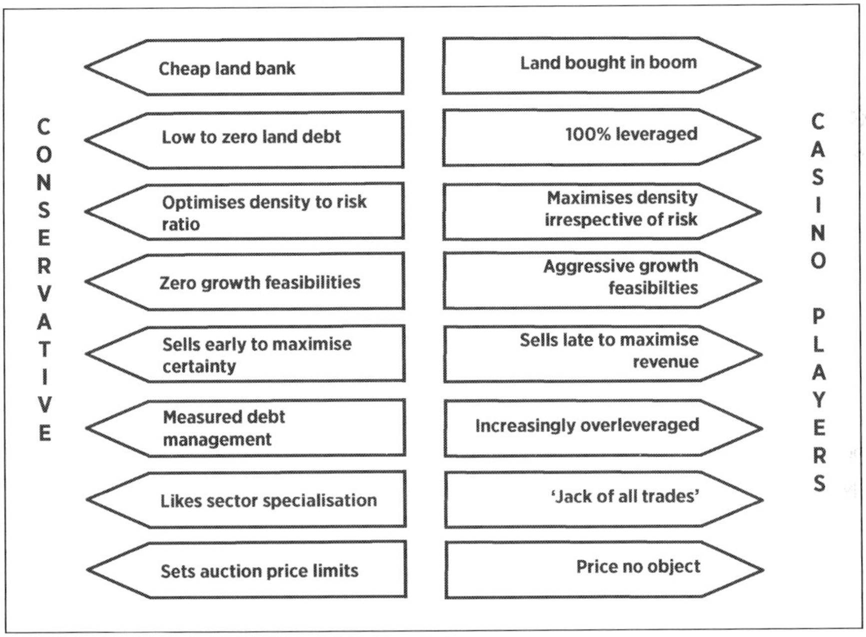

Figure 7.6 is an indicator of the different characteristics evident between the more conservative type of developer and higher risk players that have a much lower chance of surviving beyond one property cycle.

The ability to get many difficult things done as quickly as possible is the key developer characteristic, above prudence. Incurable optimism helps. Some cite their educational background as the university of hard-knocks. As a result, most successful developers are extremely bullish with a *can-do, knock-any-barrier-over* attitude. Consequently, when market conditions cool, warnings of adverse market change may be considered to be just another barrier to be knocked over, but the reality that is ignored is that no one can beat the market.

The likelihood of a developer being able to retain possession of development land in downturn is driven by land capital structure on acquisition. The lower the leverage, the safer it will be:

100% leveraged	**Distress** ↑
Leveraged loan	
Cash payment in full	
Structured payments	
Option	**Safety** ↓

The chances of a 100% leveraged land loan avoiding distress and repossession are virtually zero.

A growing, insatiable appetite for more land is contagious as values rise. However, buying land as prices rise is a bit like playing Russian roulette. If they want to stay in the game, they must eventually take a bullet. Most developers have no choice but to reduce profit margins or dip into future sales growth projections in order to gain a competitive land purchase advantage. For developers, land is a finite precious commodity. It is effectively their lifeblood and without it they perish.

The problem then is that long lead-ins make property development extraordinarily sensitive to market and price changes. Development is financially cumbersome, with similar lead in times to manufacturing industry. Unlike manufacturing though, where a recession may just reduce sales and margins, a property downturn can lead to no sales above production cost. Developers become accustomed to operating in the luxury of a good market and are generally weak at predicting and preparing for downturn. Some find it impossible to generate profits in a flat or bear market. Others find that after markets fall, their products are either out of tune with market changes outside their control, or their fundamental pricing structure is now wrong, or both. Developers with the grandest visions generally need a boom market to link their creativity to commercial reality and achieve a positive outcome.

Branding

The idea of branding is a much misused and misunderstood concept in property development. Real estate is a highly localised commodity, so the idea of name branding as used in the consumer markets is, except for a very small number of large companies, frankly absurd. Promoting individual projects makes sense, but some developers spend an enormous amount of marketing expenditure promoting their brand. Usually the two reasons they do this are, firstly, egotistical, and secondly, to promote their name to banks and funders so they can borrow more money. Lenders beware.

Assessing development property

The greatest risk in property development is over optimism and lack of knowledge. For developers to be able to grasp a large number of vastly different assumptions and then execute them simultaneously is extremely challenging, and it is no coincidence that many development companies do not last beyond one property cycle.

Development assumptions can be divided into basic assumptions and advanced assumptions. Basic assumptions include factors like:

1. **Market size risk**: is it big enough to absorb the product?
2. **Design**: is it right for the market?
3. **Costs**: risk of increase and mitigators.
4. **Timing**: risk of development overrun or delay.
4. **Finance**: risk of rate increase and cost of delay.

Advanced assumptions include:

1. **Pricing**: accuracy and competitive market risk.
2. **Absorption**: market liquidity and downturn risks.
3. **Price rate of growth**: precedent and risk of change.

We will look at the advanced assumptions in more detail.

1. Pricing: accuracy and competitive market risk

It is relatively easy to predict price for an individual property. It is much more difficult to predict price for a **high volume** of sales within a given timescale. There are a number of industry-standard pricing strategies that are adopted in normal market conditions, but generally developers tend to be overoptimistic on pricing on the basis that you can only sell an individual property once, and they understandably want top dollar. Even if they get this badly wrong, they usually get bailed out by a rising market. However, in an unforgiving bear market the over-pricing philosophy can be counterproductive when accuracy is critical.

2. Absorption: market liquidity and downturn risks

Absorption is a function of pricing. There is a proportional relationship between sales/rental price and the rate of disposals or occupancy in all market conditions. There are two issues here though: firstly, predicting this correctly; and secondly, assuming it will continue for the life of a development. It assumes ongoing buyer fund liquidity and consistent cost of buyer funds. Competition and potential rivalry from other projects is fundamental to market supply levels, and therefore price and absorption. A unique development, without any competitors, means either it will be a market leader, or, more likely, there is no localised demand for it.

Developers also need to get their relative pricing right within an individual project. Best units usually sell first, with the least attractive units selling at the end with the benefit of heavy discounting. Relative pricing therefore needs to be heavily skewed, or stepped up, in favour of better units, in order to ensure a consistent rate of sales throughout the life of a project. Price stepping tends to need greater exaggeration in a weaker market. The unique problem facing developers in all market conditions is the need to sell all the units within a project; selling only a proportion of units does not work.

3. Price rate of growth: precedent and risk of change

The assumption of the rate of growth of prices is the most dangerous that can be used, as getting it wrong is usually disastrous. Conservative developers never use one and lenders accepting growth rates within feasibilities do so at their peril. High rates of growth can make time delays due to mistakes and incompetence look good. As long as the rate of growth is greater than the cost of funds, it gives developers unlimited scope to manipulate feasibilities.

Lending to a project that only works as a result of price inflation is extraordinarily risky. If lenders are prepared to provide facilities on this basis, then the price of credit should rise proportionally in line with the rate of price increase included within the development feasibility. In practice, lenders will mostly overlook this risk, not charge for it, and let the developer take all the upside.

In order to sell in a bear market, pricing needs to undercut clear evidence of other comparable volume sales developments by an obvious margin. When products cannot be reasonably sold or discounted, it may be worthwhile considering alternative markets and new approaches. For example, in a downturn there is usually a swing from buying to renting. The key to sales is to go back and challenge all assumptions in the light of new market conditions. The optimum situation may be re-phasing and part completion, with remaining land sold off, or placed in cryonics, awaiting market recovery.

When assessing returns on different options in a bear market, time value of money often becomes irrelevant. Return on cost (ROC) is more useful than internal rate of return (IRR) when assessing potential development returns in specific negative market conditions.

Bear investors tend to focus closely on return on equity (ROE), in other words, getting their money back as soon as possible.

Relative sensitivity analysis of assumptions

No matter how much confidence there is in market conditions and development assumptions, there is a high risk of material change due to long development lead-in times. The most obvious example is new competitor undercutting on price, such as a bank taking over a competing project and dumping units at clearance levels. Relative sensitivity analysis is therefore critical to understanding the impact of change on different assumptions. It is also important to rank the most sensitive assumptions.

The type of events for which sensitivity needs to be run include:

- Increase in interest rates
- Increase in materials costs
- New unexpected competition
- Restrictions in end-user finance

The assumptions to be tested should include impact on:

- Cost of delays
- Rate of sales
- Re-phasing options
- Sales prices

Once a development has stalled for any reason, it risks being perceived by the market as failed. This will likely have negative ramifications on saleability and revenues, and it may be very difficult to revitalise and recommence. The risk is always highest in trend-driven rather than plain vanilla needs-based developments. The risk is also higher in upscale projects.

Property development is generally most successful when developers can create products for a ready, eager and willing to occupy target audience. Hunting for occupiers after construction has been completed is the most risky strategy. This being the case, simplicity is a huge advantage, and the risk of profitably completing mixed-use developments increases exponentially with the number and variety of different sectoral components.

Responding to downturn

In normal market conditions, development company principals and CEOs need imagination, optimism, immense drive, and the ability to get things done quickly and against the odds, all held together by extraordinary courage. In a downturn, most of these characteristics need to be closeted. Development company CEOs now need to become more like a doctors, plumbers and loss adjusters with:

- The ability to objectively analyse problems, emergencies, strengths and weaknesses within their operations and accurately identify comparative risk.
- To be able to decide what can be salvaged, what should be sold off and what can still be profitable, if anything, in a worst-case scenario.

Such character and culture U-turns are extraordinarily difficult, and for developers with personality cults this is likely impossible. Few survive a downturn.

7.5 Real estate market recovery

Response to change

Real estate is relatively illiquid compared to other asset classes which makes it difficult to respond quickly to market changes. The sales process mostly takes longer to execute than most other products, which is a barrier to

The six stages of developers in property cycles

In every property cycle a number of developers seem to come out of nowhere, briefly occupy the headlines, and then disappear into oblivion. There appear to be six stages to this metamorphosis:

1. **The developer starts out being conservative with projections and assumptions. Extremely close construction cost control is exercised. At the beginning of the cycle, before land prices inflate, construction must also be profitable. As a result, all development decisions are governed by return on cost.**
2. **Leverage is increased as market rises gain traction. A tight cost control formula is maintained. Promotional expenditure is increased, paid out of land profits, as awareness of reputation, image and good design increases.**
3. **There is a shift in focus from construction and marketing to liquidity and banking relationships, in order to increase land purchases. A leverage-based growth strategy emerges and rate of expansion increases significantly.**
4. **Manipulation of time value of money is used to drive feasibilities and increase leverage. Rate of growth is the key to being able to borrow and buy more land. Developers usually discover that it is easier to negotiate with bankers than experienced building contractors. They can quickly become expert at robbing banks legally and keep borrowing more in order to demonstrate confidence to funders. For some, brashness is unavoidable, on the basis that any perceived reticence might spook the banks and hamper their existing credit lines.**
5. **Unlimited access to debt enables purchase of trophy assets and land auction invincibility. Some develop personality cults and believe themselves to be infallible. Continuing price increase assumptions are critical to everything they do.**
6. **The developers are now hopelessly overleveraged. As soon as the market corrects and prices stop rising the rate of growth strategy disintegrates. Swamped by debt, collapse is inevitable.**

impulse-buying. This issue, and the fact that a high percentage of owner-occupying Western consumers have a vested interest in the housing market, makes it difficult for governments or other interested parties to create confidence for recovery traction through spin and public relations exercises, as may occur in other capital and commodity markets.

Consumers are at their most confident when house prices are rising and, conversely, cut expenditure when prices fall, which has consequences for the economy as a whole. Recovery in real estate requires market confidence based on genuine fundamental sustainable performance. The most effective way for governments to practically influence the speed, timing and pace of recovery is either by decreasing interest rates, providing tax breaks, or increasing available liquidity for purchasing property.

In a rising boom market virtually anything sells. Buying decisions are no longer governed by user needs and as a result exotic and unusual properties sell relatively easily. Markets are driven by speculators not end users and sellers lose track of market reality demands. Unrealistic asking price spreads are bailed out by rising prices. Buyers accept low standards just to get into the market and have little concern over being highly leveraged.

In emerging markets where there is limited planning or development control, once it is obvious that a market is rising, everyone piles in. Anyone who owns land or can acquire land and wants to build, does so. As soon as possible after a new demand segment is identified, it is oversupplied. The rate of prices rising slows considerably and sometimes grinds to a halt. A spate of special offers and a flurry of new initiatives are introduced by developers; a proliferation of properties for sale appears, together with widespread reductions in offers for sales or rentals. Clearly, the greater the amount of oversupply, the more the effect of a crash will ultimately be magnified.

In mature markets, where development is more strictly controlled, the special offers discounting transition period between boom and burst will be much shorter. The same early warning signs are usually also clearly evident, but the downturn may appear to be more abrupt.

Market inefficiency

The inefficiency of real estate markets make them sluggish to respond to change, and sometimes change can occur in delayed steps, say region by region, or by district. After major downturns, it normally takes a period of time to pass before the market is prepared to abandon a state of denial and reluctantly admit to bad news. Once this is accepted, players regroup and adjust their strategy.

Some have no alterative but to lower prices to fire-sale levels. Others withdraw properties from the market altogether with the remainder carrying on as best they can. Banks normally pull back from providing liquidity which further compounds decline. Recovery usually doesn't occur until the ready provision of new liquidity facilities by financiers materialises.

In the housing market, it is not unusual to see a post-crash shortage of homes appear after widespread withdrawal of homes from sale. This may cause a short upward spike in prices, as the small number of remaining buyers chase even less properties for sale. When this occurs a recovery is hailed and vendors, not least banks, with stocks of repossessed homes place homes back on the market. The market is immediately oversupplied and prices fall back again, whereupon commentators may claim that a double dip has occurred.

Three liquidity risk categories

Individual jurisdictions vary from place to place, but generally after downturn property sectors fall into three clear liquidity risk categories:

1. High occupancy demand assets

- Primary homes
- Prime retail
- Prime distribution
- Prime storage
- Core offices
- High-occupancy hotels
- Prime infill home plots

Properties in this category generally have reasonable sales prospects at lower prices according to new markets levels.

2. Limited occupancy demand assets

- Holiday homes
- Luxury speculative apartments
- Non-core offices
- Secondary retail
- Hotels with lower or seasonal occupancy
- Factories with special users
- Developments close to completion but short of cash

Properties in this category will require creative sales strategies in tandem with extremely heavy discounting.

3. No occupancy demand assets

- Embryo developments requiring substantial expenditure to complete.
- Large speculative raw land tracts.

Property in this category requires innovative strategies such as structured sales. Otherwise, selling prices are likely to be extremely low, close to option values. Therefore if structured sales are not possible, properties with upside should be kept in cryonics until markets recover, which may take years to occur.

How different real estate categories and sectors recuperate

Different real estate categories and sectors have different individual characteristics and tend to recuperate in different ways at different recovery rates:

Land

The land market is one of the most difficult real estate sectors to predict in the short and middle term. Land supply is governed both by natural geography, in terms of its proximity to locations where demand for space is highest, and also government controlled use and timing restrictions. The long-term value of land is mostly upwards.

Where there is no planning control, markets should rise and fall fairly consistently in response to demand and supply. This is illustrated in Figure 7.7.

Figure 7.7 – impact that an absence of planning controls has on land supply

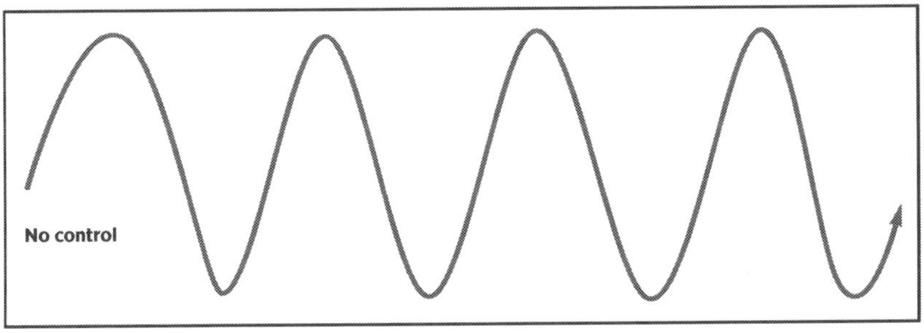

Demand is driven by market conditions within the specific use class for which land is designated or zoned. Connecting these strands is then compounded by a delay, or time lag, in transmitting demand for end user products through to the raw land market.

Extreme boom and burst cycles, as a result of supply shortage, are exacerbated by land owners, who understandably prefer to sit on land rather than sell it immediately after downturn at a discount. Waiting until market conditions improve and prices recover is common sense, if they can afford the delay. This effect tends to be exaggerated in jurisdictions with stronger planning controls and stricter supply of land for development. This cycle is illustrated in Figure 7.8.

Figure 7.8 – impact of planning controls on land supply

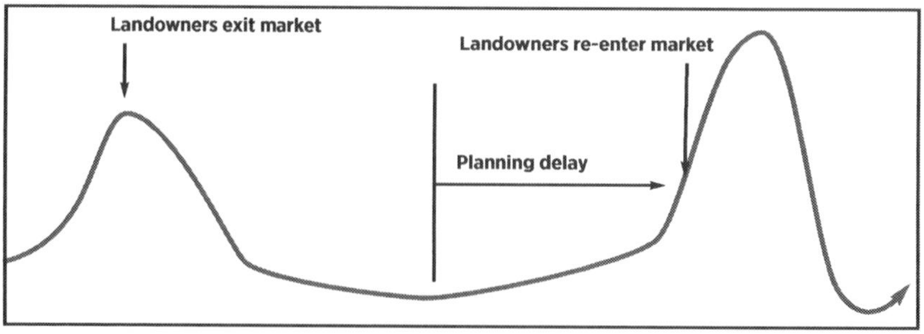

Planning delay extends the downturn and causes a much sharper recovery up-spike. As a result, the land market, of all the property sectors, is the most extreme in terms of boom and burst cycles.

The disruption caused by delay or time lag transmission from end user through to the raw land market further distorts demand and supply, and causes pricing complication and uncertainty. Housing land prices generally follow behind house prices, as demonstrated in Figure 7.9. House prices are shown with the dotted line and land prices with the standard line.

Figure 7.9 – the land market recovery time lag

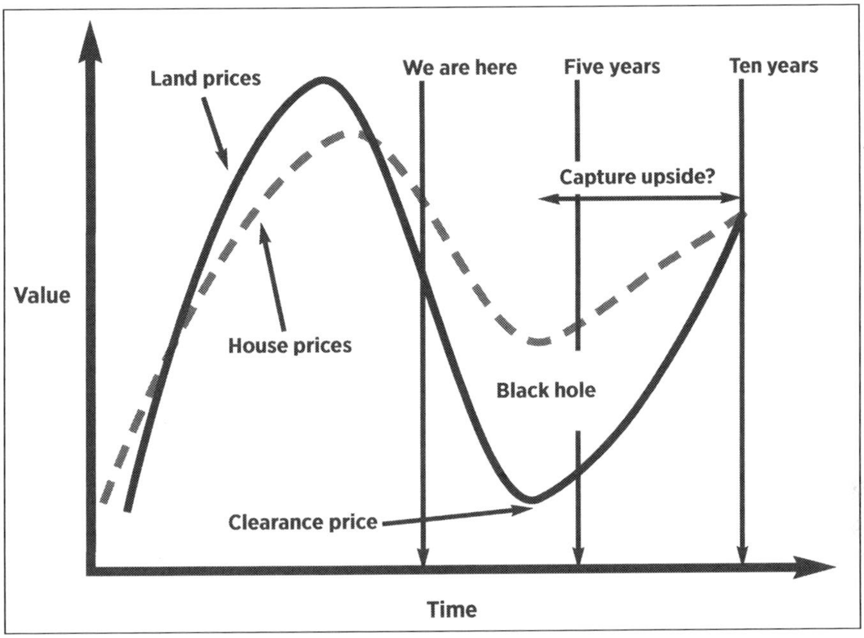

This transmission delay issue may cause land prices to increase well after the housing market has peaked. As a result of this distortion, once housing markets go into freefall, land prices are effectively sucked into a black hole, where they may remain for many years.

Holding raw land in a downturn is difficult because:

- If home prices fall below construction costs, then land has zero or negative value.
- Any sales that occur may do so at very low prices, e.g. 10¢ to 25¢ on the dollar.
- Buyers balance the risk of holding cost against longer-term windfall profits after recovery.
- If costs of funds are low it is generally better to hold land and wait for upturn.
- A good use of time during longer holding periods is investigating planning upgrades.
- A partial structured sale can be a useful halfway house for sellers that:

- Provides some cash in the short-term.
- Retains the opportunity to share in future windfall profits.

Investment property

Commercial property investment is mostly undertaken for income, with the tenant usually responsible for expenses and repairs.

Residential property investment is mostly undertaken for capital appreciation, with the landlord usually responsible for expenses and repairs.

Investment entry rationale is unique for each property, so it is critical for lenders to fully understand:

- Ownership structure
- Capital expenditure: history and ongoing requirements
- Property management
- Rental alignment with the market
- Leases
- Tenants

In recent years, Western markets have benefitted from an overall downward trend in interest rates. Property yields have tracked interest rates downwards fairly consistently, which has resulted in a proportional increase in capital values. After a crash, capital values fall, so yields increase relative to a fall in values. If interest rates remain low, so the widening spread between interest rate and yield becomes increasingly interesting to investors, which invariably attracts them back into buying again. The risk they then run is that a prolonged downturn may ultimately lead to a further loss of confidence and a double dip in market values.

As long as interest rates remain low, investment properties with strong cash-flow will likely benefit from an accelerated rebound. If interest rates rise, investment property will probably be hit. Looking to the future:

- A continuing low interest rate environment is good for investment property.
- A low inflation environment is good for long commercial leases.
- If inflation rises, yields will likely increase and capital values will fall.

- If markets remain weak or continue to decline:
    - Cash flow will likley be more important than capital values.
    - For investment property, it is critical to keep cash flowing at all costs.
    - All but essential capital expenditure should be avoided if revenues dip.
    - Landlords should expect tenants to lower overheads in response to downturn and weaker market conditions. They should therefore be prepared to actively soften rents in return for future cash flow commitment. However, commitment is irrelevant if the tenant doesn't have the money to pay the rent.
    - Good landlords know their tenants: some tenants are in trouble and need help whilst others are immune to downturn. Understanding this can avoid unwelcome surprises.
    - For tenants, high fit-out costs are an incentive to keep occupied space.
    - For landlords, high fit-out costs are an obstacle to filling vacant units.
    - Owners should pressure lenders to soften credit terms.
    - Owners should pressure all service providers to reduce real prices.
    - Best-in-class property management is a huge advantage in downturn.
- If markets continue to decline, the pace of price falls slow when:
    - Prices fall below replacement cost. Replacement cost is a key factor in a bear market as investors feel comfortable buying property below this point.
    - A similar tipping point occurs when mortgages become cheaper than rents.

Globalisation has stimulated much more inter-jurisdictional investment

- Demand for trophy investment properties in Western markets remains strong.
- This will continue as long as Western currencies are weak, or until prices start increasing again.
- Many Asian buyers are hedging overheating risk in their own jurisdictions by investing in Western property.
- As a consequence of increased interjurisdictional investment, FX hedging is becoming more important due to increasing currency volatility.

Lenders repossessing property need to be more proactive

Lenders repossessing investment properties and portfolios should always be on the look out for investment restructuring opportunity and alternative approaches that will increase their recovery proceeds. Multi-use properties, particularly, are likely to have different yields, risk and upside potential amongst separate component parts. Slicing and dicing property, keeping and improving parts, and selling off others, are the angles that investors look for, and from where they take additional upside.

Investors are always on the look out for special buyers, to whom they can flip part of their investment at a premium, thereby increasing yield on the part they retain. Just because properties are held within a particular loan, it doesn't mean their combined value is being optimised by the borrower. Lenders should always be investigating ways such as these to keep the future upside for themselves.

Hospitality

Hotel development financing risk

There is an expression amongst hotel credit providers that only the third person in makes any money. The first owner often underestimates the additional costs and delays involved in hotel development. They may be blinded by the prestige and glamour of a trophy brand and run out of money. The second one in sees the prestige and glamour, but ignores the fact that the first owner has overspent and cannot service the debt. Therefore, funders should always be wary of financing the first or second one in.

The third owner benefits from a discount, either on the equity or debt, or both, and makes money on the discounted price. Financing risk is increased by the fact that repayments to banks and funders are usually relegated below operators' management fees on cash waterfalls. As a result, a lot of funders rate hotel financing as one of the riskiest real estate sectors and many avoid it.

High costs of developing and operating hotels

People generally underestimate the cost of developing and operating hotels successfully, especially trophy and luxury brands. Behind the glamour and prestige, hospitality is basically a tough, competitive, personnel-sapping business. In a text-book, well-operated hotel model, 60% of revenues may be absorbed by operating expenses before debt service or equity. In addition to market downturn and economic conditions, hotel occupancy can be extraordinarily sensitive to unusual events such as political upheaval, pandemics, hurricanes, tsunamis or transport accidents.

Owners are often self-made entrepreneurs who are used to being involved in operations and getting their own way. Operators may see this as negative interference. As a result, owner and operator friction that diminishes performance is common, which is especially difficult when they are bound together by a 30-year management contract that is difficult to break.

There is a tendency for some owners to see a trophy brand as something to admire, rather than a common sense, commercial investment. Trophy management brands demand substantial additional development expenditure for a hotel, before they will agree to manage it. Generally, the bigger the star rating the more this costs. It involves significant additional running and staffing costs. Management contracts frequently give the operator the right to incur, in theory, any additional expense that they consider necessary to operate and maintain the brand.

In order to justify development feasibility, it is normally necessary to include aggressive projected room rate increases that in practice may be impossible to achieve. As in other property sectors, rate of growth assumptions are notoriously dangerous. Extended development periods leave new hotels exposed to market change and are therefore extraordinarily risky; more so, the higher the star rating. The concept of refinancing linked to rebranding is also full of risk, other than at the start of a new growth cycle.

The knack of hotel development is in building a property that can achieve a higher star rating than it is designed or specified for. An example of this is building a three-star property and achieving four-star room rates through smarter design and best in class management. Currently, the main hospitality growth area and highest yields overall appear to be in the three-star category, linked to the global explosion in the number of budget airline carriers.

Hotels in a downturn

In theory, hotels are the most efficient way of maximising property rental income, given the rental rate adjusts on a daily basis. This is highly advantageous in a boom or inflationary market, as rooms are chased by occupiers. However, in a downturn, hotels are handicapped by short-term occupancy, unlike other commercial property types, which benefit from the income certainty of longer leases.

Also, in a downturn big names have to protect their brand and cannot shed expensive staff to reduce overheads, unlike smaller operators. In a recession, business travellers especially will likely move down-market and stay in cheaper or lower star-rated hotels. A big brand does not necessarily equate with smart management, top staff or well located and positioned hotels, and downturn reveals the true strength of the brand. In some of the more competitive markets it is not unusual to find three-star properties performing at the same level as five-star hotels. Star-rating is just the window dressing; yield is all that matters.

The effect of new technology on the sector

Previously, big brands were able to demonstrate strong marketing muscle, but in recent years the internet has tended to level out the playing field in favour of independent operators. New technology is changing the concept of branding and distribution. Since 2008, smart operators have increasingly used internet technology to counteract downturn, sometimes through the use of social networking and chat sites. The use of communication technology in the hospitality sector is likely to grow exponentially and operators need to ensure that they are in touch with the leading edge of new technology, both in terms of attracting customers and reducing costs.

A new wave of technology based online travel agents (OTAs) is fundamentally changing the way hotels operate and their pricing structures. OTAs demand rate parity with hotel operators and can offer the customer a wide choice of hotels and rates. They effectively do the rate shopping for the consumer. OTAs have developed their own brand following because customers believe they will always get best value and choice through this channel. They have also introduced their own loyalty programmes that work on similar lines to traditional hotel programmes.

Given they are largely technology based, OTAs are extremely profitable. As they have grown in size, their increased marketing muscle has enabled them to demand higher commission fees from hotels, usually somewhere between 15% and 25%, which is a significant step up from the traditional travel agent average of 17.5%. This may also be the OTAs weakness though. As they demand greater commissions from hotel operators they eventually start costing the customer more, not saving money for them. OTA customer loyalty has been built on price, not brand, and at a certain point they run the risk of defeating themselves.

The battle for distribution between independent technology driven OTA channels and the traditional hotel branding channel is likely to become even more competitive as technology develops. Sharing high commissions with OTAs reduces profit margins for operators and hotel owners. This issue, and a growing trend of budget travel, is changing the industry. The future trend for hospitality, in many locations, seems to be one of limited revenue growth and shrinking margins, with operators finding new ways to absorb cost increases whilst giving more value at lower room rates.

Real estate consultancies

It is sometimes difficult to obtain accurate advice from real estate consultancies in a sliding market, given they are not incentivised to convey negative market sentiment. Real estate broking is most profitable when sales occur quickest. Usually, quickest sales equate to lowest prices. In falling markets, brokers need to focus on the lowest asking prices to survive. Where brokers have multiple clients, there is a natural tendency to concentrate on lower priced properties. Whereas in a boom market, brokers concentrate on securing instructions to market properties, in a bear market they concentrate on attaching themselves to buyers who can readily execute transactions. Sellers with higher expectations tend to receive less attention unless they pay high retainer fees. The estate agent's nightmare is a client who wants to keep a property on the market for a long time in order to get the best price. Agents are not paid by the hour and want to see properties sell sooner.

The standard sales pitch from brokers is to advise buyers that the market is booming and to warn vendors that it may be collapsing. A survey of real estate brokers in Chicago over the past decade showed that brokers, on average, kept their own properties on the market for ten days more than their clients and achieved 3% higher sales prices. This puts into question the alignment between brokers' interests and those of their clients, particularly how effectively they are really incentivised. As a result, sellers with large inventories frequently avoid independent brokers and many choose to set up their own sales broking teams.

Rating agencies, bank credit officers, transaction managers or risk and product control officers should only rely on published research material from real estate consultancies at the very macro level, with allowance for a wide margin of error. The main purpose of research material is to attract more business, not provide free accurate commentaries, in order to help manage risky decisions. Each consultancy has their own agenda, and in many cases these publications are only useful for providing maps and explaining market structures. Transactional information in some reports can actually be misleading.

Market changes may complicate recovery

A recurring problem facing credit and property professionals after a market crash is not only a drop in prices and uneven timing recovery but fundamental shifts in some market features. The market as a whole or sectors of the market after a crash may not necessarily be the same as they were before. These can either be short-term, trend-driven issues, or a long-term gradual movement. In the residential market prime first time buyer homes close to cities generally rebound quickly. Conversely, some second homes may be perceived as a extravagance or fad from a particular market boom and may never recover.

An example of a longer term trend is shorter commercial lease terms in juridictions like the UK. According to the British Property Federation, the average length of commercial leases has been falling since the early 1990s when the majority of leases were 20 or 25 years, with upwards only rent clauses. In the UK, average lease lengths have dropped over the past year to 5.4 years for retail from 6.5 years, 4.1 years for office from 5.4 years, and 4 years for industrial from 4.6 years.

Generally, length of lease in terms of different types of property, from longest to shortest, ranks as follows:

1. Retail
2. Pubs and restaurants
3. Office
4. Industrial
5. Residential
6. Advertising space on land or buildings
7. Serviced apartments
8. Hotels

Appreciating these trends are critical when considering future risks in terms of saleability and ability to service debt.

7.6 Finishing incomplete real estate developments

The ultimate property challenge

A market crash is enormously challenging for developers and lenders because buyers' attitudes may have completely changed between the time a project is conceived and when it is finsished. A summary of buyers' attitudes in boom and bear markets is provided in Table 7.2.

Table 7.2 – a summary of buyers' attitudes in boom and bear markets

Boom market	Bear market
Off-plan sales easy.	Buyer must see finished product.
Easy buying decision.	Buyers must be motivated to buy.
Loose targeting.	Precision targeting.
Vague designs.	Design must be tailored to market.
Size flexibility.	Space must match market demand.
Limited detail.	Buyer must know every detail.
Poor finishing acceptable.	Total quality control.
Limited price resistance.	Expects discounts below market.
Affordability over price.	Price *and* affordability critical.
Equity windfalls.	Negative equity problems.
Loose marketing budgets.	Zero scope for waste.
Loose promotion.	A *scalpel* level of promotion accuracy.

Given the long lead-in time to finishing a project, the only effective weapon that a developer may be left with in order to counteract downturn is discounting in some form – there are limits on how far this can be used before they start making a loss. As a result most projects cannot be continued profitably.

Every property development is unique, there are no duplicates. Each project has its own unforeseen problems so the development process, by nature, is beset with unexpected additional cost and delays. In a boom market, developers tend to focus on the positives and handle problems in their stride. In a bear market, it is essential to identify and focus on the weaknesses from the outset. Identifying them in advance is critical, as any margin for error is limited and there are no rising price bailouts. There is no such thing as a perfect development, and being able to recognise and fully understand the negatives in advance is fundamental to efficient execution and a successful outcome. If a proposed development doesn't appear to have any obvious flaws, it hasn't been properly evaluated.

Repossessing incomplete development

Addressing the problem of stalled projects in a bear market

Once a defaulted loan is provisioned for and land is repossessed, clear of other creditors, then a monetisation decision needs to be made. The price that the borrower may have originally paid for the land is largely irrelevant to this decision. All the lender is focused on is maximising recovery. In a bear market, sales of raw land or incomplete development usually attract extremely low bids. Given the relatively low cost of funds for most lenders, it often makes better commercial sense to hold the land and seek alternative disposal options.

Investing additional cash into stalled or incomplete developments is one of the most risky challenges for asset managers and work-out units. There must be absolute clarity around the likelihood of success before continuing with development. It is an established fact that most failures in development, irrespective of market conditions, occur due to over-optimism or poor judgement at the feasibility or planning stage.

Securing accurate independent advice is extraordinarily difficult. Appraisals generally provide insufficient information and do not answer all the right questions. Brokers will generally only be focused on sales and marketing, and may be over-optimistic in order to secure new business. Construction, design and project management professionals will provide accurate information in their respective field of expertise, but this is insufficient to encompass the whole range of issues that need to be assessed in order to make accurate overall development decisions.

The former developer/borrower is a good source of information, but given they have failed once already taking guidance from them, now that they are considering the development with someone else's is money, is fraught with risk and complication. On top of this, the lender has now taken on the same risk as the original developer, around high risk of material change due to long development lead-in times. The only party who can accurately assess the situation and make the right decision is the lender themselves and, given it is their money at risk, shouldering this liability is appropriate. Subordinating such decisions to other parties is irresponsible, particularly so to the former developer.

During the UK property downturn between 1989 and 1993, a number of lenders took on the role of developer as an alternative to selling off incomplete projects at fire-sale levels. Larger building societies, such as Alliance & Leicester, effectively became national top 20 house builders in terms of land bank size as a result of having repossessed a huge number of development sites nationwide. Interestingly, they were able to develop out a number of sites extremely successfully using third-party development consultants.

> In the early 1990s, UK lenders that took over and completed repossessed residential developments tended to choose the wrong sites. There was a natural tendency to enthuse over the more scenic and upmarket locations. In reality, after crisis, the developments that worked best tended to be small units, in areas where demand for space was highest and property was cheapest. This often meant smaller inner city infill sites closest to amenities and transport links. Good appearance was secondary and often the ugliest sites were the most profitable.

Where lenders did build out, they generally achieved far higher returns compared to selling off the land. The markets and types of project that they were able to do this within were extremely specific, equating to only about 15% to 20% of their land bank. In other words, most projects were positioned in markets or locations where development risk in the market cycle was unacceptably high to attempt completing them and planning permissions could not be changed to more marketable alternatives. As a result, they still ended up selling parts of their land banks at knock-down prices.

Six alternative strategies available to mortgagees for selling off at fire-sale levels

Mortgagees in possession of incomplete development or land have six alternative strategies to selling off at fire-sale levels once they gain possession:

1. Selling the land at a reasonable market price
2. Developing out according to plan, usually at a lower price
3. Restructuring land holdings

4. Changing planning permissions and developing out
5. *Bob the Builder* strategy
6. Cryonic strategy

1. Selling the land at a reasonable market price

It is possible, even in adverse market conditions, to sell off some pieces of land at reasonable prices. This can occur, for example, in high demand, prime locations where there is extreme competition for space, such as city centres. There are also cases of special buyers or specific circumstances, where another party particularly needs or wants to acquire a particular parcel of land, and, as a result, are less price sensitive and will pay what it takes to acquire the asset.

2. Developing out according to plan, usually at a lower price

Continuing the development on repossessed land according to the existing plan can work in specific needs-based or high-demand market niches. It may also be possible to create or identify new market opportunities that have not been tried previously.

Effectively the lender is now the developer. In addition to making the right decisions, they have to ensure that their organisation and operations are properly incentivised to be sufficiently creative and driven to complete projects profitably. Accounting or banker mentality does not work.

The lender needs to be certain that advancing more cash is not a case of sending good money after bad. The key to a successful outcome is the market – does sufficient market exist? Can it be connected with, and does it have enough desire, motivation and purchasing power to absorb the proposed products now?

A good starting point is to always make sure the worst case scenario is covered. The worst case that must be achieved is to complete construction as close to programme as possible, in order to either sell off completed units to budget, or at a discount. Alternatively, if sales are weak, rent them and sell either space or cash flow later, when market conditions improve. In a worst case scenario, extended or lower cash flow is better than no cash flow, but in order to realise this, building works must be finished.

Fully understanding the downside risk is critical

There are two distinct situations:

1. Starting new developments from scratch.
2. Finishing off and selling units in a development that has already been started.

Generally speaking, only the second option should be tried by lenders in possession, utilising third-party consultants. The first option should only be undertaken as a joint venture, together with a solvent, competent development partner. Partnership with the former borrower has its own specific problems and is discussed later in this chapter in its own right.

If continuing with development is the preferred option, needs based niches include, residentially, homes for first time buyers or, commercially, space for previously identified and contracted commercial users. Except in special, specific circumstances, speculative commercial developments without a contracted end-user should not be considered. Residentially, market sectors that are dependant upon selling other properties should generally be avoided. This includes trade-ups and empty nester or retirement homes. The following points should also be considered:

- Plain vanilla needs-based, simple developments work best.
- New alternative buyer financing schemes will likely be needed.
- New buyer incentivisation schemes will likely be needed.
- In a boom market, marketing expenditure often gets wasted through poor targeting or on unnecessary developer image promotion. In a bear market, marketing expenses must be cost effective and good value.
- In a rising market, brokers target sellers, in a downturn brokers target buyers. Potential buyers will be few and far between, so those that are encountered need to be properly courted and looked after.
- Trophy properties and projects that win architectural awards are best developed in boom conditions where buyers are comfortable paying premiums over market. In bear markets, they are often the hardest products to sell.

High-demand niches

High-demand niches include international cities like central London where there is strong demand from buyers from other countries. London has been perceived as an international home hub since the 1980s when Hong Kong residents started buying property in order to hedge against the risk of political problems after the handover of their territory to China.

Within the past decade, globalisation has widened London's international appeal. Since 2008, a weaker sterling and the need for foreigners to hedge against potential downturn in their home jurisdictions have sustained ongoing buyer demand. The potential downside risk is global – the central London property market is now more exposed to events in foreign jurisdictions than from local influences. If there are economic problems in, for example, Russia or the Middle East, the supply of Russian or Arab buyers may immediately dry up. History shows that developed markets experience downturn every 14 to 18 years on average. Applying this statistic to Asia 1997 would suggest that there is likely to be a major correction sometime between 2011 and 2015.

New opportunities as a result of government initiatives

New market or development opportunities can be created as a result of government initiatives. For example, when Ireland decreased its corporate tax rate in the 1990s to 12.5%, it boosted employment and the property development sector too. Globalisation has now created a cash-rich, middle class in emerging markets, particularly in the Far East. Many of these people are interested in buying up property in Europe, but they lack the educational background, language skills and confidence of the former Hong Kong residents. Their interest is in buying offshore homes; they need visas and residency qualification, and are seeking educational opportunity for the next generation. If government were able to work with the development sector to harness this type of opportunity, it could potentially absorb substantial stocks of undeveloped land and unsold space.

Advances in information technology are the bridgehead. The challenge for developers is connecting efficiently with the market, language and property management issues for buyers whose main residences are 6000 miles away. The challenge for government is the issue of selling high volumes of property to foreigners. As things stand, government bail-outs are funded by sovereign bonds, most of which are purchased by overseas investors. Moving this investment down a level to hard assets is more politically challenging, even though it will probably cost less, given that hard assets can probably be sold at a premium in a bear market. If it can be done, transferring risk inexpensively like this, away from the taxpayer and government bank bails-outs back to the private sector, would be a win-win situation for everyone.

3. Restructuring land holdings

Land is a scarce commodity in most mature markets. Developers have to buy it whilst it is available and finance it as best they can. Finance pressures usually mean they have to take a *once and for all* approach to development. This doesn't necessarily coincide with what is best in terms of product supply, demand and market conditions. Sites may be too big, too small, or wrongly shaped in order to optimise development and maximise profitability. Some development sites are therefore far from ideal, either for their purpose or permitted development, in terms of a range of parameters. Just because a developer has put a site together, it doesn't mean they got it right. Indeed, given they have defaulted, there is a good chance they were wrong.

In some situations, developers only commence projects because of bank pressure. Where they have already borrowed against overpriced land and have a construction facility in place, they may have only two options: default and go home; or, go ahead building a project that they think has a limited or slim chance of success. Given they are using banks' money, this is not a difficult choice to make. Having been prepared to loan against such a project once, lenders must be careful not make the same mistake twice.

Lenders taking possession of land should therefore take a fresh view of each situation and, in addition to selling off as a whole, be prepared to chop-up, subdivide or alter land parcels in order to optimise development potential and therefore value. They then need to decide whether to sell off, develop or hold different component parts.

4. Changing planning permissions and developing out

Lenders should also keep an open mind regarding planning permissions. Markets change with time and current permissions may be anachronistic or inappropriate. In boom markets, under competitive land purchase tender pressure, developers frequently choose to overdevelop land in order to maximise revenue. Lenders should therefore consider the realistic development potential for smaller scale, lower risk versions of earlier development proposals. Sometimes these can be extraordinarily successful, taking a market-driven approach, rather than trying to justify paying too much for land. Do not make the mistake of believing that maximum density equals maximum revenue.

5. Bob the Builder strategy

Optimising revenue for some developments may include a threefold approach of selling off completed units, finishing off part-built units in an advanced state of construction, and selling off undeveloped land. If it costs $50 to complete a unit that can be sold for $100 it may be worth doing and avoids deterioration of existing construction work. In such cases, it may well be more cost effective to contract out finishing works on a low risk, individual unit basis to a smaller local builder rather than mobilise the full range of development company resources. This is known as the *Bob the Builder* strategy.

> In a number of jurisdictions we entered into JVs with solvent property developers to optimise collections. We put in the land and capital. They developed out assets on a performance fee basis. Working with former developer/borrowers usually ended up badly.

Former developer/borrowers tend to dislike this approach to completing construction works. For them, economies of scale derived from volume construction activity are a fundamental cost-savings issue. Stop-start strategies increase cost significantly, so their view will always be to maximise each construction contract. The problem for a lender is excessive sales risk in a bear market. This is overcome by completing units on a piecemeal basis, which lowers market risk. The increased construction cost is mitigated by using much smaller building contractors with lower overheads. In a construction downturn, where builders are short of work, this can be extremely effective.

When completing unfinished units that are already under contract of sale, expect existing buyers to be extremely difficult. They will likely attempt to delay completion for any reason. This needs to be counteracted aggressively with good customer services and skilled handover personnel. It may also be advantageous to offer specific incentivisation schemes to fast-track completions and handover.

6. Cryonic strategy

If building sale prices fall below construction costs, then land has zero or negative value. Under these circumstances, there is no point in continuing with any form of development, and it may be best to take a mothball or cryonics approach to the land, and put it into *cold storage* until market conditions improve. A similar solution may be appropriate if the market for a particular product or sector dries up.

If land has a very low value and no improvement potential, a lender in possession has two choices: either sell land now at fire-sale prices, which will usually end up in a windfall return for the buyer in the future; or sit on the land, wait for upturn and pocket the upside. If the lender's holding cost is low a cryonics-type approach may well make good commercial sense.

In some extreme cases, land may be incorrectly zoned, or markets may fundamentally change, in which case there is no demand for the intended development use. In such cases, there may be no option but to return the land to its original use, to agriculture or for public recreation use.

Working with former developer/borrowers

Working with former developer/borrowers can either go smoothly or be a commercial disaster. In order to work effectively, the developer needs to recognise that he is now an employee and no longer in charge. This can be impossible for some characters to handle, particularly those who always like to be right. Motivating former owners to take things seriously and work hard is extremely challenging. Some developers retain an emotional attachment to their assets, which makes it extremely difficult for them to make sound commercial decisions. Some see a joint-venture (JV) work out as a means to finishing off their development dream, even though it will likely be a commercial disaster.

Some points to bear in mind include:

- Asset managers need to be absolutely certain that working with the existing developer and investing more cash or resources will work. If in any doubt, don't do it.
- Does the developer have any prior experience of operating in a downturn?
- The developer may have been operating on funding arbitrage and may be completely out of tune with the market in downturn.
- Does the marketing entity have any experience of operating in a downturn?
- Using former contractors and service providers can be a win-win situation as they already know the project and it may provide an opportunity to make up for previous losses. Given prior knowledge and experience, they

should be pressured to accept lower margins and reduce prices, but in reality most contractors see mortgagees in possession as *easy meat*.

Whether the original developer or a new partner is utilised in order to develop out sites, a development agreement needs to be written that clearly specifies, in addition to other standard legal contractual requirements:

- Specific development services
- Timing
- Authorities, procedures and controls
- Consents and approvals
- Development costs
- Construction obligations
- Contractors and consultants warranties
- Development decisions/committee
- Insurance
- Completion, handovers and defects
- Assignment, transfer and sales
- Proceeds
- Fees

Central to managing such arrangements effectively is a lock-box account whereby all sales proceeds are kept. Development partners can make recommendations for cash drawdowns in accordance with agreed budgets and third-party agreements, but have no authority to control or manage cash, other than receipt of monthly development management fees. Development partners should also be able to benefit from an appropriate incentivisation structure, which allows them to share in upside, as gauged by agreed performance benchmarks on time, costs and revenues.

PART III

PAST LESSONS, FUTURE IMPROVEMENTS

8. LESSONS FROM PREVIOUS CRISES

The traditional response to crisis

It is nearly 200 years since the US experienced its first financial crisis. Since then, crises have become increasingly common as global trade has spread. In more recent times hardly a year has gone by without a financial crisis of some kind occurring somewhere in the world. In the past 100 years, many crises have been associated with some kind of banking panic, leading to a breakdown in the credit system. This is generally followed by a huge increase in distressed loans, which banks historically would work out in-house.

Traditionally, institutions preferred to internalise problems as best they could, within the prevailing regulatory and reporting requirements. In more recent times, the capital markets, analysts and investors have demanded more transparency and sharing of information, linked to advances in communication technology. Banks that clean up their balance sheets promptly, openly and efficiently are looked upon favourably, whilst institutions that do not clean up are criticised and financially penalised. Recycling assets and resolving non-performing loans is the core of this process.

The 1989 US Savings and Loans Crisis

The concept of selling distressed debt portfolios outright to third parties was established in the aftermath of the 1989 US Savings and Loans Crisis, when over half America's savings and loans institutions failed. Whilst these institutions were not systemically important – by comparison with the bank failures of 2008 – the extent of the problem turned it into a major threat to the US financial system. At the time this was the most expensive financial sector crisis the world had seen. Close to 750 financial institutions and $400 billion of performing and non-performing debts were auctioned or resolved over a five-year period by the US Resolution Trust Corporation.

Overall, the liquidation process was efficient and effective. Assets were auctioned in a range of 20 to 80 cents on the dollar. Higher prices were achieved by providing buyer finance or participatory schemes, with shared upside. The main recurring problem with the sales process was data integrity and inability to provide up-to-date information, which caused delay, reduced buyer confidence and lowered sales proceeds. It was also noted by the US General Accounting Office that higher resolutions were achieved by separating performing and non-performing loans.

The debt resolution exercise worked well because the institutions in question were not systemically important. They were mostly small in size and some were riddled with corruption. The success of the Resolution Trust Corporation was driven by alignment between market price and disposal levels. High investor discount rates and stretched resolution periods for less liquid assets resulted in some of the non-performing loans being auctioned at extremely low prices. Some buyers reaped huge returns, which created the confidence and momentum to later develop a fledgling distressed investment business in overseas jurisdictions.

The government, as ultimate seller, was later criticised for selling assets at discounted prices, resulting in outsized returns for investors, but this is not necessarily justified. Whilst most buyers made good returns, some investors lost money on their purchase. The calculation for the criticism also excluded any allowance for the general economic benefit of an early market rebound, accelerated growth and boom that followed. Overall, the government did the right thing under the circumstances.

Recycling assets quickly created a new price foundation, from which a new era of market growth was cultivated. Increased demand for work-outs also led to the expansion or establishment of a number of new asset management companies and special servicers, which was the beginning of a new global servicing industry. For the first time in modern history, financial institutions now had a realistic and viable alternative to the hold and internal debt work-out policy that had prevailed up to this point.

The Japanese crisis

The result of the crisis also hitting Japan at this time was for the government to provide bailout funds for the banking industry and undertake nationalisation. In 1988, a US$500 billion bailout fund was set up, with US$200 billion designated to buy stock in banks, and US$150 billion to nationalise, restructure, and liquidate failed banks.

Unlike the US Savings and Loans Crisis, where the market dealt with unsound banks by allowing failures, mergers, acquisitions, and restructuring, the Japanese government went to great lengths to prevent the liquidation of the bad investments made in the prior boom. Nationalisation and bailout funds propped up unsound financial institutions and delayed the restructuring to their balance sheets that was necessary. Lending that did not reflect consumer preference was extended and the process of deleveraging was delayed, thereby extending the time for which the banks were unable to function as efficient financial intermediaries.

The result was a decade-long balance sheet recession, the legacy of which still lingers 20 years later. Despite zero interest rates and expansion of the money supply to encourage borrowing, both Japanese consumers and corporations in aggregate opted to pay down their debts, rather than borrow to invest, as typically occurs in other jurisdictions. Banks were not forced to recognise the condition of their balance sheets and were encouraged to continue lending to firms that were themselves unprofitable. Technically insolvent banks continued to direct capital to technically insolvent firms, with the result that the once-powerful Japanese economy was stagnant for that period. Despite all the criticism though, Japan was able to manage substantial recovery in property prices and the stock market, with minimal periods of GDP reduction and only modest escalation of unemployment.

The Scandinavian crises

Each country reacts in its own particular way to financial crisis and they have very different experiences as a result. Elsewhere in the 1990s, Scandinavian nations also had major financial problems. The Swedish crisis was set off by conditions very similar to those experienced in the US. Their response was to quickly recognise the problem banks, protect the institutions but not their shareholders, isolate bad assets in a separate fund, and eventually re-privatise the banks. The approach was painful and costly for the Swedish economy, but was followed by a speedy and robust recovery.

Crisis in Finland was triggered by a collapse in the former Soviet Union, their biggest trading partner, but it had its roots in the aggressive expansion of credit in the 1980s, deregulation of the financial sector and an asset price bubble. There, the central bank responded by injecting capital and taking over the savings banks, which it later privatised and sold. Finland also recovered well, albeit less spectacularly than Sweden. What these episodes showed is that, in terms of recovery, the reason for a crisis occurring is less important than the reaction to the shock by the banking sector and, in particular, the government.

The 1997 Asian crisis

Perhaps the biggest surprise of the 1997 Asian crisis was that it came as such a surprise, after a lengthy period of prolonged growth. After the currency and banking crisis struck, economies contracted by as much as 15% within a year and currencies lost between 30% and 70% of their value. Throughout the region, government policy following the crisis was primarily focused on monetary stability. In some jurisdictions, persistent resistance to fundamental economic and legal reform prolonged the recession before recovery could begin.

Signs of revival were first experienced in jurisdictions where the IMF had imposed tight fiscal, monetary and credit policies, but once the signs appeared, it seemed to encourage foot-dragging on reform, in the belief that things would continue to turn around on their own. Illogical nationalist concerns about ceding valuable assets to outsiders, weaknesses in bankruptcy laws and government cronyism towards favoured companies, blocked outside takeovers and recapitalisation with foreign funds.

> Public or organised gambling is illegal in most Asian jurisdictions, and largely operates under cover within the control of politically connected underworld individuals. Sporting leagues are frequently operated for the benefit of gamblers, not the participants. Stock markets and real estate are perceived as some of the few legitimate and legal forms of gaming. This contributed to the scale of the 1997 Asian Crisis and will have a significant impact upon the next correction too.

It was soon apparent that waiting for Asian banks to recover using market forces, without central intervention, would be too slow. The majority of financial institutions were technically bankrupt, with the cost of recapitalisation estimated to be as much as 40% of GDP in some jurisdictions. The measures eventually taken to recover from a crisis varied from country to country. The important common elements included immediate closure of insolvent institutions, government-funded recapitalisation of the banking system, outright sale of bad assets and implementation of regulatory reforms. Within three years of the crisis, some economies had embarked upon a sustained recovery.

Inadequate legislation can hold back deleveraging and asset monetisation. For example, Philippine banks were extremely slow to sell NPLs after 1997 because of excessive taxes and fees that applied to debt transfer. It was not until after the enactment of their SPV Act in 2002 that things eventually got moving.

Some new features of globalisation and the advances in computer technology were apparent during the Asian crisis; firstly, a tendency for good or bad news, however small, to instantly spread contagiously throughout neighbouring capital and currency jurisdictions; and, secondly, the entry of Western investors, effectively globalising the NPL industry with substantial foreign investment inflow and technology transfer, which eventually spread back around the world to eastern Europe and South America.

Common themes from recent financial crises

After two decades of widespread distressed portfolio disposals in all parts of the world, a number of common themes and trends have appeared. Historically, on average, deleveraging commences two years after crisis and continues for four years afterwards. The US Resolution Trust Corporation took 19 months to sell its first assets after the Savings and Loans Crisis. After the 1994-5 currency crisis, it took Mexico 31 months to start selling assets. In Asia after 1997, Thailand took 12 months to commence widespread asset deleveraging, whilst the Philippines took six years. More recently, Turkey took four years to bulk-liquidate assets after their 2001 currency meltdown.

Real estate markets usually don't recover until loan deleveraging is completed and sufficient quantity of property is recycled in order to create pricing confidence, upon which a robust upturn can be founded. There is clear evidence that after the Asian crisis of 1997 a direct relationship developed between the timing of NPL clean-up and market recovery. Economies within jurisdictions that deleveraged and recycled assets quickest clearly recovered fastest, ahead of their peers. A strong economic rebound and sustainable ensuing growth generally requires additional triggers to be set in motion. Asia 1997 was assisted by currency devaluation, the Western dot-com crash by lower interest rates, or in the case of Turkey, a manufacturing boom helped the turnaround, driven by its proximity to a thriving credit-driven European regional market.

Until the debt clean-up exercise is completed, it is very difficult for banks to halt deterioration in their balance sheets. Given that non-performing loans are mostly sold or monetised at a substantial mark-down, this creates a dilemma for institutions: whether to hold and wait for upturn or take the loss early, move on, and focus on new business. On top of this, financing a potential loss on asset mark-down is difficult, distracting and time consuming.

Distressed debt has similar charcteristics worldwide

Distressed debt tends to have some similar characteristics worldwide. Government-owned financial institutions have a proclivity to be over-scrutinised and over-litigatious, and may be reticent to make controversial commercial decisions for fear of criticism. A tendency for relationship-based loan origination is common in some jurisdictions, particularly in publicly owned banks in emerging markets. For many non-performing loans being sold, credit decisions that made sense when originated can appear to be illogical, after market conditions change. Credit standards can be low or critical information may be missing, more so with longer-dated loans. Procedural or legal errors with distressed loans that no-one in the originating credit team seems to have noticed earlier may not show up until it is time to sell the debt to another party.

> There is a tendency to want to punish bigger debtors after a market crash, particularly in situations where taxpayers foot the bill. This is usually counter-productive to maximising recovery. Sometimes, working with the borrower achieves the highest return and should be actively encouraged.

The main issues for sellers

For sellers, *double discounting* is a recurring commercial problem. As market prices deteriorate, banks are forced to mark down or discount the value of assets on their balance sheets. In the event they then propose to sell, the new lower book price is the level at which a buyer would base their underwriting. Given that investors need to make a profit on their outlay, the collateral ends up being discounted for a second time by the purchaser upon sale. This situation is illustrated in Figure 8.1. This is difficult. A bank's main concern is protecting their balance sheets, so selling discounted assets in the knowledge that they are leaving upside on the table may not be acceptable to shareholders.

Figure 8.1 – the double discount problem

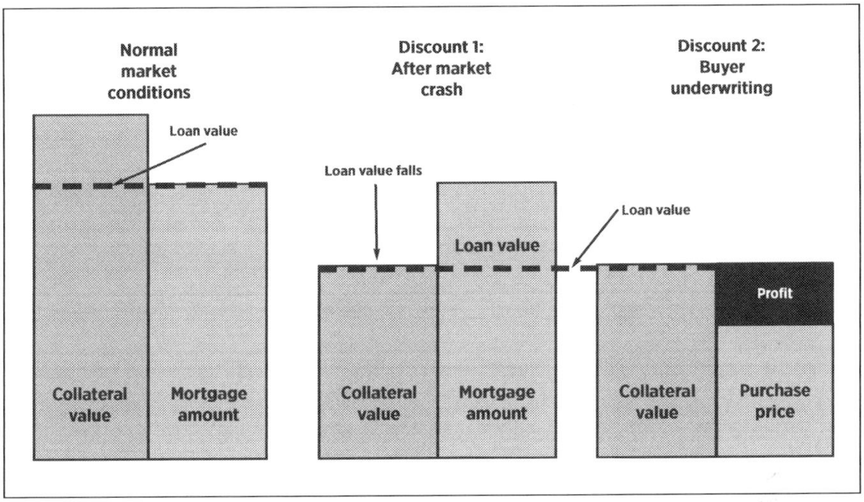

Balanced against the need to sell assets is the knowledge that slow work-out postpones market recovery. This has fiscal, economic and social costs and consequences, as well as prolonging contagion risk. It also hampers banking sector recovery and credit revival. As a result, widespread monetisation of bad assets necessary to promote a faster recovery rarely occurs, unless promoted by government. Influential organisations like the World Bank or the IMF generally encourage governments to adopt the principles of timely closure of insolvent institutions, recapitalisation of the banking system and outright sale of bad assets.

First ground-breaking transactions, either in a new jurisdiction, or under changed market conditions, are generally the most challenging transactional situation. Market confidence generally improves once a number of transactions have been consummated and both buyers and sellers better understand market pricing levels. Once servicers and asset managers get a feel for market conditions, confidence and certainty increases for investors and risk-weighted return premiums tend to adjust downwards accordingly. Transactions also tend to be executed faster.

The bid-ask spread problem

For buyers, pricing drivers for different types of loan portfolio vary. For unsecured credit card and consumer loans, pricing is determined by the age of the loan and the cost of money. The main transaction pricing drivers for secured loans are the underlying price of the loan and collateral, the projected resolution timescale, the collection costs and the cost of money.

Typically, after a major crash, property prices can fall between 40% and 60%. Prospective buyers underwrite loans within a range of 10 cents to 60 cents on the dollar, dependant upon whether the underlying collateral is illiquid, like land, or is a cash flowing asset. Poor quality data, missing information, ambiguity and uncertainty have a drastic impact upon pricing and in cases may cause loans to be marked at zero by bidders. Buyers' revenue is typically conservatively underwritten, with a substantial safety margin, on average between 40 cents and 50 cents on the dollar.

Figure 8.2 – average NPL global clearing price: value erosion steps

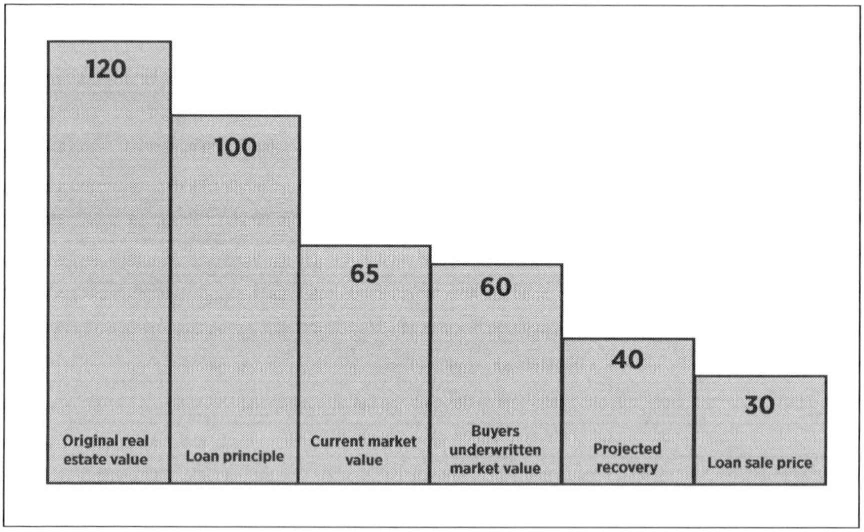

Figure 8.2 shows the usual NPL value erosion steps of clearing prices. From a starting position of, say, 120 cents on the dollar for collateral and loan principal of 100 cents on the dollar, the value of the loan gets whittled down in stages by investors. They tend to trim market values to provide an extra safety margin, before projecting recovery amounts and discounting this to present value.

Average global clearing price for the straight sale of non-performing loan portfolios over the past 20 years is 30 cents on the dollar. As much as 10 cents on the dollar, in terms of value, can sometimes be attributed to poor documentation or bad records.

A wide price gap between seller and buyer is frequently quoted as the most common reason for transactions not closing. Differentials are attributed to different views on base loan pricing, timing and costs. Real estate collateral valuations will often be disputed between buyers and sellers. Timing is usually the biggest problem – appraisal by definition is backward looking, whilst sale transactions occur in the present or the future. In a weak market, this can lead to extreme differences. Buyers will also project forward valuation to a point in time at which they expect the property will actually be sold, which in a sliding market can create extreme gulfs in pricing.

> The Lehman NPL strategy was, where possible, to be the first one into new jurisdictions after a crash. In many cases, the first one in gets the best deals. A big NPL portfolio is a relatively safe and cheap way of entry, learning how local markets work and pricing risk. Once you know your way around the market, you start buying assets at a low price. Once the local banks get back into action prices rise and you start selling equity and financing out the remainder of your investment. By the time the market is in full swing and approaching the top of the cycle, you pocket multiples of your original investment and move to another jurisdiction at the bottom of the cycle.

The investors' sweet spot

In the past, hitting the sweet spot for wholesale distressed debt buyers has been driven by accurate, preferably low, entry pricing followed by efficient monetisation. Investors have made particularly outsized returns when:

- A wide-scale need for urgent disposal of distressed assets abruptly drives down prices.
- There is an ample supply of debts for sale, and banks are psychologically at their weakest, in terms of ability to negotiate.
- Competition is limited.
- The buyer can immediately access and benefit from top-flight servicing and monetisation skills.
- The purchase is made close to the end of a sliding market.
- An economic rebound or market upturn occurs.
- Discounted, poor documentation, or enforcement regulations and laws works in the buyer's favour.

Since 2008, distressed debt in Western markets has been widely touted as an obvious potential home run for investors, but so far there is scant evidence of factors like those above coming into play, in the aftermath of crisis.

Ruthless attacks on deteriorating bank balance sheets, closely tracked by an unforgiving media audience, were also an important feature of the 2008 financial crisis. The opportunity for investors to take short positions on institutions with weakening balance sheets had dramatic and dire consequences on capital and equity, whereby merely the suspicion of insolvency could eventually become a self-fulfilling prophecy. This new development looks set to continue and escalate. For financial institutions, the future will be marked by ever more critical market analysis and commentary around efficient balance sheet management, capitalisation and deleveraging.

The Four Big Lessons from the History of Financial Crises

1. **The quicker that individual banks can sort out their loan books and clean up their balance sheets after a financial crisis or correction, the better it will be for them. The longer they delay, the greater the decline in the underlying loan collateral assets is likely to be. The more time spent on sorting this out, the longer it will be until they can return to the business of banking again – generating profits and shareholder value from traditional business lines.**
2. **Until the banking sector as a whole sorts out its individual loan books and recycles the underlying collateral, the markets lack the confidence to recover and commence a new growth cycle. Therefore, the sooner the overall banking sector puts its house in order, the faster the real estate sector will recover, and everyone else involved in property will benefit as well, including owners, professionals and especially the construction industry. When home prices are rising, consumer confidence increases and they are motivated to spend more money, which benefits the economy as a whole. Common sense dictates that in a market with a high proportion of owner-occupiers, halting decline in the overall housing market is fundamental to public confidence.**
3. **If they can afford to, banking institutions are better off finding alternative solutions to outright sale of NPLs at fire-sale prices to vulture funds, trading on fear. Investors in distressed debt have become accustomed to receiving outsized returns for their investment, sometimes with huge windfall profits, whilst paying the lowest prices.**
4. **Where governments are pressured by international financial watchdogs to sell insolvent bank NPLs, this is best achieved by a competitive sale process whereby either the government or the selling institution retain an ongoing interest in the assets. Markets can sometimes recover remarkably quickly, once everyone recognises that the underlying cause of the original correction has been halted. This being the case, it is reasonable to expect that the sellers should also benefit from the upside.**

9. NEW INITIATIVES TO PRESERVE CAPITAL AND INCREASE RETURNS

The 2008 crisis coincided with the end of a 30-year long period of gradually reducing interest rates and credit growth in most Western economies. Interest rates can no longer be reduced further so, unlike the last correction, there will be no credit-pricing boost to drive market rebound.

Unassisted, a sustained recovery within the real estate markets may therefore take much longer than previously experienced, which makes the task of cleaning up distressed debt especially challenging, and the longer it will likely be until the recovery process is completed. Given this added uncertainty, alternative approaches that produce better monetisation and ways of preserving capital should theoretically become increasingly important.

Initiatives that could be explored further

Some of the initiatives that might be improved or explored further could, for example, include the following areas:

1. Engineering more sustainable loan restructurings.
2. Better asset management: less capital destruction and more upside creation.
3. Alternative methods of resolving and holding real estate.
4. Selling loan books in joint venture structures with upside sharing.
5. Creating new ways of absorbing bank loan book losses that are not dependant upon taxpayers.

1. Engineering more sustainable loan restructurings

At the simplest level, the term *distressed* in terms of debt has two meanings:

1. The loan balance is higher than the value of the underlying collateral.
2. The borrower is unable to make the loan payments.

In normal market conditions lenders would forclose or restructure loans that failed to meet either of these two conditions. However, given a potential longer-term weakness in the real estate markets, lenders are reluctant to foreclose on distressed loans, particularly in situations where a loan is in default purely because of negative loan-to-value ratios. As long as interest payments are made, banks have recognised that they may be better off looking the other way and holding otherwise distressed loans until real estate markets return to growth.

Pretend and extend measures

The result of this policy change is that forbearance measures, otherwise known as *pretend and extend*, have recently entered the popular vernacular – the idea of banks holding off on foreclosure in order to have a more orderly liquidation, or in the hope of being paid out in full in the future, rather than take a loss now. The key to successful loan forbearance is sufficient cash flow, or ability to service debt; loan to value is secondary and sometimes immaterial.

The media and specific interest groups have been highly critical of pretend and extend schemes but, overall, the banks probably have little choice but to pursue such policies. With accurate underwriting and solid judgement, pretend and extend schemes are good business. However, the problem for some institutions is inadequate underwriting and poor judgement, which can make a bad situation worse.

Properties may behave completely differently after a market correction. For mortgage-backed securitisations, pretend and extend is much more complex, given that senior note-holders will generally favour liquidation and early pay-out, whilst junior note-holders want the cash flow to continue as long as it can, as they will likely be wiped out in a liquidation scenario.

Artificial subsidies, or incentivisation that attempts to achieve above market prices, can be extraordinarily risky, and may even end up being counterproductive and delaying recovery. In the housing markets, some lenders now prefer to restructure home loans rather than foreclose and destroy value. A number of loan modification options have been tried, including changes in interest rates, extending the maturity of the loan or reducing principal.

In spite of these initiatives, a substantial proportion of loans default again later. One of the prime causes of this is negative equity, the situation where the outstanding principal balance of the home exceeds its market value. Under these circumstances, the motivation of the borrower to continue making payments is limited. Given the choice between defaulting on, say, a credit card, or a negative equity home mortgage payments, they may well choose the latter.

Also, in the event that the housing market levels out and starts growing again, a borrower would be better off defaulting, abandoning the home and investing in another property, where they would immediately and directly benefit from equity gain. Negative equity also discourages home owners from keeping up to date with repairs and maintenance expenditure, critical for protecting future value.

Shared appreciation schemes

A better solution may therefore be to reduce the loan balance to current low market value. This is a win-win for the lender too as in the event of foreclosure costs and fees would reduce eventual net realisation to a significantly lower figure. Provided the borrower has the capacity to make monthly payments, then the new loan agreement would also include a provision for upside equity sharing. In this way, the borrower is motivated to make payments, create equity and will benefit from market rebound. In the event of default, the borrower would lose their equity stake and all upside would revert to the lender. *Shared appreciation mortgages*, as these instruments are called, go against the traditional view of pushing losses into the future through pretend and extend schemes, but in reality are a more realistic commercial alternative.

Strategic defaults, where some borrowers deliberately default in order to benefit from a reduction in principal, may be an issue. This highlights the need for sound personal judgment by special servicers. The chances are that, even with strategic defaulters, banks may still technically be better off. The biggest obstacle with this type of initiative may be that it is not possible to implement for some securitised mortgages, where there are restrictions specifically prohibiting amendments to principal.

2. Better asset management: less capital destruction and more upside creation

Banks now have the option of seeking advice from a wide range of experienced competent individuals from within the global distressed debt industry. Greater resources are now available within this specialised area than have ever been there previously. Special servicing is best outsourced to established experts, allowing banks to fully focus back on core profit generating activities. Banks are frequently reluctant to outsource special servicing on the basis of cost and control though, with many preferring to set up their own in-house work-out divisions, maybe under the control of seasoned, trusty, veterans (sometimes approaching retirement) from within the institution. Asset management is like anything else; you get what you pay for in terms of results. Professionalism, hands-on relevant experience, entrepreneurial creativity and the ability to invest additional cash to create more profitable resolutions are the key to optimising distressed loan books.

Successful outsourcing of loan servicing is achieved through alignment on fees and shared performance-driven upside. Servicers who expect to have all their costs covered without taking any risk, i.e. receiving all the upside with no downside, are not properly aligned. At the very least, servicers should shoulder some operational risk. The key to performance alignment is driven by mutual agreement on commercial issues, valuation benchmarks and performance standards. Outsourced servicing is generally more expensive than in-house work-out teams, so in return for outsourcing, the lender should expect to recover **at least** the same net amount after deduction of outsourced servicing costs. Performance upside is then a win-win for both parties.

Government asset management entities are one step even further removed from the NPL world than internal work-out departments and historically have been at their most effective concentrating on investment facilitation or regulatory roles only. Cumbersome, publicly sponsored entities run by civil servants are generally viewed by distressed borrowers as intransigent, difficult to deal with, excessively bureaucratic, insensitive to risk and commercial factors, and overly concerned with veiling themselves from criticism and deflecting political censure.

3. Alternative methods of resolving and holding real estate

Traditional ways of resolving real estate secured NPLs

The established methods for resolving NPLs secured by real estate are threefold:

1. Refinancing the loan through a third party
2. Restructuring the terms of the existing loan
3. Asset liquidation either voluntarily or through court execution

In recent times a fourth alternative similar to restructuring – the concept of pretend and extend – has come into play.

These approaches are insufficient for optimising collections though, particularly the concept of widespread auctioning of collateralised assets where loan defaults cannot be cured, or loan payments cannot be made. In a severely depressed real estate market with extreme volatility it is extraordinarily difficult to realise reasonable prices on disposal. For example, if the land market has collapsed and is unlikely to recover for five to ten years, simple mathematics dictate that selling to investors demanding a 20% discount rate will result in sale levels close to option value.

Alternative approaches in unusual circumstances

Institutions that want to optimise collections, particularly if they can benefit from low cost of funds, should therefore look at other ways of profitably holding real estate until market conditions are stronger and sales proceeds improve.

Assets for consideration in this way could include:

- Cash flowing properties
- Cash flowing properties where cash flow and management can be improved
- Properties capable of producing cash flow where income is created
- Properties capable of improvement that can be improved profitably
- Illiquid properties with future upside

Retaining and maximising upside for these categories of properties not only mitigates loss, but creates a future profits pipeline. Banks building a real-estate-backed loan book are process-driven. Smart asset management, on the other hand, is exit-driven. Where collateral is taken over, assets should be warehoused, tranched and held according to future recovery timing, cash flow, yield, and a comparison of bank holding cost versus investor discount rate. Properties that are illiquid, with no upside, and incapable of improvement, are the only assets that should be *wasted* by selling at auction into a weak real estate market.

Given that holding assets will involve the investment of additional cash, and needs specialised skills, it is best undertaken within a partnership or joint venture structure. The key to success is to find partners, not only looking to invest into these types of asset classes, but preferably with the ability to add value. Risk and profit sharing mechanics need careful consideration though. Negotiating with a partner on price alone in entrepreneurial upside situations like this is insufficient. The parties need to be fully aligned, totally transparent and fully understand one another's investment goals, in order to maximise proceeds for both of them. This means not only coordinating and negotiating on price but also on areas such as:

- Timing
- Funding costs
- Discount rates
- Cash waterfall priorities
- Sharing formulae variations or adjustments
- Additional leverage or investment

Careful attention also needs to be given to diverse types of investment. Different investors have different needs and requirements, in terms of holding periods, or how actively they want to be involved in future management. Lumping inappropriate properties together will water down returns, whilst getting it right will optimise them.

The types of assets listed above have different holding period horizons and different additional investment requirements, as shown in Figure 9.1. Matching this up with the correct investor is the key to squeezing out every last piece of upside.

Figure 9.1 – better matching investor's investment horizons to property cash flow

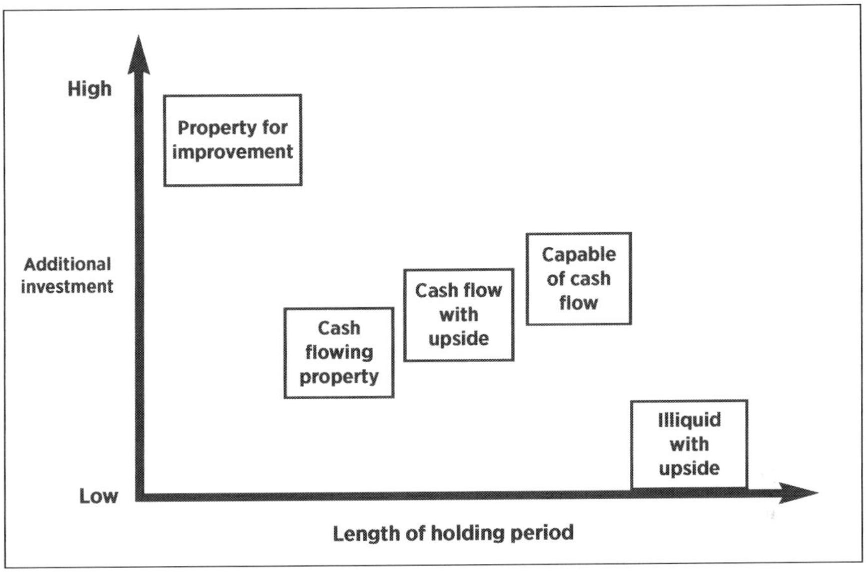

Properly executed and managed, this type of upside venture is capable of producing extremely valuable future income pipelines for institutions, which can substantially mitigate previous losses.

4. Selling loan books in joint venture structures with upside sharing

Overcoming price disparity

Interested distressed debt investors now quote pricing as the biggest obstacle to executing new wholesale NPL transactions. For investors, returns in the sector are dictated by opportunity plus skilful execution and, in the past, investing successfully has been more about opportunity and less about execution. As long as investors view opportunity to mean easy pickings by purchasing at fire-sale levels, banks know from past experience that they are better off retaining bad loans and taking their chances.

A paradigm shift in distressed debt investing is therefore occurring. If investors want to be substantially involved in the future they need to change their approach and dramatically upgrade their execution in order to compensate for finding ways of paying higher prices for loans. Vulture pricing in Western jurisdictions is, for now, an anachronism.

Current transactions will likely be executed at higher levels whereby investors can still make solid returns but there is unlikely to be a flood of easy *home-run* investments, where assets can be double, treble or quadruple discounted. Servicing can continue to be an extremely profitable business, albeit the greatest returns, both for servicers and investors, will be achieved by adding value to assets through creativity and top-flight real estate investment skills.

The four negotiable parts of an NPL portfolio bid

There are four core negotiable parts to an NPL portfolio bid:

1. The costs and expense incurred in making future collections.
2. The underlying value of loans, enterprise and collateral.
3. The projected timescale for making collections.
4. The assigned discount rate or applied cost of money.

Section (1) – the costs of future collections – is difficult to adjust significantly and is generally not disputed between parties. Otherwise, the main reasons for bid-ask price disparity between buyers and sellers occurs in sections (2), (3) and (4).

Section (2) – real estate valuation – is frequently disputed between buyers and sellers. Sellers' numbers are usually historic, whilst buyers project values forward to a point in time when they expect asset resolution to occur. In a sliding market, this can reduce numbers dramatically. Buyers may also tend to discount values to create additional deal comfort. Institutions and investors will generally have an opposite view on value in use against open market value.

Within **section (3) – timescale for making collections** – sellers and buyers usually have vastly different horizons. NPL investors usually take a shorter term view on investments. Typically a three to four-year horizon has been market standard. Financial institutions, on the other hand, generally take a longer-term view of their loan book, up to ten years. One of the reasons why they can afford to do this is their lower cost of funds.

Within **section (4) – discount rate** – sellers and buyers also have diametrically opposed views. Typically, a financial institution has a low cost of funds, on average around 2% to 3%. Investors will typically have a much higher return requirement, between 15% and 20%. Except in unusual circumstances, or unless other parties are involved, this misalignment makes it difficult to match the parties on price if a traditional straightforward sale is envisaged.

Divergence on investment return timing and discount rates

Divergence on the value of underlying loans and collateral is generally driven by differing opinions and needs to be looked at on a case-by-case basis. Divergence on investment return timing and discount rate is more fundamental. The crux of the problem is investors having a short-term horizon with high discount rates, which makes it difficult for sellers to maximise NPL sale proceeds. This is summarised in Table 9.1.

Table 9.1 – institution and investor divergence on return timing and discount rate

Institutions	Investors
Long-term view	Short-term horizon
Low cost of funds	High discount rates

Overcoming the divergences

It may be possible to overcome these divergences by structuring a sales transaction with future seller participation through profit and revenue sharing arrangements that optimises the return requirements of both parties. Investor needs could be satisfied by giving them their profit return requirements for the first three to four years, then reversing the revenue priority in favour of the seller for the remainder of the portfolio work out. This type of revenue sharing scheme, as shown in Figure 9.2, can work because the portfolio retains greater value in the latter stages for the seller, due to their lower discount rate.

Revenue sharing arrangements of this type would also give the seller the greatest advantage from any future market recovery, both in terms of collections and new lending opportunities. Special servicing is best undertaken by a third party, in order to avoid any possible bias as revenue priorities switch and transfer.

Figure 9.2 – typical profit and revenue sharing transaction structure

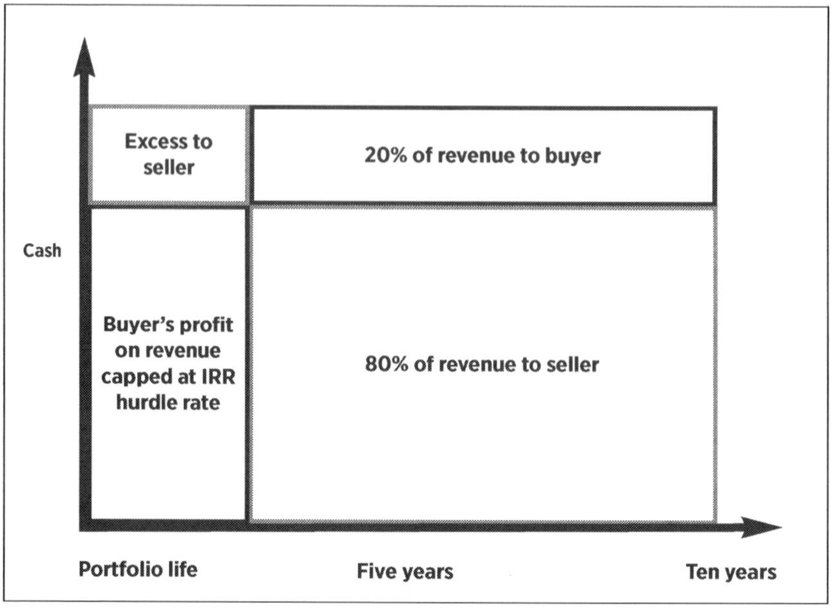

The benefits of this structure to a selling institution include:

1. Immediate cash injection at the prevailing market price.
2. Immediate balance sheet clean-up with corresponding positive publicity.
3. Immediate resource free-up enabling them to concentrate on core activities.
4. Minimising windfall profits for the buyer, at the seller's expense.
5. Substantial future collection revenue.
6. Seller retains profit from any future market recovery in asset prices.

Additional bank seller upside may also be achieved through charging client fees to the buyer after closing, for undertaking collection and custodian services on their behalf. In addition to increasing future fee income, the buyer may also be a source of future lending business for the seller.

Overall, this kind of approach to transaction structure will enable the smarter selling institution to dispose of NPLs at markets price now, with significant additional future revenues, and greatest upside potential. It provides an optimum solution by immediately solving short-term balance sheet problems, whist minimising loss to an institution and maximising sales proceeds. It immediately counteracts the traditional negative image of the vulture distressed debt investor.

Participatory structures like this, allied to the principle of more creative resolving and holding of real estate, may well become a new global template for future NPL sales, as opposed to the plain vanilla outright sale method prevalent after previous Western crises.

5. New ways of absorbing bank loan book losses that are not dependant upon taxpayers

The need for bank reserves to increase under Basel III will constrain liquidity and restrict credit distribution levels. The new regulations include some fresh ideas, such as the concept of contingent capital. These are debt securities that convert to equity in the event of specific negative capital ratio triggers occurring during the future lifetime of the securities. They are designed to phase out current hybrid bank securities which generally do not have a convertible component. The idea is that the conversion to equity will exempt the need for future taxpayer bail-outs, in the event that a market crash is big enough to cause extreme damage to bank balance sheets.

There is no reason why similar types of security could not be used by banks if they need or want to sell NPL loan books below book value. The difference between book value and sales price could be covered by the issuance of contingent convertibles, purchased by institutional investors. These could also be linked back to the concept of selling loan books into a participatory structure, as outlined in the previous section. In this case, the securities issued to cover the shortfall could be structured to have a priority over future cash flow receipts, otherwise designated for the selling bank from the sale of the loan book.

In the 20 years since the 1989 recesion the mainstream banking market has changed considerably. The distressed debt industry has also changed significantly in the past two decades, but less markedly so, given that market crashes have been largely confined to less financially innovative emerging markets. Most of the less mature capital markets lacked the infrastructure, confidence or expertise to create or implement sufficiently sophisticated, structured solutions to overcome some of the issues that might produce pricing differentials between buyers and sellers, or generate additional seller upside.

The legacy of 2008 in Europe and North America is huge stocks of distressed debt in need of resolution. Within these jurisdictions, ongoing financial innovation is to be expected. In the past decade, financial engineering has proved to be particularly effective in creating new, or improved, products that widened marketplaces and provided yield pick-ups.

There is no reason why this expertise cannot now be extended to the distressed sector, in order to help banks remove bad assets from their balance sheets, without having to revert to outright selling to investors, with outsized return requirements, at fire-sale levels. Previously problematic areas between buyers and sellers of NPLs, such as double discounting, or timing, or cost of money differentials, will be structured around, potentially with the use of new types of securities like contingent capital. As a result, the distressed debt industry will probably enter a new era of catch-up in terms of financial innovation that will likely impact transaction structuring and engineering, both for simple loans and more complex debt securities that impacts both institutions and investors.

10. RECENT DEVELOPMENTS IN DISTRESSED DEBT

A number of long-term global economic and political shifts have occurred that have their origins in the removal of trade barriers, deregulation and the global spread of IT. The original idea of globalisation was to connect the world, improve efficiency of movement of goods and people, and thereby grow the size of the world market. This aim has been fulfilled but, in addition, there have been a number of major, unintended consequences that are still unravelling. The financial sector in particular has been transformed over the past decade. The result of new innovation running ahead of itself was an enormous build up of hidden risk in mature, Western markets that has metamorphosed into distressed debt. The response to this will continue to shape the banking industry for the foreseeable future.

Financial globalisation

Trade globalisation has been evolving since civilisation began and is well understood. Financial globalisation, driven by new technology, is still in its infancy and, not surprisingly, it has produced unexpected consequences, resulting in destabilising trade and currency imbalances. Rebalancing, adapting and responding to this will preoccupy governments for some time, which will have a significant impact on capital flows, the financial markets and ultimately distressed debt.

After 20 years of international banking expansion a reverse-globalisation rebound, including localisation and downsizing, is demanded by governments in the West in response to the scale of the 2008 crisis. The central theme is that national tax-payer support conflicts with the principal of overseas risk-taking. However, change, where it can be implemented, is occurring slowly in order not to threaten stability in the financial sector.

Banks in emerging markets will continue to refrain from innovation or development of new complex financial products. Their governments will cite the 2008 Western meltdown as an excuse to avoid new Western technology imports and liberalisation that would impact their capital markets. There are also likely to be many calls, but limited action, for cross-jurisdictional regulation in order to eliminate accounting inconsistencies. The new contemporary global banking model will be one of hedged, low risk, conservative operations, focused on traditional, uncomplicated distribution and the facilitation of movement of capital.

Globalisation within the distressed debt sector has enabled technology transfer to spread everywhere. The USA continues to be the clear market leader in loan servicing, but the past decade has seen the migration of dedicated servicers to all parts of the world. Governments can now easily compare notes on systemic financial risks, or share debt clean-up experiences. Investors now scour the world looking for NPL deals as a result of having executed many international transactions. The appearance of both domestic and foreign buyers within individual jurisdictions has enabled sellers to connect with the widest possible audience and maximise sales revenues. Reverse-globalisation has also impacted distressed debt negatively, in the situation where a multinational institution has global NPLs, but its government will only provide subsidies or guarantees in its home jurisdiction.

As a result of uncertainty and volatility, governments, institutions and investors will increasingly try to spread risk and balance things out by cross-jurisdictional reciprocal investment. This will leave their markets even more exposed to overseas events, out of the control of their own government policy. *Inter-jurisdictional market contagion* is a relatively new term that is likely to become a frequent occurrence.

Technological changes in the Western banking system

Consolidating or rationalising?

Domestication will drive rationalisation in the Western banking sector. Smaller institutions, coupled with a prolonged Western slump should, in theory, increase the risk of takeover and consolidation in the banking sector. However, the *too big to fail* lobby is counteracting any move towards consolidation and the creation of bigger institutions.

Weakness in the banking sector will hinder any attempt to return to traditional balance sheet lending. The ability to effectively trade or gamble with taxpayer's money, under the umbrella of central bank guarantees, is viewed as moral hazard and may prove to be politically unacceptable. If the narrow banking lobby prevails, banking, dealing and trading activities may be separated in some jurisdictions. If this occurs, it will cause a further reduction in the size of institutions. Outsourcing, cost-cutting and head count reduction will dominate until such time as institutional credit starts expanding again and these policies reverse on the basis that when volume increases it is cheaper to do everything in-house. In the meantime, financial and technological innovation will likely occur outside the traditional credit world, with new ideas confined to trading, dealing and investing.

Changes in distribution

Building on the success of telecoms and the internet, the growth of the social web is the type of initiative that will likely drive future credit distribution. Greater use of information technology and further development in this area is inevitable and will continue to change the way things operate. Financial institutions have the opportunity to become more accessible than before. Social networks, and the new generation of smart-phones, enable customers to use and interact with banks whenever they want and from wherever they may be. The ability of information technology to store data is increasing exponentially every year and banks will harness this opportunity. People will expect unparalleled levels of accessibility, and banks will improve their services by providing a regular flow of interactive and easily shareable information for anyone who wants to access it.

A new paradigm facing the traditional banking model is that opening up the credit markets further with information technology also opens up the door to distribution competition from new and unexpected sources. In the past, financial institutions have been seen as the one of the most efficient method of linking borrowers with investors. Whether their monopoly can be maintained in the future is uncertain, and we may see increased credit distribution competition from, say, mainstream retailers against traditional branded banks, which will further change the way the finance industry interfaces with consumers. The longer credit-impotency caused by weakened balance sheets prevails, and the longer banks and government treasuries continue to bail each other out instead of returning to riskier credit origination, the greater the danger of market share erosion from stronger competitors or new entrants will be.

Since the millennium, the pace of financial innovation has been too fast for governments and regulators to keep up with, and they will continue playing catch-up for the foreseeable future. Typical is confusion over banks' risk management. Common sense dictates that there is a conflict between maximising profit on risk capital and somehow trying to limit the same risks with internal controls. As a result, internal risk management ends up as a toothless PR exercise. The reality is that investors manage risk through the investment choices they make and the price they are prepared to pay for securities or other products. The key point here is investment driven. Whether it is globalisation initiatives, technology-driven change, or distressed debt, improvements will only work properly if they are something that people want to invest money in.

Regulatory intitiatives

Ways of protecting banks from sinister elements such as speculative runs are being investigated, but this seems difficult to implement effectively. A vast array of financial and economic numbers are now available, together with the processing power to crunch them, but no-one is certain on how to interpret them correctly and implement them. The authorities have noticed that the more profitable banking strategies prior to the last crisis have also turned out to be the most risky. Regulatory proposals, whilst desirable in terms of their intent to control leverage, do not go anywhere near far enough. The problem of large, dealer, banks posing a systemic risk to economies has not been solved. It is not just the leverage, but the scale of financial innovation and the creation of new structures and securities itself, that needs regulatory attention. The insoluble problem of national regulators and international markets will also continue to stoke inter-jurisdictional risk disparity.

Whilst all these regulatory initiatives are laudable, they miss the point that maybe the way that regulations are now approached is out of touch with the pace of commercial and technological changes in the financial services sector. No set of rules can guarantee the solvency of the banking sector in a crisis. The rules of ordinary competition demand that banks must seize any new opportunity to increase their return on capital. In order to police them effectively, though, means that regulators would need to be dynamic, highly responsive to change and ahead of the curve, which is not what they are designed or set up for.

The advent of Basel III should in theory have added to deleveraging pressure. Banks need balance sheet expansion in order to grow their way out of 2008 problems, but the increased capital reserve requirements under the new accord would normally absorb additional capital that would restrict their ability to lend, by comparison with past levels. Because of the weak state of bank balance sheets, implementation of the new accord has been delayed until 2019, so it should be business as usual for now for the banking sector, which gives them plenty of time to sort their house out.

Has anything changed with distressed debt in the last 20 years?

Different responses from governments

Whilst technology in the past decade has fundamentally altered the way that credit markets operate, only modest change has occurred in the distressed debt industry since the last major Western property correction in 1989. Distressed loan e-trading platforms and exchanges are, for example, one of few initiatives. The big difference between the response to 1989 and 2008 is in the nature of government involvement. Twenty years ago, the institutions that crashed and were liquidated were not systemically important, so selling their assets quickly at fire sale prices had a limited negative effect upon the economy as a whole. The clean-up task was, in essence, an exercise in rebuilding market confidence.

The 2008 recession is completely different. Risk of insolvency has blighted most big Western institutions, which has cast doubt on the banking system as a whole. The scale of the downturn and damage to loan collateral is so big that government could not afford the cost of bail out at the asset level. This is driving distressed debt recovery in a completely different direction.

This extraordinary government involvement has allowed banks to postpone widespread monetisation of distressed debt and enabled them to avoid further damaging their balance sheets. After the Lehman collapse, $600 billion was immediately wiped off global equity markets. As a result, central banks and governments are wary of releasing debt figures that might spook the markets. The exact numbers are a closely guarded secret, but the problem that is now appearing in its place is the risk of rating agencies downgrading sovereign debt, due to the provision of excessive banking sector support. This may eventually increase the cost of national borrowing, which could ultimately become the overriding reason for extensive NPL monetisation.

Finding sufficient resources to help tackle the problem

The enormous size of the 2008 problem has made it especially difficult to find a sufficient number of qualified advisory resources. The result is a sort of pyramid pretend and extend scheme from government level down through the regulators to banking level. Banks continue to use traditional credit resources to advise on work-out issues and everyone goes through the motions. Once again, the need to cover decisions made with someone they can blame is overriding. Whether NPL resolution is being optimised is doubtful. Some bank work-out divisions now freely admit that, when they use them, the name and reputation of the advisor is more important than the quality of output.

Since 2008, a small number of institutions have hired high quality managers with proven expertise, but these tend to be the exception, rather than the rule. Banks overriding preference still seems to be *do it yourself*. As a result, flimsy, cheap resolution platform structures and demotivated staff are common occurrences. There is now a much bigger pool of global talent within the distressed debt industry for banks to tap into, but their inclination seems to be to keep things local.

Restricting outsiders because they don't know local markets is a cop-out. The ability to step in from outside, particularly after a market correction, can be a huge advantage. Keeping things local limits fresh ideas or approaches, and blunts resolution performance. Going back to the car manufacturing analogy, broached in the first chapter, too many institutions seem to be content selling off the old models on a localised, piecemeal basis from the adjacent vacant land plot. Market recovery must ultimately occur and many banks seem to be content, passively waiting for this to come around again. The difficulty that may arise is that this may take a lot longer than originally envisaged.

Having been publicly pilloried by the authorities for the 2008 crisis, banks are likely to be doubly careful to cover themselves in their clean-up decisions. This mind-set is not necessarily producing the best results though. A case in point is a European government, hiring one of the biggest global retail banking names to advise them on their 2008 distressed debt problem. The issue that was ignored is that the institution involved, whilst reputable and solvent, had no experience of buying distressed debt at the wholesale level, or taking over any other substantial loan portfolios. Their experience of NPLs is many years of working out limited numbers of delinquencies from their own loan book, which is largely extraneous, by comparison with the scale and nature of what they were supposed to be advising on. Returning to the car theme again, this is a bit like a highly regarded car dealer advising on the setting up and running of a truck servicing division.

So far, no one seems to be looking too far ahead. Regulators and governments have focused largely on bank liquidity, and ways of mitigating the next down cycle at the asset level are very low down the political agenda. The system moves on relentlessly with ever greater challenges and a new by-product of globalisation is the likelihood of borrowers spreading risk by hiding assets in overseas jurisdictions.

Asian borrowers are now hedging the likelihood of correction in their home markets by buying assets in Europe. Domestic banks in their home jurisdictions should be tracking this carefully, as it is likely to become their new work-out challenge at some time in the foreseeable future. It will then also be interesting to see how banks in Asia change the way they approach things in comparison with their 1997 crisis when their markets eventually correct.

Resolving the distressed debt problem

The massive scale of the problem

The problem that continues to drag on Western markets is the scale of collateral damage from the 2008 crisis, together with the length of time it will take to get to the bottom. With extreme public scrutiny and pressure on the banking sector, distressed debt has tended to be pushed into the background, which means it is not receiving sufficient attention or resources. *Too big to fail* could be construed as *too much debt to monetise quickly, or in an orderly manner.*

Resolving hitherto unseen levels of non-performing legacy loans is therefore the single greatest challenge facing the financial sector. Banks have experienced a significant weakening in their balance sheets, which is having a dramatic influence on their ability to work their way through the recovery phase. The situation is complicated by state guarantees, which have overcome banking sector liquidity risk but have not addressed the solvency issue.

State guarantees have influenced bank ratings since the 2008 crisis and there are concerns that their removal will result in downgrades and higher cost of capital. There is also a risk of moral hazard, whereby some institutions may take the view that the taxpayer should foot the bill for cleaning up, which removes the pressure to maximise recoveries in a timely manner. It is also apparent that in situations where government has guaranteed or purchased distressed obligations, banks have overpriced NPL book values.

Some distressed debt work-out has occurred, but at a modest rate. In the USA, the Federal Deposit Insurance Corporation (FDIC) has been the principal seller of assets of failed financial institutions. Left alone, banks are understandably concerned about selling into a declining market, which would further erode the value of their balance sheet, and are disincentivised from taking losses on their loan books. Institutions that contributed to their own downfall through poor credit decisions may also delay their own recovery through poor asset management choices and waste further money unnecessarily.

A securitisation solution

Structured finance was one of the main contributory reasons why the market crashed in 2008 and is potentially one of the best escape routes. Securitisation of cash flows from non-performing loans has been used successfully after other financial crises in the world, starting with the US Savings and Loans Crisis. It has even been used in newly emerging markets, as a means of early debt monetisation, albeit from seasoned portfolios with high degrees of over-collateralisation. Confidence in the underlying collateral market and a clear understanding of recovery rates and timing are key.

Technically, there is no reason why this could not occur all across Europe and North America, as a widespread means of recapitalising and strengthening balance sheets, and to lessen reliance on taxpayer bail-outs. The main stumbling block is confidence – there is a lack of trust in bank balance sheets, their transparency, their asset quality, and not least, in their ability to resolve high volumes of distressed debt profitably, which is the main topic of this book. A lack of belief in Western bank balance sheets not only hampers recovery generally, but prevents banks from finding widespread technical solutions to monetising their debts.

Probably, the only way that debt securitisation might work in the short term is with the addition of government guarantees. Even though the taxpayer is already on the hook for bailing out the banking system, any new initiatives like this that involve transfer of risk, even if cosmetic, are probably politically unacceptable. Trust in banks and their ability to spawn new initiatives are at an all-time low, which is contributing to an overall loss of confidence within mature Western economies.

Once Western real estate markets return to sustained and robust growth, there will be a rebound in the creation of structured credit or similar distribution vehicles. Their efficiency should ensure their survival, provided their future treatment in terms of risk-weighting is not disadvantaged. For securities holding property, though, their accounting treatment needs to be reviewed. Specifically, marking them to market at zero after a crash is absurd, given that the underlying collateral has substantial value.

More structured securities would require an increase in the need for third-party independent master servicers and special servicers, and as a result, the asset management industry may be a beneficiary from future developments in the financial sector. If the huge amount of distressed debt in need of resolution is factored in, putting money into loan servicers may present an excellent investment opportunity.

The last US crisis in 1989 established the template for monetising NPLs for the subsequent 20 years. The credit world is now watching and waiting to see how the latest Western distressed debt clean up evolves, which could then be the new global template for the next generation of NPL work-outs.

The downward deleveraging spiral

The 2008 financial crisis was not unique. A downward deleveraging spiral, as shown in Figure 10.1, is a common occurrence after a crash, which postpones recovery in real estate and credit markets. An over-reliance by banks on legal execution and auction into a falling real estate market drives recoveries down even further. Consumers lose confidence and prefer to hoard cash and avoid taking on additional credit risk. New buyers sit on the sidelines and avoid putting their money down, patiently waiting for market prices to fall further. Many assets need to be recycled, in order to lay the ground for market recovery.

However, widespread monetisation of assets continues to depress property prices, which drives down bank balance sheets further. The banks get stuck between a rock and a hard place, and can do very little about their predicament without outside assistance. Many of them become too weak to lend, and lack the capability to monetise their loan books creatively in order to generate additional lending profits and upside. Ultimately, some will be forced to sell.

Halting a cycle of value destruction is extremely difficult without bold, aggressive, concerted action. Widespread subsidisation of assets and borrowers just slows things down, and postpones the time when recovery can occur and growth can recommence.

Figure 10.1 – real estate deleveraging: cycle of value destruction

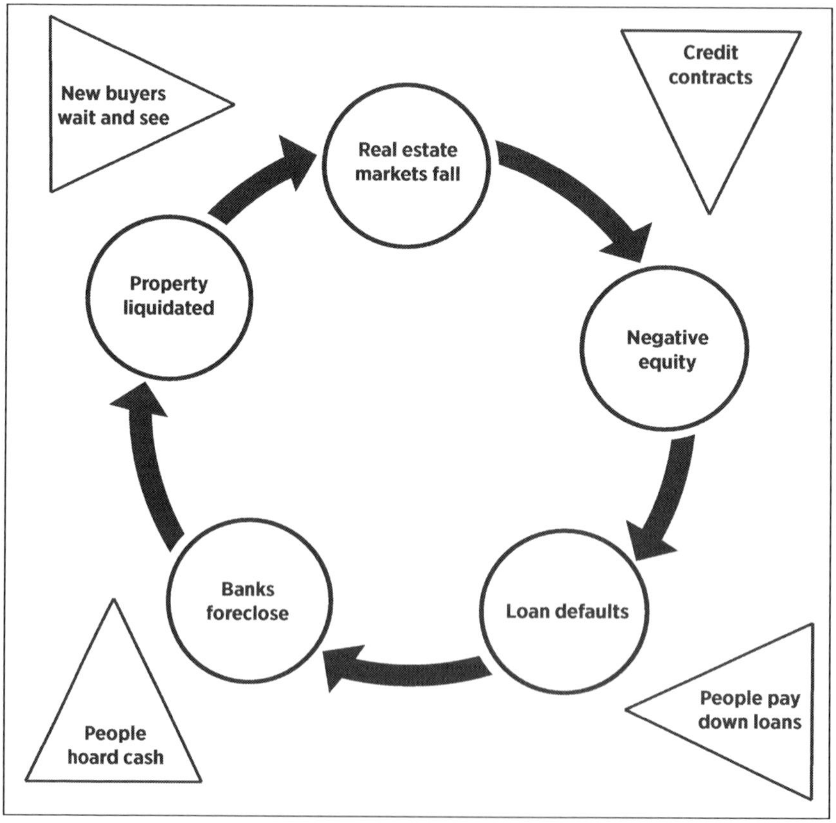

Until it is stopped, the downward spiral continues to erode confidence and destroy value. However, adversity for the market is joy for the wily, vulture-like, distressed debt investor. Cycles of value destruction, credit contraction, people hoarding cash, buyers waiting rather than acting, all contribute to increasing the vultures' potential rewards. To them, a downward deleveraging spiral is a sort of stairway to heaven and the longer and deeper it falls the greater their future upside ascent will be.

When the market at large is busy paying down their loans, distressed debt investors will open their war chests and spend their money. When people hoard cash and become defensive, this will be the time when the distressed investor starts leveraging up. As the cycle of value destruction gathers momentum, the vulture prepares for his cycle of opportunity. This cycle is shown in Figure 10.2.

Figure 10.2 – distressed debt investment: cycle of opportunity

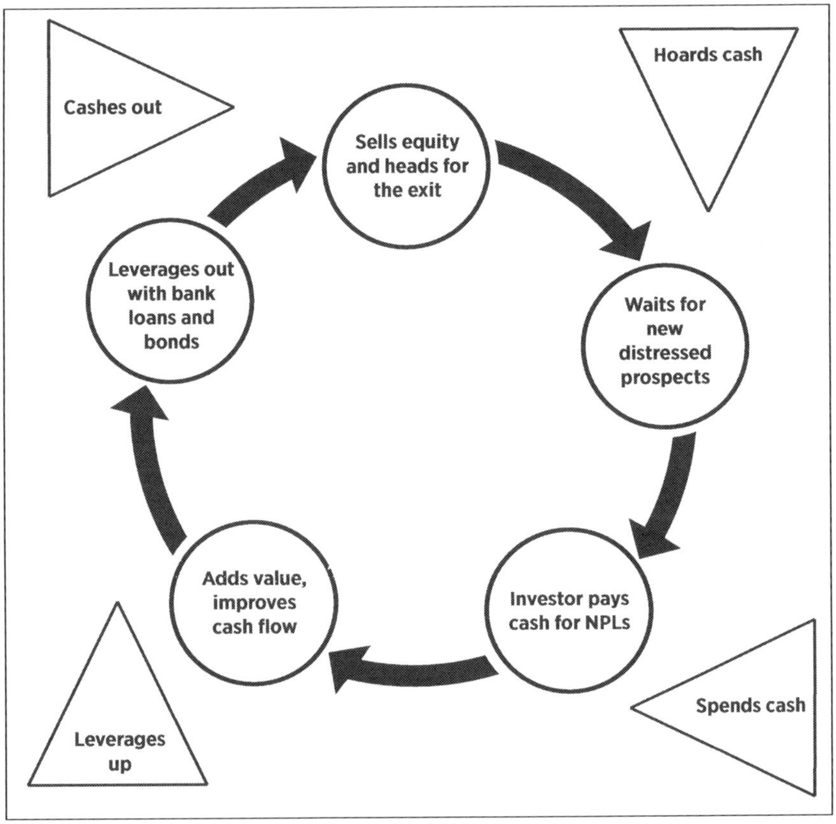

With patience, good timing, a deep pocket, deft application and strong execution, the potential for the distressed investor to make outsized returns is enormous.

Optimising distressed loan books

Investors will always beat the banks

Returning to the central question posed in the introduction to this book, it is inevitable that specialist investors will be better than banks at working out loan books because they are fully focused and committed to the goal of maximum recovery. The specialist methods that investors use to achieve this have already been detailed in earlier chapters, but simply put: debt collection is not the banks' main business and they are limited in what they can do in work-out situations. Banks detest NPLs. They are not set up for work-out, nor to engage in entrepreneurial activity, and have neither the capacity nor the budget to tackle new alternative strategies.

Distressed debt investors, on the other hand, are determined, motivated and incentivised to make the most of work-out situations. Their vision is the Midas touch, to turn bank waste into gold, and they will do whatever it takes to make this happen.

Banks go furthest off track when they succumb to the attitude that they have failed; their punishment is selling assets at a loss, and they need to erase the memory of crisis as soon as possible and move on. They should also resist the urge to park NPLs in a remote, obscure corner of the institution where they don't have to look at them, best resolved through a gradual, controlled fire-sale.

Instead of being embarrassed by bad loans, banks should aggressively exploit them and seek good, independent, professional advice. In many cases, the optimum outcome will be achieved by setting up a new independent bad bank, moving the bad assets out of the good bank and appointing experienced, expert special servicers to manage it. Banks should be looking to keep as much of the value in their distressed loan books in their own pocket. If they need to raise cash, they can invite investors in. If the bad bank enters into leveraged, joint ventures with partners that can add value to assets, this is a ready and easily controlled method of growing a new good loan book. They should also stay away from securities and derivatives that risk being marked-to-market and promote instability.

Banks' failure to take advantage of the situation is their own choice

One of the most bizarre things about the distressed debt industry is that the party with the greatest natural advantage is often the seller themselves. Firstly, banks already know the assets; and secondly, their low cost of funds, usually around 2% to 3%, is a fraction of the discount rate required by investors. Banks should therefore recognise NPLs as an opportunity to re-price loans, take equity-scale, uncapped upside, boosted by the advantage of their low cost of funds, and reap all the rewards for themselves.

Such innovative solutions rarely happen though and banks mostly prefer to maintain the status quo by persevering with assets that they consider toxic, and believe they are not very good at resolving. Their rationale is threefold:

1. In the aftermath of crisis, doing nothing avoids the need to make difficult, bold decisions that may come back and haunt them later.
2. By keeping distressed loans in-house, they can best manage the potential negative impact of bad loans upon their balance sheet. As business recovers, and pressure on their balance sheet eases with time, they may then consider more radical solutions, such as selling off their bad loans outright.
3. They will justify weak collection performance by calculating less money will be lost by working loans out themselves, rather than selling their loan book off early at rock-bottom prices to vulture investors.

Internal work-out is generally the banks' favoured method of resolution because it is simplest and cheapest. Bad banks generally only get established where market or public opinion demands stronger action, with widespread, outright sale of loan books usually only occurring as a result of government pressure or intervention. Public outrage over subsidising bank losses is understandable but governments need to be careful not to be swayed into making poor commercial decisions if they intervene.

In the turmoil of a major market crash, the focus tends to be on the amount of bank loss and recovery whilst the cost of an early or delayed economic recovery may be unnoticed. Calculating this should be given far greater emphasis as it impacts everyone. In debt clean-up, market recovery and economic rebound, speed is king. Whether the banks lost money, and if the government then achieves disappointing clean-up results or makes a profit, is minor by comparison.

Can government-sponsored asset management companies do any better?

The halfway house between a bank and an investor that is sometimes created in extreme cases is a government-sponsored asset management company. These are usually set up under, or linked to, government bank deposit guarantee organisations, in order to orderly manage asset liquidation. A table summarising the respective metrics that influence collection performance for banks, government AMCs and distressed debt investors is included in the Appendix.

The huge advantage that government entities have is the potential for virtually unlimited statutory power. This enables them to force banks to do more or less whatever they want. This makes them highly suitable for taking over distressed assets from banks, but, given their other handicaps, they are not necessarily the best option for resolving debt at the asset level, if maximum recovery is the aim. Alternatively, there is nothing to prevent government AMCs entering into work-out joint ventures with specialist work-out investor-servicers, whereby they share in the upside, similar to the type of transaction discussed in Chapter 9.

Government AMCs, like investors, have the timing advantage of approaching the clean-up situation after a crash and are also set up for the specific purpose of asset management, with 100% focus on recovery. The first hurdle they encounter though is an overriding need for public accountability. Entrepreneurial flair is then dampened by submission to the civil service. They can be established in a way that caters for alternative strategies and budgeted in a way that allows additional investment, but this must always be limited by public accountability controls.

One of the unique features in maximising distressed debt is that you frequently never really know what you have until you get into the middle of things, and actions constantly shift in response to changing circumstances. The commercial realities of life that accurately reflect the divergent views and horizons of different parties cannot always be accurately documented in, say, a current-day valuation report, that fully satisfies public examination. Optimising distressed debt revenue involves brinkmanship and horse-trading. Quick, immediate decisions are required, many of which deviate from previously tabled business plans and strategies. This is extraordinarily difficult to manage with the encumbrance of civic answerability, the glare of public scrutiny and the risk of political interference.

Public opinion can become a major handicap, particularly where government AMCs needlessly set themselves up to be profitable. If this occurs, the biggest setback facing the AMC is paying too much for assets, which can easily happen during the chaos that follows a major crash. If this is the case, it is extremely difficult for the AMC to be effective, and it can induce a state of siege mentality due to criticism of their overall performance, or lack of it. As a result, many government asset management companies end up spending a disproportionate amount of their time protecting their position and covering their actions, rather than creatively maximising recoveries.

Returning again to the theme on the first page of this book, successful optimisation of loan books demands specific focus, expertise and execution. However, no matter how capable we are, if we pay too much for an asset, we will always struggle to make a good return. Whether it is a government AMC or the most talented investor – **in distressed debt, we create our profits when we buy, not when we sell.**

11. CONCLUSION

Since the 2008 crisis, the shape of Western financial centres and the global financial system has changed immensely. The enormous scale of the downturn has taken everyone by surprise. The problem is vast, fascinating and complex. Responsibility has been pinned on governments, regulators, banks, rating agencies and speculative investors. Wasting time on blame is counterproductive though. Taking everything into consideration, it is probably the system that has fallen too far behind technology and evolution, and is out of touch with the times. Whether those in power have the motivation or the ability to fix the system still remains to be seen, and the least politically damaging way out of the problem seems to be to create another bubble and inflate the debt away.

The rest of the world is bracing itself for the next correction and the threat of a new wave of distressed debt hitting emerging markets. The shock of a crisis, both on Western institutions and markets, has now worn off. The financial sector as a whole has adjusted; it is recognising reality and is trying to move on. However, recovery will not be easy. Not only is there no interest rate solution available to boost revival, but there is a real risk that Western inflationary pressure may cause lending rates to rise and hamper recovery. Western markets will probably take much longer to recover. This being the case, the management of distressed debt and resolving the underlying assets needs greater care and attention than previously has been considered. Moving the debt mountain this time around represents a far greater challenge than we have seen before.

Many books have been written about the 2008 crisis, but very little has been said around the mechanics or practicality of resolving bad loans. The Western banking sector's ability to replace distressed assets with a new wave of performing assets in a rising market may still be some years ahead, in which case, the need to extract the absolute maximum value from every NPL and preserve precious bank capital is theoretically more pressing that at any time in the past. Government subsidy and guarantee has changed the dynamics though and most people seem to be assuming that the taxpayer will ultimately pick up the monetisation bill. As a result, no one is drawing too much public attention to the scale of the debt predicament and Western governments' policies of printing money seem to be removing the pressure to act quickly on resolving the issue.

The regulators seem to be completely disinterested in the legacy debt overhang. Reversing unemployment and returning the economy to growth in anticipation of a new boom cycle appear to be top of the civic agenda. Politically, the easiest way of addressing the distressed problem is to let it gradually fade from the voters' memory. For now, the banks have enough problems with their core business without being overly-distracted by distressed debt. Their hands are full deflecting political criticism, defending their balance sheets, raising capital in preparation for new capital adequacy rules, guarding the most profitable parts of their business and protecting their traditional, credit distribution hegemony from attack.

Eventually, the bad assets will be monetised, by which time the banks will be busy growing their balance sheets again in the next cycle. As yet, it is not clear on exactly who is most likely to earn the next round of luxury yachts, private jets, castles and tropical islands from the clean-up. When it comes to the waiting game though, the banks have a tendency to run out of patience and usually lose out. Once that milestone is reached, the chances are that the patient, wily, distressed debt investor will probably be the one who ultimately triumphs again.

Glossary of Terms

AMC: Asset Management Company.

Bid-ask spread: The difference in price between the highest price that a buyer is willing to pay for an asset and the lowest price for which a seller is willing to sell it.

CDO: Collateralised debt obligation.

CLO: Collateralised loan obligation.

CMBS: Commercial mortgage-backed security.

Cryonics: The process of preserving life at very low temperature with the purpose of future revival. Applied to assets, it would mean keeping them in cold storage until market conditions improved and they could be resold at a higher price.

Distressed debt: Loans in default or at immediate risk of default.

Loan book: An inventory of loans held by a financial institution.

Mark to market: Current market value of an asset, as demonstrated by, for example, its market price on a trading exchange.

Moral hazard: When a party insulated from risk behaves differently than it would behave if it were fully exposed to the risk. Similar to having a free insurance policy.

Narrow banking: The move to separate bank deposit taking and payment activities from financial intermediation activities.

OPB: Outstanding principal balance, the total unpaid principal balance for a loan, excluding interest.

NPL: Non-performing loan, i.e. a loan in default.

RMBS: Residential mortgage-backed security.

Structured finance: The processes of moving loans and other receivables into securities that can be purchased by large numbers of investors.

Valuation benchmarking: Analysis of a number of property valuation reports that enables them to be readily compared with one another.

Zero carbon: Achieving net zero carbon emissions from production, operations and building occupancy.

Appendix

Table A1 – Relative performance metrics table

This table summarises the respective metrics that influence collection performance for banks, government AMCs and distressed debt investors.

Performance metric	Bank	Government AMC	Investor
Statutory power	None	Maximum	None
Timing advantage	Crash victim	Post-crash advantage	Post-crash advantage
Aim of business	Banks, not debt collectors	100% focused on debt collection	100% focused on debt collection
Compatibility of aim & business structure	Not core business	Core Business, but part of civil service	Core business
Profit incentivisation	Focused on loss minimisation & balance sheet impact	Focused on public accountability	Focused on maximum profit return
Staffing skill set	Mostly amateurs	Mixture of civil service, amateurs & professionals	Professionals
Entrepreneurial appetite	Low	Limited by public accountability	Limitless
Alternative strategies	Limited by budget & capability	Limited by public accountability	Open to everything
Additional investment in assets	Difficult	Possible, but limited	Keen to invest more
Additional investment in other creditors loans or liens	Difficult	Difficult	Keen to invest more
Attitude to borrowers	Inflexible	Tend to pillory them	Maximum profit opportunity
View of loans after crash	Need to protect their balance sheet	Need to protect public interest	Maximum profit opportunity
View of loans later on	Risk of distressed debt fatigue	Need to protect public interest	Maximum profit opportunity
Political intrusion risk	Medium risk	Very high risk	Low risk
Risk of adverse public opinion	Can be high	Very high	Immaterial

INDEX

26287228R00145

Made in the USA
Lexington, KY
25 September 2013